CATHOLICISM AT A CROSSROADS

Catholicism at a Crossroads

The Present and Future of America's Largest Church

Maureen K. Day, James C. Cavendish, Paul M. Perl,
Michele Dillon, *and* Mary L. Gautier,
with William V. D'Antonio

NEW YORK UNIVERSITY PRESS
New York, New York

NEW YORK UNIVERSITY PRESS
New York
www.nyupress.org

© 2025 by New York University
All rights reserved

Please contact the Library of Congress for Cataloging-in-Publication data.

ISBN: 9781479832170 (hardback)
ISBN: 9781479832187 (paperback)
ISBN: 9781479832217 (library ebook)
ISBN: 9781479832194 (consumer ebook)

This book is printed on acid-free paper, and its binding materials are chosen for strength and durability. We strive to use environmentally responsible suppliers and materials to the greatest extent possible in publishing our books.

Manufactured in the United States of America

10 9 8 7 6 5 4 3 2 1

Also available as an ebook

To Jerome Baggett, for everything. —M.K.D.

To my mother, C. Joann Cavendish, and her siblings, whose faith has always been a source of inspiration. —J.C.C.

To my fellow researchers and friends at the Center for Applied Research in the Apostolate. —P.M.P.

To the prophetic sociologists who launched this project more than thirty years ago: Bill D'Antonio, Jim Davidson, Dean Hoge, and Ruth Wallace. —M.L.G. & M.D.

To my wife, Lorraine, for her steadfast support and inspiration over many years, and to Mary G., and the rest of the team who continued the work I started years ago with Jim D. and others. I'm gratified to have played a part in the origin of this work. —W.V.D.

CONTENTS

Introduction

If you were a very active Catholic in New Mexico's Diocese of Las Cruces, odds are you would know either David or Veronica, who are about to meet for lunch.[1] David—a White man in his mid-sixties—stands up from his chair, waves, and calls out to Veronica—a Mexican-American woman in her mid-thirties. She smiles broadly and walks quickly over to him for an affectionate hug. Observers might assume they have some sort of familial connection; this is reasonable because at first blush, and even more so when considering a few demographic markers of the pair, their friendship is unlikely.

In addition to their generational and ethnic dissimilarities, a few other differences mark Veronica and David. David grew up in a working-class family but attended a high-ranking Catholic university. Veronica also has working-class roots, and went to her public college's Newman Center. David nearly always votes for Republican candidates and Veronica is a consistent Democrat. Even though they are both Catholic, those aware of the diversity within Catholicism might say this is more likely to be a dividing than a unifying factor for them given their respective proclivities. As far as their connections with Catholic lay groups goes, David enjoys the conferences that the Napa Institute offers and reads the posts on CatholicVote and *National Catholic Register*. Veronica likes to pray the rosary at her local Catholic Worker house and follows politics through *America* and, the other NCR, *National Catholic Reporter*. Veronica is closely following the Catholic Church's efforts at racial reconciliation and David is concerned that the church is neglecting anti-abortion efforts. Again, while active Catholics in their area would probably know one of them, it is unlikely they would know both, given the differences in their demographics and Catholic circles.

On paper, their friendship does not seem likely, but circumstances brought them together about six years ago when they were both asked by their respective parishes to assist a diocesan-wide effort to improve parish faith formation programs. Even with two dozen other potential friends on this commission, David and Veronica clicked from the start. Although they are marked by important differences, the diocesan commission always began and ended in prayer and faith sharing. This allowed David and Veronica to get to know each other as people, appreciating each other's sarcastic but good-natured sense of humor, and especially their passion and dedication toward their faith. They grew more empathetic toward their differences, at times even appreciative. They continued their friendship—and additional collaboration—well beyond the conclusion of the commission.

Over the years, Veronica has learned that David, a father of seven, is a congenial fellow with a quick wit and a big heart as well as a man of tremendous integrity. His faith is the foundation of everything he does. He is a retired manager and business consultant and will often serve as a volunteer coach for the boys' and girls' basketball teams at his parish's high school. A few years before the pandemic, his faith was deepened during his pilgrimage walk on Spain's Camino de Santiago. He and his wife have been hosting two Sudanese refugees—a mother and daughter—in their home for the last three years; David is just telling Veronica how elated everyone is that the daughter got accepted to a Catholic university with a full tuition and housing scholarship. Veronica is amazed and praises David for all the work he did in helping her navigate the college application process, while she unashamedly steals a French fry from his plate.

David appreciates Veronica's considered opinions—always grounded in church teaching—and her welcoming and optimistic nature. She has a graduate degree in theology and teaches at the local Catholic high school. Her job allows her to bring her faith to her workplace as well as spend summers with her two school-aged children. She loves David's stories of the Camino, and he made her promise to walk the Camino with her husband once they are empty nesters. Both Veronica and David are deeply concerned with the polarization in the church; they are not disturbed by differing perspectives, but they are worried about the growing numbers of people who are being pulled into increasingly hostile factions.

Veronica and David exemplify our survey respondents in some ways, but they are atypical in others. They help illustrate the wide diversity of

Catholic lay people in generation, ethnicity, gender, doctrinal proclivities, and political views, among other factors. However, they are extraordinarily involved in their faith, which is not typical; just over a quarter of American Catholics (26 percent) attend church weekly, and only 20 percent of Catholics qualify as "high commitment" (more on this label below). Yet, Veronica and David's commitments and concerns give us glimpses of Catholics more deeply engaged in their faith. Their shared friendship and their personal dedication to their faith paints a piece of a larger picture as well as raises some questions regarding American Catholicism. What are the ways that self-identified American Catholics understand and connect to their faith (or not)? To what extent do Catholics feel priests and bishops are in touch with laypeople's lives? How do racial and ethnic differences matter among Catholics? What impact has the sex abuse scandal had on Catholics? How aligned are lay Catholics with official church teachings on matters related to sexuality? How are they connecting their faith to their political commitments, if at all? Is American Catholic polarization a real issue or an exaggerated specter? What do trends from the last thirty years tell us about the historical arc of American Catholicism and, modestly, about the future? How are ordained and lay leaders suggesting that parishes, dioceses, and lay organizations respond? These questions and more animate the analyses within this book.

This book is the sixth in a series of volumes reporting survey findings on American Catholic laity since the 1980s. Readers familiar with previous titles will recognize some of the questions we have asked consistently through the decades—questions that are helpful not only for snapshots, but also in tracing longitudinal trends. Collectively known as the American Catholic Laity Surveys (ACLS), prior surveys in this series were conducted in 1987, 1993, 1999, 2005, and 2011. The most recent survey includes new questions, such as the sorts of resources Catholics turn to when facing important moral decisions. Most distinctive about this book is its inclusion of interview data with 58 Catholics who work in important roles, whether in the church hierarchy or across a variety of Catholic organizations. In different ways and especially together, these two distinct data sources help us to understand the American Catholic experience and the challenges entailed in revitalizing the church.

Methods

The survey team—William V. D'Antonio, Michele Dillon and Mary L. Gautier—conducted a survey of U.S. adult Catholics in April 2017 using a representative national sample of 1,507 Catholics, including an over-sample of self-identified Hispanic Catholics. The survey was administered by GfK Custom Research (formerly Knowledge Networks), a polling company that conducts academic-quality surveys online using appropriately-screened, internet-based panels of respondents. To determine eligibility for the survey, adults were asked what their present religion was. Anyone who volunteered that they were Catholic continued the survey. Our sample, therefore, does not include those who were raised Catholic, but no longer identify as Catholic. The questionnaire was available in either English or Spanish, depending on the respondent's language preference. The survey intentionally over-sampled Hispanics of multiple generations, yielding a total of 706 Hispanic respondents. Roughly 150 completed the Spanish language version of the questionnaire. Analyses presented in this book use statistical weighting so that race and ethnicity, as well as other background characteristics, match the best national estimates of Catholic demographics.

The survey contains questions on respondents' faith beliefs and practices, their attitudes toward moral authority and pastoral leadership, the relevance of church teachings for their lives, respondents' political and civic beliefs, and their experiences of liturgy. The data were analyzed using SPSS statistical software, and differences of ten percentage points or more between subgroups of respondents can be considered substantive. When percentages in tables or figures do not total 100, unless stated otherwise, this is due to rounding.

The 58 interviewees are not intended to be nationally representative, but are a purposive sample of people whose work in and around church matters gives them particular insight into the American Catholic context. The interview team—James C. Cavendish, Maureen K. Day, and Paul M. Perl—identified and interviewed individuals in leadership positions in regional and national Catholic organizations, Catholics who are popular authors or with specific academic expertise, and others who are lay or ordained ecclesial ministers. The interviewees also include bishops who chair committees and less-known lay Catholics who nonetheless hold or held important positions within the United States Conference of Catholic Bishops (USCCB) and other ecclesial structures. Care was taken to generate a list that reflected gender, racial, generational, and doctrinal diversity.

Rather than using a standardized interview schedule for all our interviewees, we designed separate interview protocols for each of the topics our study explores (i.e., church, authority, race, sex and family, citizenship, and longitudinal trends) and revised them for individual interviewees based on their particular expertise. Because of this topically focused approach, when we write that "many" or "most" of the interviewees were of a certain opinion, this refers only to the subset of interviewees for that topic and chapter, not to the sample of interviewees as a whole. We used a semi-structured format, allowing the interview to pursue emergent strands in the conversation that variously engaged the study's overall themes. The interviews were conducted from November 2021 to July 2023. The transcripts were lightly edited for grammar, clarity, and readability (e.g., removing false starts and filler words like "um").

Given our interviewees' prominence and the responsibility they have for their institutions, some sociological protocols used when interviewing the general public were not followed. Rather than aiming to protect the confidentiality of our respondents, we asked them if we could use their names and identify their roles to help demonstrate the competence and authority of their observations. Everyone agreed. However, so that they could speak more openly to us than they might in public, we told them that at any point in the interview they could tell us something confidentially, and, if we used their statement, we would not attribute the statement to them. A handful availed themselves of this option. More rarely, interviewees told us things that they wanted completely off the record—not to be used in the study at all—but revealed these things to us because they believed the information would be helpful to the larger context of our analysis; we honored these requests. Given their institutional roles, nine of the interviewees requested to see their transcripts to make any revisions or redactions. We allowed this.[2] Most interviews were conducted over Zoom, but there were also a few in-person interviews, as well as interviews conducted via email with people who requested this option.

In total, we had 57 interviews,[3] yielding 2,572 minutes of recordings and 2 emailed responses. These 57 completed interviews represent 58 percent of the total number (98) of individuals whom we initially identified and invited to be interviewed for our study. When a potential interviewee actively declined (as opposed to not responding), the only reason given was that they were too busy. Given the immense responsibilities of the interviewees, it is not surprising that some chose to opt out of a 30-minute interview.

The interview team knew at the outset that we wanted to hear from a diverse range of individuals to ensure we would capture the broad range of perspectives and concerns of those in influential roles in the Catholic Church. We succeeded in interviewing men and women, people in a variety of religious states (i.e., ordained, vowed religious, and lay people), many Catholics of color,[4] and a spectrum of other important aspects of diversity. Although we did not ask our interviewees to self-identify politically or theologically, given their diverse roles, experiences, and organizational affiliations within the church, we are fairly confident that their responses reflect the wide range of perspectives that can be found among engaged and influential Catholics today. We provide a list of interviewees and their affiliations in the appendix to illustrate their diversity.

Some Terms

There are some terms used throughout this book that warrant clarification. First, the survey gathered the attitudes and behaviors of what we refer to as "everyday Catholics." Previous books in this series drew only upon survey data and referred to respondents as "lay Catholics" or similar. To continue to use this term for our respondents might create undue confusion for the reader, as many of the interviewees are also lay Catholics. In order to distinguish the survey respondents (and the "ordinary" Catholics they represent) from the interviewees, we use the term "everyday Catholics" to refer to the survey respondents. We find this phrase useful in describing the wide breadth of experiences, attitudes, and practices that characterize the range of self-identified Catholics across the nation.

Second, in the above story with Veronica and David, we describe them as "high commitment Catholics." In our analyses, Catholic commitment is a composite variable created using three questions from the survey: how frequently respondents attend Mass, how personally important the Catholic Church is to them, and their likelihood of remaining in the Catholic Church. If respondents stated that they attend Mass weekly or more frequently, that the church is the most or among the most important parts of their life, and they chose a 1 or a 2 on a 1–7 scale (in which 1 indicates they would never leave the church and 7 says that they might leave), they are considered high commitment Catholics. Those labeled low commitment respond to at least two of these questions with the following: 1) they attend Mass seldom or never, 2) that the Catholic Church is not very important to them, or 3) that their likelihood of leaving the church is a 5, 6, or 7. Those who do not qualify as high or low commitment are classified as moderately committed. To set the stage for the coming chapters, we begin by offering an overview of the stability and change we have documented on demographic factors since 1987.

Thirty Years of American Catholic Life

Although some characteristics of the U.S. Catholic population have remained stable since the first survey was conducted more than thirty years ago, much has changed. This section explores these patterns of stability and change, recognizing that these demographic patterns—and the demographic characteristics of our respondents—have an influence not only on the structures that shape American Catholic life, but also on the beliefs, experiences, and practices of everyday Catholics. This discussion sets the foundation for what we will see throughout this book: in many ways Catholics today do not live, think, act, or look like Catholics did thirty years ago. This is not surprising, given that the Church itself and society at large have undergone considerable change since 1987.

The Size and Share of the U.S. Catholic Population

When the first American Catholic Laity Survey was conducted in 1987, it was estimated that between 62 and 64 million U.S. adults identified as Catholic.[5] By 2020, shortly after our current survey, that number rose to approximately 72.4 million, and in 2022, the most recent year for which data are available, approximately 73.5 million

American adults self-identified as Catholic.[6] Although this represents an increase of nearly 10 million Catholics over the last thirty-five years, because the overall U.S. population has grown at roughly the same rate, the actual proportion of the U.S. population that is Catholic has remained fairly stable, remaining between 21 and 25 percent throughout this period.[7]

The fact that the Catholic share of the U.S. population has remained stable over the last few decades is remarkable, given the dramatic increase in religious non-affiliation over this same period. Between 1990 and 2014, for instance, the percentage of Americans who are religiously non-affiliated (i.e., people who, when asked their religious affiliation, say "none" or "nothing in particular") increased from 7 percent to approximately 23 percent.[8] This relative stability in Catholics' share of the U.S. population amid broader trends of religious disaffiliation is largely due to post-1960 waves of new immigrants, many of whom migrated from countries and regions where Catholicism is strong—Mexico, Central and South America, parts of Africa and Southeast Asia.[9] Their arrival on U.S. shores has helped to stabilize Catholics' share of the population and secure Catholicism's ranking as the largest single religious denomination in the United States. This is not to diminish the fact that Catholicism has lost a sizable number of adherents through religious switching and disaffiliation. It has. But the loss of Catholics to other religions or to no religion at all has been offset by the influx of immigrants.[10] These new waves of immigrants have changed the racial and ethnic composition of the U.S. Catholic population over the last few decades.

Age

In terms of age, Catholics surveyed in 2017 are a bit older, on average, than those surveyed in 1987 (figure I.1). The average age of respondents in 1987 was 42, compared to an average age of 48 in 2017. This is a substantial difference, and not likely due to sampling error. But what does it mean? The primary reason why the average age of Catholic respondents has increased over these thirty years is because the average age of the entire population has also increased, and this shift in age is primarily due to the nation's largest birth cohort, the so-called baby-boomers, moving through the lifecycle.[11] Moreover, just as life expectancy has

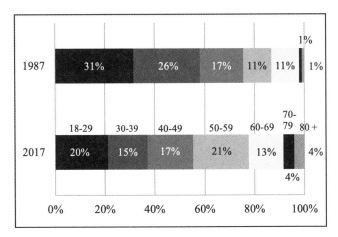

Figure I.1: Age Composition of U.S. Catholics, 1987 and 2017.
Sources: 1987 and 2017 American Catholic Laity Surveys (ACLS).

increased for the entire population, so too has it for the Catholic population. The surveys merely reflect these realities.

Generations

Sociologists have found generational comparisons to be among the most powerful tools for examining changes in beliefs and practices of everyday Catholics. In our analyses of generational differences, we used standard generational categories common in demographic research, but we modified them somewhat to reflect the cultural experiences common among Catholics.[12] These categories allow us to examine differences in the distribution of Catholics across generations between the first wave of the survey in 1987 and the current wave.

The leading institutional and cultural event in the life of the Catholic Church that distinguishes the experiences of different generations of Catholics was the Second Vatican Council (Vatican II). This was a global synodal convocation of Catholic bishops, consisting of four sessions lasting several weeks each, that took place from 1962 to 1965. Pope John XXIII convened it to open the church's windows to the modern world (i.e., an "*aggiornamento*," meaning "bringing up to date"). Vatican II summoned the largest and most multicultural group of bishops in the church's history to deliberate about what they deemed were the most pressing issues for the Catholic Church and the world. The discussion and documents that emerged led to a variety of wide-ranging theological and liturgical reforms, including renewal of Catholics' vision of what it means to be a participatory and relevant church, increased lay involvement and shared governance, and reform of the liturgy so that the Mass, which had been celebrated in Latin with the priest's back to the congregation, would henceforth be celebrated in each culture's vernacular language with the priest facing the people. Because these changes in theology and liturgy were so pronounced, Vatican II is a watershed event in the experiences of everyday Catholics.

Consequently, the earliest waves of our survey set a precedent for drawing comparisons between three generational categories—pre-Vatican II Catholics, Vatican II Catholics, and post-Vatican II Catholics. Pre-Vatican II Catholics are those who were born in 1940 or earlier and whose childhood and early adult experiences were shaped by the characteristics of the church before the Council. Their experience of the church during their formative years included attending Masses in Latin presided over by a priest with his back to the congregation. Although those attending Mass were usually passive observers, outside of Sunday Mass parishioners were often engaged in a variety of devotional and social activities, as parishes often served as centers of hospitality and welcome, especially for newly arriving European immigrants. Many of this generation supported the reforms called for by Vatican II, and worked hard to implement them. Many embraced, for example, Vatican II's renewed understanding of the church as the "People of God," its call for greater lay participation in the life and liturgy of the church, its creation of more formal roles for lay pastoral ministry (eventually known as lay ecclesial ministry), and its restoration of the diaconate as a permanent and stable order of ministry within the church. Some of our analyses of old survey data break this generation into two groups, the "older" and "younger" members of pre-Vatican II. The former are those born before 1928, and the latter are those born from 1928 to 1940. The older group corresponds to the "Greatest" or "GI" generation in many pop-cultural generational schemas. Few survive today. In the 1987 survey, one-fifth of the sample were older pre-Vatican II members. There are just 6 such respondents, out of the total sample of 1,507, in the 2017 survey.

The second generational category, Vatican II Catholics, are those born from 1941 to 1960, and came of age as the Council was unfolding. In comparison to pre-Vatican II Catholics, these Catholics were more intensely engaged with, and more strongly affected by, the reforms of Vatican II. The oldest in this generation were twenty-one years old when the Second Vatican Council opened in October 1962, and the youngest were just five when it closed in 1965. Most of this generation had some experience or memory of the Mass in Latin before the switch to the vernacular. Their experience of Catholicism was radically different from that of previous generations. Rather than experiencing the church as hierarchical, unchanged, and unchangeable, as did their parents, Vatican II Catholics witnessed a transformation. They were among the first to volunteer for the new positions as lay ministers and permanent deacons, and they gradually assumed many of the pastoral responsibilities previously performed by religious sisters and brothers. Thus, this generation witnessed a transformation in the church from a hierarchically structured, clergy-dominated institution, to one that was more participatory, collaborative, and consultative.

The third generational grouping, post-Vatican II Catholics, are those who were born between 1961 and 1978, and thus have no lived experience of the pre-Vatican II church, and little or no memory of the tumultuous years immediately following the Council. Their experience is almost entirely of a church that had gone through *aggiornamento*. The church they grew up in celebrated Mass almost exclusively in English (or another vernacular language, if they were immigrants), with the priest facing the people, and the assembly expected to actively participate in the liturgy. Smaller in number than the generation that preceded them or the generation that followed them, the majority of post-Vatican II Catholics grew up in the suburbs, away from the intensely Catholic urban neighborhoods of their grandparents' generation. During the formative years of this generation, divorce rates surged, women's labor force participation increased, and traditional gender role expectations were largely eschewed. In fact, because both parents were often working full-time jobs, members of this post-Vatican II generation came to be known as "latch-key kids" since they had to let themselves into the house when they returned home from school. They were less likely than Vatican II Catholics to attend Catholic elementary school, and more

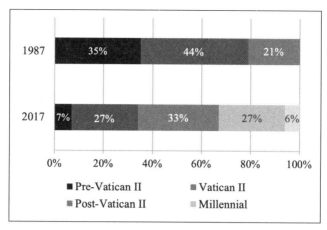

Figure I.2: Catholic Generations, 1987 and 2017.
Sources: 1987 and 2017 ACLS.

likely to have experienced parish-based, rather than school-based, religious education. These Catholics were formed under the papacy of St. John Paul II (1978–2005) and during a time of increasing polarization in American Catholicism.

When the first American Catholic Laity Survey was conducted in 1987, only these three generational groupings—pre-Vatican II, Vatican II, and post-Vatican II—were compared because they were the only generations in the survey at that time (figure I.2). Pre-Vatican II Catholics comprised 35 percent of U.S. Catholics, Vatican II Catholics comprised 44 percent, and post-Vatican II Catholics 21 percent. The smaller percentage of post-Vatican II Catholics relative to the other generational categories is understandable given that the youngest in this generation were not yet adults in 1987. In fact, only the oldest members of this generation (i.e., those born between 1961 and 1969) were included in the first wave of the survey.

By 2017, we had a different set of generations, with different experiences of church and different understandings of what it means to be Catholic. The pre-Vatican II generation, who were more than a third of those surveyed in 1987, now make up just 7 percent of survey respondents. Vatican II Catholics, who were the largest group in 1987, now make up just over a quarter of respondents. The post-Vatican II generation, who were just emerging as adults in 1987, now make up a third of all adult Catholics. And two new generations, Millennial (27%) and iGen (6%), make up the other third. By far the largest portion of American Catholic laity today (67%) are Catholics with no lived experience of the pre-Vatican II church or of the European immigrant enclaves of that period. As we shall see, compared to Catholics in 1987, Catholics in 2017 are also more geographically dispersed, suburban, educated, and racially and ethnically diverse. The Millennial generation appears for the first time in the 2005 survey sample, and the iGen appears for the first time in the 2017 sample. Thus, the current 2017 survey wave is the first time we are able to make comparisons across these five generational categories, though in some of our analyses we will merge the Millennials and iGens into one category and refer to them collectively as "young adults."

Millennial Catholics are those who were born between 1979 and 1994, and they comprise 27 percent of our 2017 sample. One of the chief historical events that defined this generation was the September 11, 2001 terrorist attacks. Because many in this generation witnessed these terrorist attacks during their formative years as teenagers or young adults, they helped shape their worldview. A significant ecclesial event at this time was the revelation of sexual abuse and subsequent episcopal coverup within the Archdiocese of Boston in early 2002. Compared to older generations, Millennial Catholics are less likely to have attended a Catholic elementary school, and their understanding of Catholicism was influenced primarily by the second half of the papacy of John Paul II and that of Benedict XVI.

The oldest iGen Catholics were just entering adulthood in 2017, and as a result they comprise only 6 percent of the 2017 sample. Those included in the 2017 survey were born between 1995 and 1999. These Catholics have been shaped by the pontificates of Benedict XVI and Francis. Compared to previous generations, they are even less likely to attend Catholic schools, and they are more racially and ethnically diverse. They are the first generation to enter adulthood as the number of religious non-affiliates in the U.S. has surpassed that of Catholics.

Geography

Another major demographic shift over the thirty years of our surveys is the geographic location of American Catholics (figure 1.3). The most

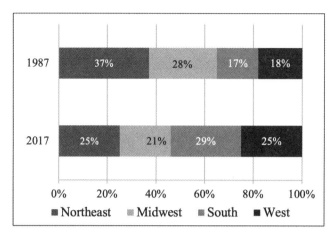

Figure I.3: Percentage Distribution of U.S. Catholics across Four U.S. Census Regions, 1987 and 2017.
Sources: 1987 and 2017 ACLS.

noteworthy geographic shift has been the movement of Catholics from north to south, and from city to suburb. In 1987, Catholics had already begun migrating away from the urban ethnic enclaves that had characterized major metropolitan areas in the North during the first half of the twentieth century. According to our surveys, in 1987 about two-thirds of all Catholics still lived in either the Northeast (37%) or the Midwest (28%), with the other third mostly concentrated in the suburbs around major cities in the South (17%) and the West (18%). By 2017, the picture looks much different. In that year, less than half of Catholics were living in either the Northeast (25%) or the Midwest (21%), and over half were living in either the South (29%) or the West (25%). In other words, over the course of these thirty years, the proportion of Catholics living in the Northeast and Midwest dropped by a total of 19 percentage points (by 12% in the Northeast and 7% in the Midwest), while the proportion residing in the South and West climbed by 19 percentage points (by 12% in the South and 7% in the West). This geographic redistribution of the Catholic population has had a profound influence on everyday Catholics and how they experience their church.

One of the chief ways this geographic shift has influenced American Catholics' experience of their church is in terms of access to Catholic schools. Since 1987, the total number of Catholic schools and Catholic school enrollments has declined by nearly 40 percent at the elementary level, and 20–30 percent at the secondary level.[13] Although the reasons for this decline are numerous and complex, one important contributing factor has been the migration of Catholics from the Northeast and Midwest to the South and West, and from city to suburb.[14] As Catholics moved into areas with sparse Catholic populations and weak Catholic infrastructures, few or no Catholic schools were available to serve them. Bishops and pastors in those rapidly growing areas were hard-pressed to provide liturgical and sacramental services to the flock, let alone build and staff Catholic schools. As Catholics left urban centers behind, many of the Catholic schools located in those settings were forced to close. The net effect was fewer Catholics attending Catholic schools.

This is evident in our survey data. Table 1.1 shows that attendance at Catholic elementary school was highest for younger members of the pre-Vatican II generation (born 1928 to 1940) and Vatican II Catholics (54% and 55%, respectively). It declined to 36 percent of post-Vatican II Catholics and 29 percent of Millennials. Although less dramatic, a similar decline is evident in Catholic high school attendance, from about a quarter (27 percent) for Vatican II to about one-sixth (17 percent) for each of the younger two generations. In contrast, the proportion of all Catholics who have attended a Catholic college or university has remained relatively stable across the generations. However, this is partly because the proportion who have attended *any* college has been steadily increasing. When examining only Catholics with at least some college education (the final row in table 1.1), the percentage who attended Catholic college has fallen noticeably. As we will see, this decline in access to, and enrollment in, Catholic schools affects the formation of children in Catholic faith and culture. With fewer Catholic children receiving faith formation outside of whatever their families provide, the likelihood of faith being transmitted to the next generation is diminished.

Education

While a declining proportion of Catholics have been attending Catholic elementary and secondary schools, the overall educational attainment

TABLE I.1: Estimated Percentage with Catholic Schooling, by Generation.

	Pre-Vatican II (Older)	Pre-Vatican II (Younger)	Vatican II	Post-Vatican II	Millennial
Attended Catholic grade school	40%	54%	55%	36%	29%
Attended Catholic high school	19	24	27	17	17
At least some college education	23	29	48	55	59
Attended Catholic college	7	8	9	6	8
Attended Catholic college (among college attendees only)	28	26	20	11	14

Sources: Multiple waves of the American Catholic Laity Surveys. Note: There are too few iGen respondents for reliable estimates.

of Catholics has continued to improve, a trend that really took off after the implementation of the G.I. Bill following World War II.[15] Comparing the American Catholic Laity Surveys to U.S. Census data shows that Catholics are similar to the general population with respect to educational attainment. Comparing our 1987 survey findings to our 2017 findings reveals that Catholics' educational attainment has been increasing at a pace similar to that of the general population.

In 1987, 21 percent of American Catholics surveyed reported that they had not completed high school, and almost eight in ten (79%) reported they had attained a high school diploma or more (figure 1.4). Nearly four in ten American Catholics (39%) had at least some college education. Twelve percent of Catholics possessed a college undergraduate degree, and another 7 percent had pursued or attained a graduate or professional degree, bringing the total portion who had attained a bachelor's degree or higher in 1987 to 19 percent.

By 2017, the percentage of U.S. Catholics who had not completed high school dropped to 16 percent, and the percentage with a high school diploma or higher rose to 84 percent. By 2017, the percentage of Catholics who reported having attended at least some college rose to approximately 53 percent, with almost three in ten having attained either an undergraduate degree (16%) or a graduate degree (12%). This increase in educational attainment has been shown to influence a variety of

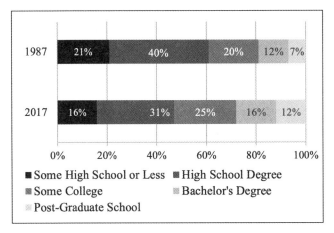

Figure I.4: Educational Attainment of U.S. Catholics, 1987 and 2017.
Sources: 1987 and 2017 ACLS.

Catholics' beliefs and behaviors with respect to the church, as seen in previous books in this series.

Race and Ethnicity

Another important trend over the course of these thirty years is the increasing racial and ethnic diversity among Catholics (figure I.5). White, non-Hispanic Catholics were 86 percent of respondents in 1987,[16] Hispanics were 10 percent, non-Hispanic Black Catholics were 3 percent, and all others (including Asians, multi-ethnics, and those of some other race or ethnicity) were about 1 percent. In 2017, White, non-Hispanic Catholics are 56 percent of respondents, and Hispanics are 35 percent. Black, non-Hispanic Catholics still make up 3 percent of respondents, but all others now make up 6 percent of respondents.

This increasing diversity is most striking when viewed across generations. Remember, two in three adult Catholics today are members of the post-Vatican II, Millennial, or iGen generations—the bottom three bars in figure I.6. Unlike the older two generations, these younger Catholics are strikingly diverse, with the youngest generation, iGen, being majority Hispanic.[17] These three younger generations also include a slightly larger proportion of other, non-Hispanic Catholics. As seen in previous

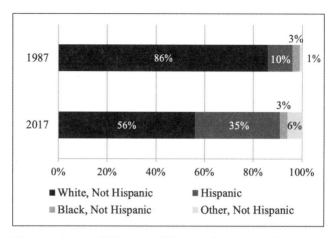

Figure 1.5: Race and Ethnicity of U.S. Catholics, 1987 and 2017.
Sources: 1987 and 2017 ACLS.

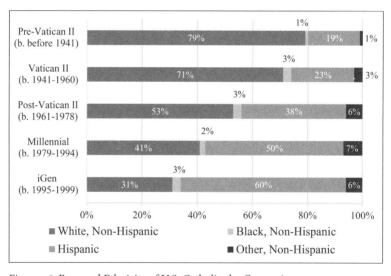

Figure 1.6: Race and Ethnicity of U.S. Catholics by Generation, 2017.
Source: 2017 ACLS, supplemented with data from the Pew Research Center.

books in the series, and as we will see later in this volume, this increasing racial and ethnic diversity among American Catholics has had a profound effect on how Catholics view themselves and their church.

Income

In 1987, nearly one in five respondents (19%) reported earning less than $10,000 a year in annual household income, and just 9 percent reported earning $75,000 or more. Adjusting for inflation, that $10,000 in 1987 translates to about $22,000 in 2017 dollars and the $75,000 translates to nearly $165,000. By 2017, just one in ten respondents (11 percent) reported less than $20,000 in annual household income and 17 percent reported earning $150,000 a year or more. It appears that, in 2017 dollars, U.S. Catholics are doing substantially better financially than they were in 1987. However, the average household income for Catholics in 1987 was about $25,000 (or about $55,000 in 2017 dollars). In the 2017 survey, respondents reported a mean annual household income of about $60,000, which suggests that the average annual household income of Catholics has actually stayed about the same over the last thirty years.

Order of the Book

The chapters that follow each open with a vignette to put a more "everyday" face on the statistics and interviews that comprise the bulk of each chapter. Each chapter also closes with an "Implications" section, which offers theoretical, methodological, or practical analysis of the data. Chapter 1 looks at multiple levels of the Catholic Church, from parish to national body, to understand both interviewees' and everyday Catholics' experiences and observations of Catholicism. Chapter 2 examines data from a variety of sources that demonstrate the declining moral authority of the Catholic bishops in the United States. Chapter 3 examines the ways racial and ethnic identity shapes Catholics' experiences of their church and world and also discusses ways ministers and leaders are responding to this increasing diversity in the Catholic population. Chapter 4 explores everyday Catholics' political and civic attitudes and behaviors as well as interviewees' concerns with a less than robust public Catholicism. Chapter 5 turns to everyday Catholics' and interviewees' perspectives on issues connected to family and sexuality. Chapter 6 looks at larger longitudinal trends to better understand the changing directions of everyday Catholics' beliefs and practices and what these mean for the institution. Finally, we conclude by looking at key themes through the lens of personalism, that is, a person-centered method of analysis that has import both sociologically and theologically.

We now turn to our first chapter: Church.

1

Church

In the Diocese of San Diego, the synodal process is highly participatory. It is early 2022, and the diocese is in the parish stage of the Synod on Synodality, called by Pope Francis in October 2021 and which altogether is a three-year (2021–2024) global process and, like previous synods, is marked by listening and dialogue focused on a particular theme. The theme of the synod, "For a Synodal Church: Communion, Participation, Mission," is amplified by its epigram "Enlarge the space of your tent" (taken from Isaiah 54:2). An important aspect of this synod is to discern what the Catholic Church is called to be in this moment, and what it means to go forth as an ongoingly listening church at all levels. With this backdrop in mind, on this mild, March evening, parishioners at Church of the Epiphany slowly begin to fill their parish hall for the first of three synod listening sessions—two in English and one in Vietnamese. Participants are a variety of ages. They make name tags for themselves—stopping by a table of cookies, juice, cheese, and wine—and make their way to the eighty or so folding chairs that face a large screen.

About five minutes past the official start time, a parishioner approaches the front and formally welcomes everyone. She thanks everyone for coming and outlines how the evening will proceed. She plays a video produced by the diocese that begins each of their listening sessions. It opens with their bishop explaining Pope Francis's hopes for the synod, and how their participation tonight helps inform that. Next, their chancellor describes the importance of being a church that listens, and the longer-term scope of the diocesan plan. The third person to appear is the Director of the Office for Life, Peace and Justice, and he details how the evening will proceed, emphasizing the importance of both listening and confidentiality. He says that the discussion will center around the themes of joy (the question being "Tell us about a time when you experienced joy with the church."), disappointment ("Tell us about a time when you experienced disappointment with the church."), and hope ("As you leave this experience, what is a hope you have for the church?"). He explains that participants will soon gather into small groups of six to eight people to be led by a designated facilitator as well as a trained note-taker. Before they do, the bishop gives his closing message. Then the in-person host invites the participants to move into their pre-assigned small groups.

In one small group, eight people gather. The facilitator prompts them to share a time when they experienced joy in the church. A theme that is nearly universal among the participants is the sacramental life of the church, whether their own reception of the sacraments or that of children and other family. Two participants mention the priest and deacon and the closeness they felt to them in these moments. Another theme is community. Although lighter memories—like making friends in Bible study groups—are common, one participant mentions how touched she was by the parish's support when her husband passed. They also emphasize how welcome they feel each Sunday.

People also share disappointments. A few people bemoan the church's inability to engage children, teens, and young adults. One opines that Protestant churches do much better in this respect. And although one parent is thankful that he could afford to send his three children to Catholic school, he notes that there was little to no economic diversity there. Several also comment on the sense of betrayal from decades of priests' sexual abuse and, especially, the bishops' coverup. This disappointment is exacerbated because it was a tragedy on a global scale; across the board, leaders had failed. One notes how difficult it is to evangelize about the beauty of the church given the reality of this sin. Another theme is a desire for the church to be more welcoming and inclusive. The participants believe that the dominant pastoral approach of the church is one of rigidity, and this turns many people off. As changes they wish to see, participants name female and married priests and a more widespread welcome of LGBTQ+ Catholics.

Little do these participants know, but twelve miles away at St. John Vianney, another listening session is voicing concerns rooted in a different theological perspective. Several are concerned that church leaders are slipping into moral relativism and believe a stronger statement reinforcing the church's position on same-sex relations and the place of LGBTQ+ Catholics in the church is needed. Two worry that Pope

Francis as well as their local bishop are making moral ambiguity a facet of Catholic moral teaching. One says that a stronger separation between Catholicism and secular society would reinvigorate the church; several people nod their head at this. And not too far from St. John Vianney, the parish demographics become more low-income and racially and ethnically diverse. At St. Peter Claver and down the road at Holy Redeemer, participants express a range of emotions—sadness, anger, and apathetic acceptance—when they recall being treated as second-class members due to income, legal status, or their racial identity. These experiences of marginalization have not only happened due to prejudicial actions on the part of fellow parishioners, but also on the part of parish leaders and even higher levels of church authority.

A final disappointment is negative pastoral experiences. Returning to Epiphany, participants talk about priests who were insensitive, or who denied sacraments to people in critical moments. Another person remembers when the parish priest was not available to make a sick call for her dying husband. But it is also the day-to-day experiences of church that leaves them disappointed, with a few feeling that the quality of homilies is quite low, specifically needing them to be more pastoral and uplifting. One criticizes the bishops as a national body, again citing the sex abuse cover-up and adding clericalism; the group nods. Many prioritize poverty, race, immigration, and the environment. A few miles away at St. John Vianney, the participants say abortion should be the church's top priority. Both groups feel polarization in the church.

Turning to the hope question, much of what was stated in their disappointments is reiterated, with a desire for resolution appended. Yet, something else also emerges. Many people state their gratitude for the openness and listening of those in their small group. They say how thankful they were to meet other people in the parish and discover they had so much in common with them. One of the small groups that evening decides to keep meeting monthly as a faith sharing group. The groups close in prayer. A few amble by the snack table for one last cookie before heading out to their cars.

The above is a composite vignette of the synodal process in the Diocese of San Diego.[1] It describes the efforts of one diocese—out of the 194 in the nation—to respond to Pope Francis's global convening of a Synod on Synodality. The confidential discussions that emerged in each parish's listening sessions were submitted to the diocese. The diocese, in turn, brought a cumulative report to the national body of bishops. The U.S. bishops, along with bishops' conferences in other nations, submitted a report to the Vatican, for the cumulative insights to be discussed, deliberated, and voted upon. This synod, from the pope's perspective, must be characterized by the three key tenets of communion, participation, and mission.[2] In his remarks opening the synod in October of 2021, Francis reminded listeners that being church required the participation of all the baptized. As in the other synods he convened, ordained leaders would need to listen closely to the lay faithful at all levels of the church. In the United States, this meant that an estimated 700,000 people added their voice to the process, either through a listening session or an online survey.[3]

Despite the abiding hope Pope Francis expresses at the opening of the synod, he also identifies three risks. First, he is concerned with formalism. That is, that the church undergoes a significant process and names areas in need of change, and yet this change is only superficial, and real changes are never made. The second risk is intellectualism, which keeps the discussion abstract and removed from the concrete lives of human persons. The final risk is complacency; he warns that, "'We have always done it that way'—is poison for the life of the Church." He cautions against applying old solutions to new problems and encourages everyone to take "seriously the times in which we are living."

The pope's address also includes three opportunities. His first opportunity is mentioned quite briefly, but its impact could be enormous: "[M]oving *not occasionally but structurally towards a synodal Church*, an open square where all can feel at home and participate" (italics in original). The second opportunity is to become a listening church. He contends that Catholics need to take more time to listen to God, to their brothers and sisters, and to those enmeshed in the realities of everyday life. Finally, Pope Francis believes the faithful have an opportunity to build a church of closeness. He claims that Catholics have a chance to better imitate God's compassion and tenderness for one another, to be a church immersed in and bringing healing to the world. He closes by citing theologian Yves Congar, "There is no need to create *another Church*, but to create a *different Church*" (italics in original).

This chapter examines Pope Francis's central synodal focus: church. We examine church from several perspectives, from the beliefs and practices of everyday Catholics to the parish to the larger institution of the Catholic Church in the United States. We begin by looking at the salience of Catholic beliefs among the faithful. Next, we explore parish experiences and concerns. Third, we review a theme that surfaces among our interviewees: the often too-fragile relevance of the Catholic Church. Finally, we close by considering some implications of the data.

Religious Beliefs and Practices among Catholic Laity

Official Catholic teachings are multifaceted, complex, and plural. They are also often open to interpretation—both in prudential application and in understanding—and can have a "both/and" or paradoxical quality to them that requires believers to stand in the tension. When we write that official Catholic teaching on a position is *clear*, this does not mean that it is *simple* or *settled*.[4] Still, teachings are typically quite clear. For instance, theologians, leaders, and Catholics with sophisticated knowledge of church teaching understand how to engage this; they are aware of the official position of the church, how much prudential space a teaching might provide, and why they might disagree with the church's position. Teachings are clear even while being complex and, at times, contested. However, rather than examining official beliefs, this section instead examines the centrality of beliefs and practices for everyday Catholics.

We asked everyday Catholics about nine different beliefs and practices (figure 1.1). For each, there were three response categories: "essential to the faith," "somewhat essential," and "not essential at all." Five elements of Catholicism rise to the top, receiving a response of "essential" or "somewhat essential" from more than 80 percent of Catholics. The element deemed most essential—belief in Jesus's resurrection—is unsurprising; this is a central Catholic dogma, and its relevance is emphasized each week in Mass through various creeds. However, there is no simple pattern explaining the centrality or marginality of the other elements. For example, some high-ranking items are particular to Catholicism, such as devotion to Mary and having a pope. But the four seen as least essential—participating in devotions, obligatory weekly

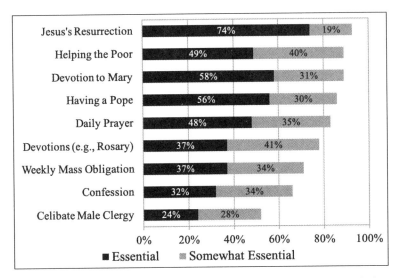

Figure 1.1: "Essential" or "Somewhat Essential" to What It Means to Be Catholic. *Source:* 2017 ACLS.

Mass attendance, confession, and priestly celibacy—are also particular to Catholicism.

Lastly, 83 percent of Catholics say that daily prayer is essential or somewhat essential to their vision of what it means to be Catholic, as do 66 percent for the sacrament of confession. While Catholicism has no formal expectation as to how often a Catholic must pray, prayer is seen as a very important aspect of faithful living. When asked how often they pray, 15 percent of Catholics pray more than once per day, 36 percent pray daily, 35 percent pray occasionally or sometimes, and 14 percent pray seldom or never. The Catholic Church expects the confession of serious sins at least annually.[5] Four percent participate in the sacrament of confession monthly or more often, 12 percent participate several times per year, another 12 percent confess yearly, 16 percent go to reconciliation less than once per year, and the majority—56 percent—seldom or never go to confession. It is striking that although two-thirds claim that confession is somewhat essential or essential to being Catholic, only 28 percent confess at least annually. As this section demonstrates, the salience of Catholic beliefs, practices, and identity varies considerably among Catholics.

We also asked Catholics to indicate their agreement with four items connected to Catholic beliefs and identity (figure 1.2). In alignment with Catholic teaching on the primacy of conscience, nearly nine in ten Catholics agree that Catholics can disagree with church teaching and still be considered loyal Catholics.[6] Just over three-fourths believe that "divorced Catholics who remarry without an annulment should, in consultation with a priest about their situation, be able to receive Holy Communion." Although we cannot determine why some disagree with this—it may largely be driven by their own, or awareness of others', personal marital circumstances (divorce), or it may be due to a misunderstanding of church teaching—it is, nonetheless, a pastoral possibility.[7] Either way, this view is embraced by a large majority of American Catholics, and has been for several decades, as documented in our prior surveys.

Catholic leaders—most visibly the bishops—expressed much concern when the Pew Research Center reported that only one-third of Catholics believe in transubstantiation.[8] This will be revisited in the implications section, but for now we note that our 2011 survey asked whether "the bread and wine really become the body and blood of Jesus Christ" or "the bread and the wine are only symbols of the body and blood of Jesus

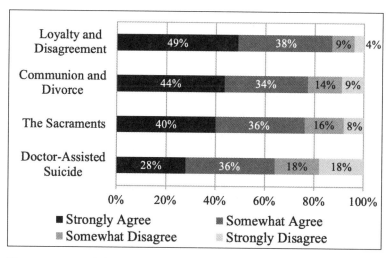

Figure 1.2: Lay Catholics' Religious Beliefs.
Source: 2017 ACLS.

Christ."[9] Our findings are reversed compared to Pew: 63 percent believe the former statement, aligning with Catholic teaching on the Eucharist, and 37 percent believe the latter, departing from teaching. Postponing the question of whether Pew's or our findings more accurately reflect everyday Catholics' understanding of the Eucharist, 76 percent of Catholics find the sacraments to be spiritually important. This signals that even when Catholics are unaware of or even knowingly disagree with the church on the specifics of a sacrament of the church, roughly three in four imply a deep spiritual encounter through participation in the church's sacramental life. That is, even if the cognitive dimension among Catholics is less than what leaders might want to see, the sacraments still speak to Catholics in a deeply affective way, so much so that three-fourths find them "essential" to their relationship with God. The final question in this series is the only one in which agreement goes against official teaching; a substantial majority agree that individuals who are terminally ill and in great pain should have a right to physician-assisted suicide. We now turn to how Catholics experience the most central institutional carrier of Catholicism in the United States: the parish.

Parish Experiences

When asked about what makes a strong parish, Paul Wilkes—retired journalist, founder of Homes of Hope, and author of *Excellent Catholic Parishes*—highlights the centrality of the parish in the American Catholic experience. "The parishes that are vital, you want to be there," he writes. "That's the key. Those are the places that people really feel wanted, needed, and appreciated. . . . You want to be on a winning team that's really making a difference. . . . When you talk about the Catholic Church, you talk about the parish. . . . When that parish is vital, people are vital." When later asked about what he thought might revivify American Catholicism, Wilkes continues with this thread: "It's so obvious and so difficult. It's obvious that people need and want it, and it's so difficult as to how to do that." This section begins by looking at some of the observations of parish life that interviewees share, especially in their desire for a more relational experience for those attending Mass. Next, we turn to both interview and survey findings to explore the reasons why people attend Mass. We close this section by exploring interviewees' thoughts on liturgy.

Importance of Relationship

Interviewees have much to say on the ways parish staff can foster greater relationality in parishes. Echoing Wilkes, they insist that the parish is the most vivid and regular encounter Catholics have with institutional Catholicism. As such, it is imperative that this encounter be relational, positive, and meaningful. Many believe parishes too often fail to provide this to members, especially in key moments. They articulate the desire to provide a more relational parish experience through two main themes: community and hospitality.

Beginning with community, our survey findings show that the relationship Catholics have with their parish is complicated, with some questions revealing great satisfaction and others showing that many Catholics are more loosely tethered to or disconnected from their local parish. Most Catholics report at least some parish connection, with 60 percent registered at a parish. Forty-four percent believe Catholic parishes are too big and impersonal; clearly a large minority of Catholics would like a more relationally meaningful church experience and feel that parishes have room for improvement. Further, 60 percent of Catholics who attend Mass monthly or more say that seeing parish members is a personally significant reason for attending; as parishes foster relationships, they foster compelling reasons to attend.

Some of the interviewees are deeply touched by experiences of community in their current or previous parishes. Dr. Timothy O'Malley, academic director of the Notre Dame Center for Liturgy, recalls from his childhood, "[Our family's] cash flow wasn't exceedingly high, and one of the things I remember is how present the parish was when we needed it. So that is my first awakening to the power of the church. It was in this solidarity that a bunch of people from a parish actually care about us." This experience not only had social consequences for O'Malley; it also shaped his ecclesiology: "I think that awakened me to what I call, theologically, the church as a communion. A communion that brings all men and women into a love, a love that is not created by them. . . . And through that [childhood experience] I was attracted to a communion of men and women dedicated to a love that they do not create, a love that comes to them first as gift: the love of Christ." O'Malley demonstrates with his own biography something discussed by many leaders:

the power of caring relationships in leading people to a strengthened religious commitment. Further, communion is a powerful image in Catholic theology. It is both a mystical unity that believers share with one another in this world and the next (e.g., the communion of saints) as well as being another word for the Eucharist, the "source and summit" of the Catholic faith.[10] These words are not used lightly among Catholics, revealing the significance of relationships in parish life.

Dominican sister Theresa Rickard, president of RENEW International, an organization that helps to revitalize parish life, discusses her organization's success in forming community in parishes by training small group facilitators, something she notes that is especially important as parishes are growing in size: "[Dioceses are] merging parishes, parishes are getting bigger and bigger. So, I think the whole thing about the parish as a community of small communities becomes a vision that thriving parishes are beginning to adopt." Although the Catholic population is fairly stable, the number of priests per Catholic is declining.[11] This is forcing many dioceses to merge two or more parish communities into one. This reorganization troubles Catholics on a variety of levels, from losing their parish building to feeling that they are being forced to abandon their historical way of worshiping, socializing, and "being church."[12] Nonetheless, barring cases of significant attrition from those who oppose the merge, parish mergers result in larger parishes. Small groups are one way that newly growing parishes create a sense of connection between parishioners.

While community focuses more on the regular members of the parish and the bonds they share, hospitality signals an intentional welcome of new or otherwise marginal members. One of the challenges parishes face in being places of welcome is staffing shortages. John Michael Reyes, lay parish minister who works closely with the United States Conference of Catholic Bishops (USCCB) staff on parish related projects, sees this among his colleagues: "That's the challenging thing, where our parish staff members are overworked and too busy to take notice." Catholics are not especially generous givers, donating to their parishes about half what Protestants give.[13] This usually means that parishes are understaffed and ministers are spread thin with programs and other job duties; introducing themselves to a newcomer might fall off their cognitive radar on a frenetic Sunday.

Others noted that it is not the size of parishes or even busy staffs that are the problem. Indeed, some interviewees noted that the professionalization of the parish leads many Catholics to take a more passive role in their faith. As society becomes more credentialed, people can feel that they are proficient in one area, but then defer to pastoral leaders in spaces where they have not been formally trained. Jason Simon, president of Evangelical Catholic, an organization that helps form lay people, discusses the need for Catholics to play a more active role in parish life. "Parishes are big," he notes. "The problem, though, is not really the size of the parish. The problem is that there aren't more apostolic laborers in the parish among the lay people. . . . If we have more laborers in the pews, the parishes—no matter how big they are—won't feel big because there will be more people in the pews equipped for this kind of personal engagement." Catholics in the pews take inadequate responsibility for the spiritual care and formation of one another. But whether a particular parish is understaffed or has a more passive assembly, the result is the same: Catholics do not have vibrantly welcoming worship communities, and they fail to build relationships among members.

A second hospitality-related concern is failing to offer pastoral support to loosely tethered members at key points in their faith journey. There are moments, like wanting to become a godparent, that require Catholics who do not typically engage with parish life to approach parish staff in a one-on-one or small group setting. We have personally heard countless stories of Catholics describing negative parish experiences; these are familiar to the interviewees, as well. Nicole Perone, National Coordinator for the Leadership Roundtable's ESTEEM, a program for Catholics in college, uses the phrase "gateway moments" to highlight encounters that have the potential to lead marginal Catholics into a deeper faith life:

> Whether it's attending Mass for the first time or approaching the parish for a sacrament, like, "We want to get married here and baptize our child here." Or, "I never received the sacrament of confirmation so how do I do that?" And those moments of encounter are, more often than not, at best impersonal, at worst very detrimental and off-putting. . . . How we respond in that moment of encounter can make the difference between someone saying, "Oh, parish life is just so impersonal, I don't fit in here,

it's so unwelcoming," or, "Wow, they made me feel so seen and included, and everyone was so gracious!" That's what we should be going for. Jesus calls us to Disney-level hospitality . . . just this radical falling over ourselves to make you feel at home here.

She imagines that parishes could do a much better job of offering welcome and encounter in these gateway moments. But too often parishes present a lukewarm or even cold threshold.

Perone, a young adult herself, also notes that these parish-level encounters are extraordinarily significant for people's relationship to the church as a whole: "So many young adults I encounter aren't even thinking that much about [the November 2021 USCCB meeting], but they're thinking about the fact that they went to St. Mary's to try to get a certificate to be a godparent and didn't know where to go and people were kind of rude. So, they're not thinking about church as this big thing. . . . Church for them is the most local [expression] and what we do in those little, local moments." While media and some leaders might emphasize bishops and other ordained leaders as "the face" of the church—especially at the diocesan and global level—quite often it is personal experience that shapes most Catholics' understandings of church. Interviewees bemoan subpar ministry and mourn the reality that parishes, ministers, and everyday Catholics in the pews fail to offer people the meaningful encounters they need.

Mass Attendance

Our 2017 survey asked everyday Catholics how often, aside from weddings and funerals, they attend Mass (figure 1.3). Twenty-nine percent report attending weekly or more, 10 percent attend two or three times per month, 9 percent attend about monthly, 22 percent attend a few times per year, and 31 percent attend seldom or never. Catholics attending Mass monthly or more often are at least somewhat connected to parish life. Separating those who attend frequently (47% of sample) from those who attend infrequently (53%), we asked the frequent attenders about the reasons they attend Mass, and similarly asked the infrequent attenders about reasons they did not go to Mass more often.[14]

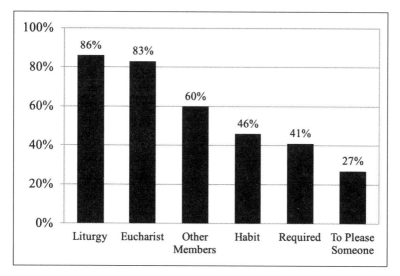

Figure 1.3: Reasons Frequent Attenders Go to Mass.
Source: 2017 ACLS.

Respondents in both groups are able to pick multiple reasons, and several rose to the top for both frequent and infrequent attenders. For frequent attenders, the liturgical experience itself and the need to receive communion each receive extraordinarily high support. These might be considered intrinsically rewarding reasons that affirm central religious teachings and meet spiritual needs. Clearly, large numbers of regular attenders experience a real need for the sacrament, which is good news for church leaders concerned with a declining significance of the Eucharist among Catholics. Enjoying fellow parishioners is also a strong response at 60 percent. Given the relational aspect of religious belonging, parish leaders might consider this response likewise meaningful and not simply social. Lay and ordained ministers may find the remaining responses to be more disheartening than these first three. Large minorities of Catholics say they attend out of habit or because the church requires they attend. Finally, just over one in four claim they attend Mass because they want to please someone close to them. These final three responses are more extrinsically motivated but are nonetheless important in building the church community.

Many interviewees were pleasantly surprised when we shared these findings with them, with some explicitly citing the Pew survey as leading them to expect that some of these reasons would be much lower. Others thought that the high percentage of frequent attenders wanting to receive the Eucharist is to be expected, given the primacy of this sacrament in the life of the church. One such interviewee is María del Mar Muñoz-Visoso, executive director of the USCCB's Secretariat for Cultural Diversity in the Church. "For the people who are high in attendance," she says, "they in general understand that it's important to be part of the community, to participate in the liturgy of the church as a community and to celebrate as a community. They know that we're made for communion, and that sharing the Eucharist is the highest form of expressing that community, if you will, the Word and the body and blood of Christ." It is not only important to gather as a community in shared liturgy and sacrament, Muñoz-Visoso claims, but it satisfies deep needs built into our humanness. Some wanted to see the community response higher. Cardinal Blase Cupich of the Chicago Archdiocese underscores the importance of liturgy, Eucharist, and community in the life of a parish: "I have dedicated my life to liturgical reform, having received my doctorate in the area of liturgy and sacraments. And so I believe that a good liturgy does in fact keep people anchored into the life of the church, as well as the Eucharist. . . . Coming to Mass is also about socialization. And it is important, I think. It's a very human need to come together, with that benefit." Cupich is representative of the interviewees; far from dualistic—with the spiritual on the one side and the earthly on the other—they see the human person as integrated in both. Effective ministry, they argue, recognizes this.

None of the reasons for not attending Mass more often receive majority support from the infrequent attenders, but two came close (figure 1.4). Forty-five percent of Catholics who attend Mass a few times per year or less frequently say they do not attend more often due to work or family responsibilities, and forty percent say this is because they are "Just not a religious person." There is a fairly large drop to the next response, followed by a gradual decline. Twenty-nine percent report busyness, 28 percent respond that it is not a mortal sin to miss Mass, 25 percent say health reasons, 22 percent answer that the Mass schedule

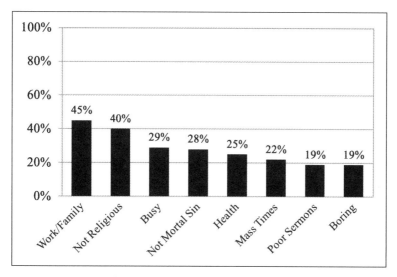

Figure 1.4: Reasons Infrequent Attenders Do Not Go to Mass.
Source: 2017 ACLS.

is inconvenient, 19 percent say poor homilies, and a final 19 percent explain that Mass is boring.

Rather than getting discouraged when shown these findings, interviewees immediately began to find insights here. First, while there is the popular "soccer" cliché that sports and other extracurricular activities have usurped family life, our interviewees were encouraged that family was a priority and were sympathetic to the time and energy that work and family require. Jason Simon saw this as a way to reach out to those more loosely tethered to parish life: "If I was a pastor and I saw this chart, then on days when I know I'm getting these [infrequently attending] people—Easter, Christmas, Ash Wednesday—I am hitting it hard how the gospel is good news for our work and for our families." Simon is pushing pastors to think more about who is coming on significant days and to counter some of these obstacles.

Looking to other responses, interviewees did not think that the forty percent of Catholics who say they simply are not religious means that people are simply more secular. Instead, many believe that parishes are not helping people discover that they are, in fact, deeply religious beings who are free to prioritize Mass over other things. Deborah Rose-Milavec, co-director of FutureChurch, offers, "When people are motivated to do something, all these things [e.g., being busy, work obligations] don't matter." Our interviewees argue that Mass experiences fail to connect to work and family, or help people tap into their own spiritual longings, or make a case that parish life is worth their time.

Sandra Coles-Bell, executive director of the National Black Sisters' Conference, believes that experiencing Mass as boring is especially common among younger Catholics: "Children really are just incredibly bored with Mass and liturgy and just don't understand the rituals that go along with it. So, I can understand that 'It's boring' response, especially for children. And I think that's how we are losing so many of our young adults. It's starting at a very early age." Coles-Bell's response indicates that "It's boring" could connect to family obligations; if children do not want to go to Mass, that makes it all the more difficult to go.

Several of these responses indicate that many do not find Mass attractive or engaging. And while Catholicism has not lessened the obligation for Catholics to attend Sunday Mass, these findings indicate that a fair number believe this is the case.[15] Parish life is tenuous or nonexistent for more than half of American Catholics, thus underscoring the critical potential of the Synod on Synodality to help recraft a more participatory and mission-driven church community, especially locally.

Liturgy

The final part of this section on parish life explores the most prominent liturgical concerns among interviewees. Liturgy, or the official rites comprising public worship and prayer, is no small matter for Catholicism. The *Catechism of the Catholic Church* reminds readers of "the ancient saying: *lex orandi, lex credendi*. . . . The law of prayer is the law of faith: the Church believes as she prays. Liturgy is a constitutive element of the holy and living Tradition."[16] How people pray shapes what they believe. The various markers of the liturgical seasons; when the community sits, stands and kneels; the words spoken at baptism—none of these ritualized external practices is inconsequential; rather, each communicates and shapes the internal beliefs and commitments of the adherents as well as affirms their communally shared identity as Catholics. There were two perspectives interviewees took when discussing quality liturgy.

The first was to emphasize what all good liturgical experiences held in common. The second was that liturgical expressions should vary considerably depending on the context of the worshiping community, what we call, in the spirit of Francis's synodality, a "big tent" approach.

Starting with what is held in common, interviewees emphasized that good liturgy is rooted in the worshiping community. Interviewees articulated an open approach as to what prayerful liturgy could look like. For example, Russ Petrus, co-director of FutureChurch, an organization concerned with inclusion issues in church life, attested that "Liturgy means the work of the people. Liturgy has to be of the people, and I think oftentimes liturgy is of the church [hierarchy]. And so we get wrapped up in things like, what materials the vessels are made out of, whether or not this song conveys an appropriate theology, or whether it's too androcentric. And a lot of energy and time is spent on postures and things of that nature that I think can contribute to good liturgy as long as the liturgical experience is rooted in the people's lived experience." Good liturgists ensure that music, preaching, environment and other elements resonate with the community of believers. Mar Muñoz-Visoso speaks about the importance of the Liturgy of the Word: "Good proclamation and a fiery homily that unites heaven and earth. That, in essence, is speaking words, God's message, but is also touching real life, is touching my reality." Good liturgy helps people see the spiritual significance of their everyday lives.

Another element interviewees believe should characterize all liturgy is reverence. Although reverence is universally lauded, interviewees displayed an openness as to how reverence could be expressed. Chris Check, president of Catholic Answers, a popular media outlet, articulates, "I'd say this is an objective truth, there are standards of beauty, and there are standards of liturgical beauty. . . . And reverence can be something that perhaps in one culture exhibits in one way or another. But nonetheless, I think there are fixed standards of reverence, where it's clear that what's underway is sacred because it conveys a sense of the sacred and of mystery." Interviewees maintain that there are objective standards of reverence, and recognize that there may be diversity in its expression. For Paul Wilkes, reverence means "the priest is involved, you can feel his emotional involvement. . . . And the people, of course, being into it, singing and wanting to be there and being friendly to one another before, during, and after." Emotional and relational affectivity on the part of the presider and community communicate reverence. Nicole Perone discusses the music, "[s]pectacularly beautiful music, but you could sing along, too, which is important; it was not just performance art." Reverence is communicated in being affectively touched and in communal participation, here in music. Dr. Timothy O'Malley emphasizes the transcendent orientation of the liturgy as well as the belief that something is "at stake" in worship: "This is what I call reverence: that there's something at stake in what we're doing and what we're doing is worshiping the living God." Reverence orients believers to God and is the community's way of saying that what they are doing matters deeply. The common thread for Catholic leaders is that reverence is important for both the community and the worshipers' ability to encounter God in the liturgy.

Although there are the common threads—being rooted in the community and reverence—of quality liturgy, as just discussed, interviewees also advocate for "big tent" Catholicism. That is, even with the specific rubrics of worship expected by Catholicism, there is a wide diversity of Catholic implementation and, in the interviewees' eyes, this is a good thing. Quality liturgy can and should vary with the local context. Important here is that, although Catholic worship may look very different in an affluent, White, New England suburb than it does in a low-income, Hispanic urban parish in the West, neither of these expressions is more authentically Catholic than the other. This big tent image—especially with its emphasis on diversity—is unifying for Catholicism.

The big tent metaphor allows leaders to see unity amid diversity in liturgical contexts. Sandra Coles-Bell previously worked in her archdiocese's Office for Cultural Diversity and Outreach, and notes the unifying thread in the big tent idea of liturgy, "Through that job I came to really understand the ritual expressed in many different cultures, in many different ways, with so many words. When I see liturgy, I know where I am within it, even while I see it expressed with a different vibrancy, different energies, a different focus. . . . It is all so rich. When I celebrate with my African brothers and sisters, I don't speak what they speak, but I understand the significance of what we're sharing." The diversity of Catholic worship is found in the particularities, which are cohered and made familiar through the universal rituals. The big tent provides an enlarged space for everyone.

Relevance

Matthew Kelly, founder of Dynamic Catholic, an organization that aims to deepen Catholics' faith, described comments he shared with some parish staff: "'Your pastor got up and he gave a homily complaining about what people wear to church. If the center of the bullseye is the most important aspect of Catholicism, how many concentric circles do we have to go out before we get to that issue?' And it's a fascinating discussion. Now we might disagree about what the center of the bullseye is. But in that conversation, most people would agree that you have to go out many, many, many concentric circles before we get to 'What do we wear to church on Sunday?'" Sometimes parishes spend their energies on things far from the center of the faith and their audiences' lives. This section examines how well church leaders demonstrate the essential relevance of the faith.

Topics and Approach

In evaluating American Catholic leadership, our interviewees most often discuss the bishops as a body. They are typically discouraged—or report that their constituents are discouraged—by the bishops. They say either the topics the bishops are prioritizing do not align with the needs of the Catholics they work with or that diocesan and parish leaders' approaches lack sufficient pastoral savvy. For instance, Sandra Coles-Bell is disappointed in American Catholicism's response to racism: "I think the biggest challenge has been the—and I'm going to just have to say the word—ignorance of certain leaders in speaking about Black Lives Matter. That it's a political organization and—how offensive—and that the church is not racist. How offensive. After all of the revelation that we've witnessed and seen not only in the past two years, but over and over again, and yet [some leaders] keep wanting to ignore and erase the sin of racism, the sin. And to make it plausible." As will be discussed further, many Catholics need a more robust response to racism from their bishops. Susie Tierney, executive director of JustFaith Ministries, summarizes the concerns of Catholics she has spoken with—the pandemic, poverty, climate change, racial justice—but her contacts bemoan the bishops' response, "The bishops just had their conference in November

[2021]. . . . And what people saw coming out, all the communications related to the bishops' conference were about whether or not Catholic politicians should be denied communion. And so for our audience, they were like, 'The bishops don't have a relevant voice because they're not talking about anything that's happening here' . . . there's a lot of launching into a void happening at that larger level." For many interviewees, the bishops as a body are not in touch with the concerns that preoccupy most Catholics.

But at the same time, there are signs of hope that a different and more pastoral approach is readily possible. Nicole Perone had much to say on this at both the national and the parish level. Beginning with the bishops, Perone recounts a reception for bishops and young adults at a USCCB meeting that gave her great hope and amplifies the importance of being reflexive about what leaders communicate:

> I asked them, "In reading that pastoral framework [for youth and young adults], what's one thing going on there where you see yourself?" And almost every bishop said more or less, "We love you and we want you here and you belong here." It wasn't any doctrinal thing. It was this heart of love saying, "Oh my God, I want them to know we love them. I want them to know that we want them here so badly, that *our hearts are for them*." And we can work with that, that's workable! We just need to keep doing that and keep making that the most outward facing thing.

If Catholic leaders want a message of love, belonging, and inclusion to be at the center of their mission, they need to make this first in all things. Perhaps more than bishops, priests play a very strong role in what a marginal member's encounter with Catholicism might look like; we turn to the survey and interview data to explore how Catholics perceive the pastoral efficacy of priests, bishops, and lay parish leaders.

Priests and Other Leaders

Several questions on our survey had to do with leadership. Looking first at parish leadership, our survey finds a mixed bag (figure 1.5). Catholics have an overwhelmingly positive impression of priests as a whole, with 88 percent agreeing that they do a good job. However, when evaluating

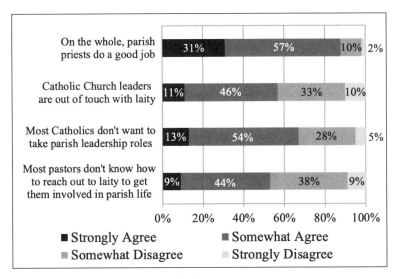

Figure 1.5: Opinions on Parish Leadership.
Source: 2017 ACLS.

"Catholic Church leaders" broadly, over half agree that they are out of touch with the laity. There is also an apparent reluctance to serve in parish leadership positions among everyday Catholics, with two-thirds agreeing that most Catholics do not want to serve their parish in this capacity. At the same time, just over half say that pastors are not skilled in inviting the laity into greater parish involvement. Although this shows that Catholics are by and large affirming of their local clergy, these findings also reveal a disconnect between lay Catholics and their leaders. The idea that leaders are out of touch in a few ways, as our interviewees indicate, seems to be the case, even while Catholics harbor a fondness for priests.

We also asked how satisfied they were with church leadership at several levels (figure 1.6). Moving from most global to most local, Catholics have an astoundingly high level of approval for the leadership of Pope Francis, with 85 percent approval, 57 percent of that being "strongly approve." Large majorities of Catholics are satisfied with other leadership; the leadership receiving the lowest satisfaction rating, the national body of bishops, still stands at 70 percent. Seventy-six percent are satisfied with the leadership of their own local bishop, 79 percent with their

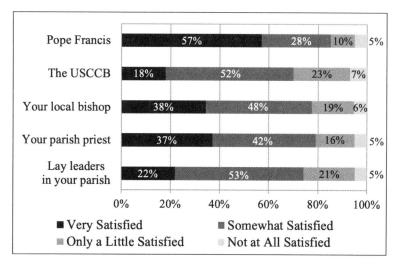

Figure 1.6: Satisfaction with Church Leadership.
Source: 2017 ACLS.

parish priest and seventy-five percent with lay leaders in their parish. These numbers reflect rather positive perceptions of leaders at a variety of levels. However, it should be disconcerting to Catholic leaders that 21 and 26 percent of Catholics are not satisfied with their parish priests and lay leaders, respectively.

Even with the reluctance of some Catholics to take on leadership at their parish, support for lay decision-making at the parish, diocesan, and global levels remains strong. The sense of a right to authority tends to be strongest for matters that have the most local impact (figure 1.7). Beginning with the parish level, 80 percent say the laity should have the right to decide how their parish spends money, 76 percent say this of selecting priests for their parish, and 75 percent say this for deciding about parish closings. Seventy-three percent desire lay voices in spending diocesan income, 68 percent say this of selecting bishops for their diocese, and 63 percent want this in deciding whether women should be ordained to the priesthood.

There have been studies on the declining number of priests,[17] the gradual historical shift in their own understanding of their priesthood,[18] and priests' wellbeing amid the sexual abuse crisis.[19] Turning to the external evaluation of priests, although figure 1.5 shows that the typical

Catholic harbors warm feelings toward priests, most of the interviewees were less impressed with priests in general. Several referred to older generations of priests who were more connected to their flock. Cardinal Blase Cupich showcases this in his own priestly emphasis, having been ordained a priest in 1975:

> I remember when I was first ordained and I came back, having studied in Rome, my good old Irish pastor said to me, "I'll just give you one piece of advice. People don't care how much you know. They want to know if you know them." And that always stuck with me. We don't go and give people the *Catechism* right away and say, "Here, learn this." They want to know if we know them and their lives and their circumstances. And this is the great mission and the approach that the Holy Father is saying when he says we need to encounter, we need to accompany, and we need to integrate people.

This idea of the priest being close to and knowing his flock is a hallmark of priests ordained in that era. Some interviewees voiced a concern that today's seminarians are caught in clerical trappings that hinder their ministry.

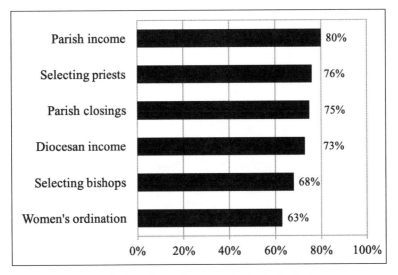

Figure 1.7: Areas in which Catholics Favor Lay Authority in Decision-Making. *Source:* 2017 ACLS.

Poor preaching is another concern voiced by several interviewees. Sister Theresa Rickard did not name her research sources—these may have been studies internal to her organization—but is confident that lay Catholics prioritize quality preaching higher than priests and deacons do, "The most important thing in the liturgy is good preaching and, quite honestly from my own anecdotal experience as well as the research, this is a disconnect because the people of God say preaching is really, really important. The preaching must connect to people's lives. It needs to be meaningful. And when you look at where it ranks among priests and deacons, it's not the top of the list, it's number five or so." Chris Check echoes this, "Most preaching is banal, very little is said . . . you get to the end of the sermon and you say, 'What did he say? What are my two takeaways here? What am I going to do this week as a consequence of the sermon?'" The interviewees believe that most preaching is not of the quality it needs to be, nor is it often relevant to the parish community. Pew data likewise show that Catholic satisfaction with preaching is lower than that of Protestants.[20]

A final piece on leadership is Christology. Christology raises a question: how does a particular understanding of Christ shape what it means to be a Christian and a church today? Jesus, understandably, is a recurring theme across all our interviewees. It is worth drawing upon a lengthy quote offered by Matthew Kelly to distill some of the central Christological themes:

> Jesus's fundamental model of ministry was to, essentially, never preach to anyone before he fed them, healed them, comforted them. He always dealt with a human need before he did the preaching. We have lost that as a church. We've lost our ability to connect and integrate the gospel with the real challenge of people's lives. And by doing that, we're losing those trigger experiences. Because if you are drowning in credit card debt and someone from the church comes and helps you overcome your credit card debt—they don't even talk about God, they don't talk about church, they don't ask you to come to church or tell you to go to church—they just say, "Let us help you with your credit card debt. Let us help you think about it, get a plan." That person is connected to that person and their church forever. It is an absolute trigger moment. It is a moment of inseparable connection. And if that person overcomes their credit card debt,

it becomes an experience of gratitude that literally never ends. And so when we don't meet people where they're at, we're not able to create those trigger moments. Because the best way to win someone to the gospel is to show them how the gospel relates to the very worst part of their life. Because if it works there, it works everywhere.

Kelly is saying a lot here. First, Jesus always began his ministry with the deeply human need of the person right in front of him. Whether that is credit card debt, poor grades, addiction, depression, burnout, or a tense relationship with a loved one, the human need is where Jesus starts. Second, this is not where ministers tend to start even though, as Cupich states above, good ministers—or Christians broadly—start by understanding the person before them. Third, the church as a whole is failing in this regard. When a person has identified a need, and a Christian presents this person with something that appears totally unrelated to that need, the Christian comes off at best as clueless, or at worst as completely insensitive and incompetent. Fourth, real encounters, even those not overtly spiritual, are capable of transforming the person in a significant way. Finally, Jesus does not back away from those who feel lost, broken, or despairing. Catholics need to dive into those spaces because God's love can work there. While this is Kelly's quote, many interviewees lifted up these ideas in whole or part. Yet, most parish ministry is limited to the expressly spiritual, such as Bible studies, that may or may not connect to human needs; in the leaders' assessment, this is a loss for both church and world. Yet even given these shortcomings, the church has substantial spaces of influence in people's lives in some areas. To better understand institutional relevance, we turn to the specific areas of strength and weakness named by the interviewees.

Church Vitality and Weakness

As far as outstanding areas of church vitality go, one was nearly universal among the interviewees: the laity. When asked about the strong areas of Catholicism, phrases like "lay ministers," "lay movements," "small Christian communities," and "lay apostolates" were common. There was a great esteem for the laity and the spaces in which they gather and are sent as Catholics. However, when interviewees discussed strengths, they tended to qualify their response. Often the strength was in a particular case or situation that revealed simultaneously a space where improvement was needed. Jason Simon's response is a good example of the "both/and" quality that characterized the interviewees' responses. Simon offered an analysis of the laity's gifts using the terms *ad intra*—referring to things internal or more explicitly within the domain of church life, such as doctrine or religious devotions—and *ad extra*, meaning things beyond formal ecclesial structures or the overtly religious, such as work or family life:

> I've seen in parishes and campus ministries where our organization worked, you get the *ad extra* mission of the church functioning through well-formed, equipped laity. . . . And it starts to form the *ad intra* in a way that supports the *ad extra*. . . . The church sees that this is transformative for the Catholic community. And now the conversation inside the church is how do we support, build up, and pour gasoline on this *ad extra* activity? And that sets our ecclesiology right. Now we are looking to support the laity in the *ad extra*. . . . In contrast, to invite people to the liturgy, I don't think that's going to be the most effective way to equip people to go out to evangelize and make disciples in the world, in their lay apostolates, and then to draw other people to the Eucharist as they themselves are drawn to receive Jesus in the Eucharist. Now, we've got an ecclesiology that's supporting the lay apostolate, serving the lay apostolate, serving the baptismal priesthood. And then the ordained priesthood is looking to support that and push it out rather than suck lay people into the parish structures, into the *ad intra*, get them all busy in church, making less time for apostolates in the world.

The strength that Simon discusses so enthusiastically is a church that forms the laity to actively bring their faith to the various other commitments in their life.

Simon continues, bemoaning that this is not the typical approach parish leaders take, "I think right now we, as a church, are making a mistake in a lot of areas. We're trying to suck lay people into the church to get involved, to build up the structures, to strengthen the structures, to offer more activity on parish grounds, which then gives the lay people less time in the world in an apostolate." Catholic laity could have a profound impact on society if more church leaders would push them to integrate their faith with their secular commitments. With many parishes understaffed, the laity are stepping into both professional and volunteer roles in parishes. This is desperately needed. However, some worry that it distracts them from what, since Vatican II, the church has taught is a primary mission of the laity, to "work for the sanctification of the world from within as a leaven."[21] For the laity to neglect life beyond the parish walls serves neither the *ad extra* nor the *ad intra* mission of the Catholic Church. To be clear, none of this is to say that the laity should not be involved in their local parish—none of the interviewees would have argued for this and all lauded the initiative and entrepreneurial spirit of the laity—but their point was that it is important not to confuse where the laity can be most generative and whether parishes are fostering this sort of influence. In fact, the exemplary parishes that were highlighted by interviewees often offered a wide range of lay opportunities for every age group, but it was a matter of whether these groups pointed the members outward to the world for mission, or inward to the parish in a self-interested way.

As for notable weaknesses named, the issues come as no surprise for those familiar with Catholic life in the United States: they pinpointed insufficient focus on racial justice, lack of healing and accountability regarding the sex abuse crises, increasing disaffiliation, financial troubles, lack of leadership by women and Catholics of color, decreasing numbers of priests, and not accompanying people well. Although this is not an exhaustive list, these weaknesses rose to the top for interviewees. And while the issues were many, there remained a common way they spoke about them: the weaknesses named tended to be areas where the church was failing itself. This was more obvious with concerns like racial justice; many interviewees believe the USCCB needs to offer a collective condemnation of systemic racism and speak out on it regularly within their respective dioceses. Similarly, many believe that the church must make genuine efforts of reparation toward sex abuse survivors. And even in discussing disaffiliation, interviewees did not put primary blame on external causes (e.g., increasing secularism); the blame remained squarely on issues internal to Catholicism.[22] An internal issue called out by interviewees was a sentiment identified as coming from a relatively small segment of Catholics: that a "smaller, purer church" was a good thing.

Interviewees who mentioned this thought nothing could be farther from the truth. Matthew Kelly pushes against this attitude, "Sadly, many people who would consider themselves faithful Catholics or committed Catholics or highly engaged Catholics are too comfortable with the church getting smaller. In fact, they have a strong preference toward the church getting smaller and believe that would be good. And that is anti-Christian. Christianity by its very nature is procreative, is expansive, is non-elitist, is non-exclusionary, is 'where is everyone?'" James Joyce is often credited with the quote, "Catholic means 'Here comes everybody.'" Kelly's closing mirrors this, but in a context of disaffiliation: "Where is everyone?" For the interviewees who named this issue, they see this smaller church movement as at least partially accountable for shrinking membership. Preference for a smaller, purer church is also antithetical to the theological and cultural pluralism within Catholicism and to the ethos reinforced by the Synod on Synodality: *Enlarge the Space of Your Tent*.[23] Also named when discussing disaffiliation were poor encounters with leaders, the loss of moral credibility with the sex scandal and cover up, and the lack of relevance of Catholicism for everyday Catholics. Each of these wide-ranging weaknesses are seen by the interviewees as something at least somewhat capable of being changed by the church.

A specific weakness also worth exploring is, as Matthew Kelly elaborates, the lack of enthusiasm Catholics typically harbor toward being Catholic, "People who don't feel good about being Catholic don't evangelize, that's never going to happen. You're never going to get someone who doesn't feel good about being Catholic to evangelize." At a time when religion attempts to distance itself from the therapeutic, some leaders may forget that Jesus promised his followers happiness and to have life abundantly.[24] St. Thomas Aquinas connected happiness with virtuous living. These examples show that it is not beyond the Catholic tradition for Christian faith to cultivate joy and wellbeing. But religious grounding aside, belonging to any group usually evokes some sense of esteem, support, and heightened affective state.[25] And there is evidence that this positive affectivity is especially pronounced in religious contexts.[26] Kelly concludes by stating the obvious: People who are not enthusiastic about being Catholic will not discuss or apply that faith in any significant way. Kelly later argues that there are ways the church could give people reasons to be excited about their faith. As an example, he says that with organizational savvy and a sacrificial use of resources, the Catholic Church could eradicate childhood hunger in the United States. He argues that this *ad extra* effort would give everyone—Catholics and non-Catholics—greater esteem for the Catholic Church. Despite the direction from Vatican II—renewed by Pope Francis—to make Catholicism relevant to people's everyday lives, our interviewees' assessments indicate that there is much work yet to be done.

Implications

Several implications stood out from our analysis. The first is methodological. In 2019, Pew Research Center reported that only one-third of Catholics subscribe to official teachings on the Eucharist, causing much concern within the Catholic community.[27] However, this was the reverse of what we found in our 2011 survey, with roughly two-thirds of Catholics (63%) aligning with Church teaching on the Eucharist.[28] First, we need to examine the way the Pew question was worded.[29] Pew respondents were required to answer in a forced-choice fashion whether they believe in transubstantiation—that the bread and wine become the body and blood of Christ—or that the bread and wine are symbols. They were also asked whether they thought Catholicism teaches that the bread and wine are transubstantiated or are symbols. The key problem with this question is that although Pew believed it was asking an either/or question, there is also the possibility that those who chose the symbolic response also affirm the true presence. To clarify, Catholicism teaches that the bread and wine are symbols as well as the true presence of Christ, and the way that the symbolic choice is worded does not deny true presence, even though Pew in its analysis assumed that it does.[30] When we asked Catholics about this topic in 2011, we asked them to pick which phrasing most aligned with Catholic teaching as well as which best aligned with their beliefs. Importantly, we asked whether "the bread and wine really become the body and blood of Jesus Christ" or "the bread and the wine are *only* symbols of the body and blood of Jesus Christ" (emphasis added). With the addition of "only," these questions set up a clear either/or in which respondents must deny transubstantiation if they select the symbolic response, rather than being able to lean into one response while still holding the other as true as the Pew wording allows. The inclusion of "only" allows us to get a much clearer picture of Catholic belief on the Eucharist. With this phrasing we find that the percentages reverse, with 63 percent believing that transubstantiation happens and 37 percent believing that the bread and wine do not become the actual body and blood of Christ. How we ask questions matters.

This brings us to a related second implication, this time pastoral. To look at the 2011 American Catholic Laity findings more closely, we can talk about four groups of Catholics. First are the knowledgeable believers—46 percent of our sample—who know that the church teaches that the bread and wine become the body and blood of Christ, and who personally believe this to be true. Second, there are the knowledgeable doubters—4 percent of our sample—who know that the church teaches that the bread and wine become the body and blood of Christ but who do not personally believe this. Third, the unknowing believers—17 percent of the sample—who believe that the church teaches that the bread and wine are only symbols of the body and blood of Christ, yet they personally believe that they become the actual body and blood of Christ. Finally, there are the unknowing unbelievers—33 percent of the sample—who believe that the church teaches that the bread and wine are only symbols of the body and blood of Christ and they personally believe this to be true. Looking at this, only 4 percent of Catholics knowingly deny Catholicism's position on the true presence of Christ in the Eucharist. Nearly two-thirds agree with this teaching, with a subset of 17 percent—the unknowing believers—doing so while mistakenly believing they are departing from church teaching. One-third, a sizable minority, believe they agree with the church teaching that teaches that the bread and wine are merely symbols.[31]

Given these findings, there are a number of approaches that the USCCB could opt for in helping more Catholics align their beliefs with official teaching. They have chosen to focus their efforts at the diocesan and parish levels in the hopes of better informing Catholics of their faith's teachings on the Eucharist. These types of efforts are most likely to touch those who attend Mass frequently. Current institutional efforts will likely not affect the lives of many of these infrequently attending Catholics. Unsurprisingly, this is the group that had the lower knowledge of church teaching on the Eucharist as well as lower personal belief, with 43 percent personally believing in transubstantiation and 66 percent mistakenly believing that the church teaches that the bread and the wine are only symbols. Without more expansive outreach, these efforts may change some people's beliefs or better educate some on church teaching, but they run the risk of essentially preaching to the choir.

In considering the ways the interviewees discuss an experience of community or communion in ecclesiological life, a third implication emerged. *The American Heritage Dictionary* defines "catholic" as, "Including or concerning all humankind; universal." Although this lens can amplify what various components share in common, it can also dismiss what distinguishes them. In missing the nuance, it risks portraying Catholicism as an institution that is ossified and monolithic. When adherents employ this lens in their more localized context, they might look to their own commonalities and falsely assume that there is something more authentically Catholic in their own beliefs and practices and, by implication, something that is less Catholic about other beliefs and practices. Matthew Kelly is concerned with Catholics' ability to understand the difference between the way Catholicism manifests in their own context and what is essential to being Catholic: "I think this is one of the biggest challenges we face as a church at the moment, is understanding the difference between something that is essentially Catholic and something that is a preference. . . . But we as American Catholics have a very localized view of church. And we prioritize according to that localization. And I think it can be very dangerous." There is a need for American Catholics to have a wider view of Catholicism, as well as understand the particularities of their own context and appreciate—rather than condemn—the particularities of others.

To bring some depth to "catholic," *The American Heritage Dictionary* offers another definition that points us to the distinctions among any grouping, "Of broad or liberal scope; comprehensive." The *Oxford Dictionary* is even more explicit in its focus on diversity, "including a wide variety of things; all-embracing." The Catholic Church in the United States—at the level of the national bishops, the diocese, the parish, and the actively engaged person—is in the midst of a struggle or a tension in navigating what is shared in common, what is distinctive, and how both cohere into an integrated whole. Catholics at all levels share some consensus around what is core (e.g., the sacraments), but there also remain elements that are contested as to where they should fall in relative importance, as well as how they might develop or be pastorally applied (e.g., teaching on same-sex relationships). This raises questions. How does a church that is so diverse name what unites the parts into a whole? How does a church that is fully united still foster and encourage distinctiveness? How can Catholics be diverse, but not fractured? And practice unity, but not uniformity? What is unequivocally core to Catholicism, what is important but can still be contested, and what is simply grounded in the particularities of time and place?

There were some insights from the interviewees that offer sparks to ignite a fruitful dialogue on these questions. Whether it was the familiarity of the liturgy even in a foreign country, the diversity of the saints even while they all imitated Jesus, or a sense of family at their parish as well as the global church, the interviewees drew upon what is best described as an "ecclesiology of communion."[32] This ecclesiology cohered believers even while differentiating and celebrating particularity. There was an appreciation of both the frailty and splendor of the human condition as well as a desire for community while cautioning against the homogeneity of "lifestyle enclaves."[33]

In paraphrasing a piece of the introduction of *Deus Caritas Est* by Pope Benedict XVI, Cardinal Cupich pulls in elements of communion ecclesiology, "Our faith is not about a doctrine or a theory or ideology, but rather it's about an encounter with the real person of Jesus." The fact that each of the leaders, in one way or another, ultimately came back to Jesus in their responses is key. The diversity of human experiences, when all grounded in Christ, come to take on a unifying quality. Further, the emphasis on encounter pushes Catholics into relationship with others; relationships can foster an appreciation of differences while forging common bonds. Elements of faith, such as the Trinity, the saints, the sacraments, and others are incredibly unifying among Catholics and bring about positive feelings toward their own Catholic identity.

That communion ecclesiology necessitates a recognition of difference is especially important in the pastoral realm. Paul Wilkes emphasizes the importance of particularity and a nuance in pastoral approaches when discussing what the American church needs right now: "It's obvious that people need and want the church, and it's so difficult to actually break through the static, the internet, and all that." There is no single solution that promises full pews. Leaders identify a universal yearning for meaning, purpose, and belonging, but no universal way to meet that need. Each person will have a slightly different way of meeting their spiritual needs, and parishes should be aware of the unique situations and needs of each person who approaches the church in whatever key moments they arrive.

This emphasis on difference and the particular helps to address some of the pitfalls of communion ecclesiology that have been highlighted by theologians, recently by theologian Susan Reynolds.[34] The communion ecclesiology, for all its merits in amplifying unity, in practice can overlook the importance of difference. She argues that a more robust ecclesiology is one that actively incorporates solidarity. Too often an uncritical use of communion ecclesiology has minimized or dissolved difference, which leaves questions of power and inequality unasked or, worse, silenced. Reynolds proposes an ecclesiology in which believers are one in Christ because of—rather than despite—difference. This approach builds bridges of affective and material relationship (i.e., love) within and across communities. Paying careful attention to discussions concerning unity and difference, and keeping solidarity at the center of these dialogues, can help ensure that difference is neither tamed nor ignored for the sake of a superficial unity.

A fourth implication is the pastoral importance of the homily and the sense that clergy do not give this the effort that it's due. The interviewees repeatedly underscore the importance of quality preaching for a fruitful and formative experience in Mass. For the vast majority of Catholics, the primary space of contact with their pastor is the Sunday homily. There is both immense potential as well as responsibility here. If a priest has a strong sense of the pulse of his parish, he has the ability to inspire and enliven his parishioners, both deepening their faith and helping them to discover ways to bring that faith to all aspects of their lives.

The need to exercise responsibility here has been discussed at a variety of levels. Considering that his apostolic exhortation *The Joy of the Gospel* is only 288 paragraphs, it is noteworthy that Pope Francis devoted a full 24 of these to the homily.[35] In this, he notes how important the homily is for lay formation as well as a way to judge "a pastor's closeness and ability to communicate to his people." He takes great care to outline what a homily is and what it is not. In his book on professional ethics in ministry, priest and ethicist Richard Gula reminds readers—many of whom will be priests—to be respectful of those who will hear the homily and that the homily is, for many Catholics, their only interpretive contact with the scriptures; he notes the homily is an "awesome pastoral responsibility."[36] The USCCB has explained that the homily is not meant to be catechetical or to feel like a scripture course, but should instead help the listener to interpret their lives through the scripture.[37] This and much more has been studied and said of Catholic homilies. Homilies are critical encounters for the faithful not only with their pastor, but with their tradition and their ability to see God in their lives. Time and care should be taken in the preparation of homilies, and regular, honest, evaluative feedback should be provided to priests in the interest of continually improving their efforts.

A fifth implication is the critical impact of key moments in the lives of the faithful, especially for those more loosely tethered to parish life. It shows the importance of instilling welcome and hospitality in the staff, as well as in volunteers and parishioners more broadly. Providing relationship-building opportunities—not just "greet your neighbor" efforts—before and after Mass, within small groups, and through service projects helps move from "welcome" to "belonging." People who are most likely to encounter estranged Catholics need to be amply aware of how critically their words, their silence, and their attitudes shape not just that person's impression of them, but of the Catholic Church.

Further, the interviewees tended to lean hard on a pastoral approach of inviting or re-inviting people into Catholicism. Some were concerned that too many parishes take a "behave this way, then we can talk about beliefs, then once you embrace those you can fully belong" approach (or "behaving-believing-belonging"). These interviewees and other pastoral resources indicate that it might be better to reverse this: extending a radical belonging at the start, which opens people up to inquire about and engage beliefs, with new patterns of behavior then following (or "belonging-believing-behaving").[38] Apologetics, catechesis, theology, and the pastoral each have their place; ministers need to know which is called for, given the person's circumstances and capacities. But, if all you have is a hammer, every person looks like a nail. Some interviewees were concerned that too often a potential returner was hammered with some teaching that excluded them from belonging. They generally agree that a pastoral, belonging-first approach that connects with people on a human level is the best way to conduct ministry; some added that this also best approximates the ministry of Jesus.

To conclude this chapter, we return to Pope Francis's discussion of the Synod on Synodality, specifically his identification of three risks—formalism, intellectualism, and complacency—and three opportunities for the church—to become structurally more synodal, more listening, and affectively closer. The risks he identified are serious. Formalism is a real disappointment and can cause demoralization and attrition. To call a synod to better incorporate the experiences of the faithful and to help clergy and laity work together raises expectations; disaster can occur when those expectations are not met. The interviewees and many of those surveyed feel a great affinity for Catholicism, even while they see clear spaces where improvements must be made. If changes are merely superficial, this could be very discouraging. Intellectualism distances church leaders from the everyday lives of lay Catholics and makes faith heady and theoretical rather than integrated with Catholics' lived realities. With the interviewees' emphasis on the personal and relational, they likewise perceive intellectualism to be a dangerous specter in the church's life. Finally, complacency—as justifying practices simply because this is the way they have been done—is not helpful. The interviewees see all the challenges the church faces, and warn that much of what is currently being done is not effective. New and innovative ideas and approaches must be proposed, tested, and shared.

Notably, each of these three risks lies in the hands of those with power; whether changes remain superficial, discussion remains in the realm of ideas, or stale practices continue and uphold the status quo, is squarely in the hands of the magisterium, that is, the bishops. The synodal process incorporated lay voices and voting, but the effort put into holding parish synodal meetings varied by diocese. Even with a fully open process and with lay representatives participating as full voters, the outcome of the synod will be shaped by the appointed participants who convened in Rome and by the pope's response to their deliberations and recommendations. Finally, the implementation of the outcomes may also vary considerably, depending on how a local bishop or even pastor feels about the results of the synod. Care, transparency, intentionality, and accountability at the levels of process, outcome, and implementation are necessary if church leaders wish to avoid these risks and to have this and future synods bear fruit in the lives of the faithful.

Pope Francis presented three opportunities. To help shape the church into an institution that is structurally synodal, not just occasionally synodal, would be a profoundly different way of "doing church" for Catholics in the United States. This would require a constant openness and solicitude on the part of ordained leaders to hear the experiences and insights of the laity. The second opportunity is to become a more listening church. Too often Catholics can become siloed into their slice of Catholicism and confuse that slice for the whole; what may be central to one Catholic (e.g., teachings on migration) may not be what is central to another Catholic (e.g., devotion to Mary). Catholics can take this as an opportunity to be less defensive, and more humble in their listening. The final opportunity identified by Francis is to build a church of closeness. This is not simply about tolerating difference, but appreciating one another as gifts. It is an affective movement toward compassion and tenderness, to love first before all else. He notes that this would benefit both Catholics and the world more generally.

John Carr, an interviewee at Georgetown University, reflects, "An organizer friend of mine said, 'If you Catholics ever got your act together, you'd be dangerous. You have ideals, you have visions, you have people, you have leaders.' The question is, can we get our act together?" The synod is one way that Catholicism is trying to regroup and become—as Francis quoted Congar above—not *another* church, but a *different* church. Thriving religious communities are found to share ten characteristics; they are adaptive, bounded, enfranchised, embodied, embedded, authentic, empathic, activated, pollinating, and networked.[39] Many of these qualities are intentionally pursued in this synod. Not all fruits will be immediate, and time will show how well Catholics avoided the risks and took advantage of the opportunities this synod offered their church. And as Catholicism begins to listen more to lay experiences, this focus on listening shifts the meaning and understanding of authority for Catholics and their leaders, the topic of the next chapter.

2

Authority

In the 1970s and early 1980s, Michael McDonnell was a boy growing up in Norristown, just outside Philadelphia, Pennsylvania. His family was Catholic, but more than that, it was a family in which everyday life was often intertwined with the life of the local parish. His childhood recalls an era prone to idealization. It was a time when parochial school enrollment was much higher, and when Catholics in a neighborhood knew most others by name and greeted one another at Sunday Mass. In McDonnell's case, though, there was a dark and disturbing side. He recalls:

> I was an altar server. I'm six foot three, so as you can imagine I was always tapped to be the cross bearer in a high Mass or procession; I was front and center. I don't think I missed a single high Mass or forty-hour devotion or Easter liturgy, or Christmas Eve Mass while growing up. I was a grade school student in the parish school. The rectory was a hundred yards from the school, across the parking lot, and I worked at the rectory answering phones, alphabetizing church envelopes, and taking messages. I was active in parish functions: Christmas bazaars and carnivals. Teachers and nuns alike always encouraged the kids to get involved—to volunteer to paint signs, clean up the playground, clean up the ballfield. And my parents were very active in the church. My mother was in the choir. My father was president of the athletic association, and I was involved in athletics. I did it all. I was always at parish activities. . . . And both my abusive priests were always there.

From 1979 to 1981, when he was in grades six to eight, McDonnell was sexually abused, separately, by two priests at St. Titus Parish. John Schmeer was a priest in residence and Francis Trauger was assistant pastor. McDonnell did not know it until many years later, but both priests were abusing other boys and young teens at the parish during that time. Like many priest predators, they chose victims deliberately. McDonnell, now in his fifties, is a national communications manager for SNAP, the Survivors Network of those Abused by Priests. He knows the pattern well:

> They targeted two types of children. They targeted a vulnerable type whose family was going through a lot of turmoil: divorce, separation, splitting of the children between mother and father, or a family needing help with tuition. . . . And they targeted the other extreme, the families that had the most devout children and the most religiously active children. They *knew* that I would not say a word because of fear. . . . I was very fearful that, had I said something, it would come back and make my parents look bad. And the priests knew it.

Trauger's crimes are especially appalling. McDonnell describes him as one of the Archdiocese of Philadelphia's worst priest abusers: "Schmeer was more of a fondling, huggy, touchy-feely type guy, but it was still always a violation. Trauger was extremely violent—he would strip you naked, masturbate you, the whole thing." Trauger sometimes attacked victims in the rectory, for example, when altar boys were changing out of vestments, or in McDonnell's case when he was working there. Often though, Trauger lured them away from the parish under pretexts, such as camping or skiing trips, which turned out to be nights in hotels where he anally raped them and manually stimulated them for hours on end.[1]

In 1981, two other victims in the parish told their parents about Trauger's abuse. The two families reported him to the pastor, who in turn reported him to the chancery. According to a later grand jury report, this was the first provable time archdiocesan officials knew Trauger was a predator,[2] but McDonnell believes they likely knew already. Less than a week later the officials reassigned Trauger to a new parish (and barely a year passed before a new victim there came forward).[3] The archdiocese would transfer him five more times before the end of his priestly career. St. Titus parishioners were told nothing by the pastor or the archdiocese. The chancery clearly realized there were likely other victims in the parish, boys with whom Trauger had been alone for long periods of time. A brief letter was typed to McDonnell's parents stating: "We believe that your child may have come in harm's way at the hands of Francis Trauger." But somebody in the chancery apparently had a change of heart about notifying families; the letter was never mailed and was discovered by prosecutors decades later, still collecting dust in a chancery file.

McDonnell, not knowing of the existence of other victims and certain his parents would not believe him, was essentially on his own. He discovered a way to cope with his growing depression: he became an alcoholic before he became a teenager. "I had found my drug of choice at age twelve, and it numbed me, and it helped me push that pain down. It helped me become another person. It helped me develop an entire facade of a life, so that I could continue in some way to be able to get married, to be able to get jobs, to be able to sit at the bar for twelve hours and not think about the horrendous acts that were performed on me and I was forced to do." At the age of thirty-five, after two failed marriages, four lost jobs, and two foreclosed houses—and at the urging of friends and family—he entered a twelve-step program. Trauger, who was not removed from ministry until 2003, finally faced criminal charges in 2019.[4] He pled guilty to abusing an altar boy in 1996 and another in 2000. The statute of limitations had run out for all other (known) victims, including McDonnell, but it afforded him some sense of satisfaction and justice: "I was able to sit in that courtroom directly behind Trauger as they cuffed him to lead him away to state prison, and my face was the last face that he saw. It took thirty plus years to put him away."

Today McDonnell says that he thinks of God more in terms of the "Higher Power" of Alcoholics Anonymous than the Catholic God of his upbringing. When asked if he still considers himself a Catholic, he hesitates and jokes that he is a "recovering Catholic" as well as a recovering alcoholic, then he adds: "But yes, I do consider myself a Catholic. I'm not a *practicing* Catholic. There are too many triggers. I've been to a lot of funerals over the past year due to the pandemic, and I'll tell you, I am absolutely triggered every time I go into a church. Just the smell of incense, the smell of candles. I did love the image of church I had as a boy. I loved the liturgy. I loved everything about it." McDonnell's tone changes when speaking about the Catholic bishops, both those in his own archdiocese and the episcopacy as a body. He is blunt, dismissive, disparaging. Asked how he feels hearing bishops speak publicly on moral or social teachings of the church he replies:

My reaction when I read anything like that, for example, on the issue of immigration, is: They really do not have any legal or any moral authority to be commenting when they have ignored a huge plague [sexual abuse] that has overtaken the vision of church that I knew. I still know many devout Catholics, but they too are starting to sway in their faith because the bishops are not taking any *action* to fully address it. So, I really don't put any weight into anything that they say publicly about any moral topic or any other moral crisis they believe is going on within their church.

It is hardly surprising that McDonnell has little desire to listen to the bishops when they speak on issues of the day. But he references something else. Other Catholics—not victims, just ordinary, everyday Catholics—may be less likely to defer to church leaders because of disenchantment and disillusion brought about by the scandal. The focus of this chapter is the teaching authority of church leaders and American Catholics' deference (or resistance) to it. We first review survey evidence as to whether the cataclysm of the abuse scandal diminished their deference. We then take a look back, examining prior changes over time in Catholics' attitudes about sexual morality and ask how it laid the groundwork for current views of the church's teaching authority. Finally, we review some more recent developments in Catholics' posture toward authority.

The Sexual Abuse Scandal and the Church's Moral Authority

The most explosive series of clergy sexual abuse revelations emerged in January 2002, when the *Boston Globe* started reporting on cases in the Archdiocese of Boston, based on files newly unsealed by a judge. The scandal spread quickly as other newspapers inquired into cases of clergy abuse in their own local dioceses. It remained headline news well into the fall of 2002, and still received semi-regular coverage two years later. During this period, polls of Catholics conducted by the Center for Applied Research in the Apostolate (CARA) found low approval for "the job Catholic bishops as a whole have done handling accusations of sexual abuse." The first poll was conducted in April 2002. Just 8 percent of Catholics rated the performance of the bishops as "excellent." Twenty-six percent said "good." More than half, 57 percent, said either "fair" or "poor" (26 and 31%, respectively). A month later, with no sign of the scandal losing steam, responses were worse. The percentage who rated the bishops' performance as "poor" had risen from 31 to 41 percent.[5] The percentage giving the bishops a positive mark (either "excellent" or "good") had fallen from 34 to 22 percent. Perhaps, if there is anything surprising about these findings, it is that such positive responses were not even lower.

The bishops gathered in Dallas in June 2002. It was a regular semiannual meeting, and they used the opportunity to draft a document outlining a procedural response to the crisis. Officially titled *Charter for the Protection of Children and Young People*, it became colloquially known as the "Dallas Charter." The procedures it enacted required that a priest be temporarily removed from active ministry when an allegation was made and that the allegation be reported to civil authorities. Every diocese was to establish a review board made up primarily of lay people who were not church employees; they were charged with examining allegations and judging their credibility. The concept of a lay review board was taken from a few dioceses that were already using this approach, most notably the Archdiocese of Chicago under Joseph Cardinal Bernardin. Review boards—in the dioceses that had them before 2002—were typically composed mostly or entirely of clergy, who may have been pliable to the will of their bishops.[6] Some victim advocates had been encouraging the laity-based alternative. The charter dictated that if even one allegation against a priest was found credible by the review board, he was to be permanently removed from all ministry ("zero tolerance"). Moreover, this policy applied retroactively. Each diocese and religious order had to reevaluate (or perhaps evaluate seriously for the first time) any allegation from the past for any living priest.

Just under a year later, in October 2003, CARA conducted another survey. Forty-seven percent of Catholics said they were aware of the new policies enacted under the Dallas Charter, a proportion little different from that for non-Catholics (50%).[7] This is a surprisingly low proportion given the extensive news coverage of the scandal and the efforts of the bishops themselves to publicize the charter in order to assure Catholics that the abuse problem was being addressed. Nevertheless, Catholics were slightly more likely to have heard about the charter policies if they attended Mass at least monthly (58%). This was likely due in part to greater exposure to informational sources, such as pastors speaking about it at Mass or coverage in diocesan newspapers.

Many of the specific policies established in the charter were highly popular. For example, CARA found that 91 percent of Catholics supported the requirement of immediately reporting sexual abuse allegations to the police, and 68 percent supported lay review boards.[8] Though few Catholics wanted abusive priests to have further contact with young people, opinion was split on zero tolerance. Forty-four percent of Catholics supported permanently removing priests from all priestly ministry for a single instance of abuse, and 47 percent preferred restricting abusers to ministries where they could have no contact with children. (Just 5 percent wanted to return priests to parish ministry after treatment.) Polls also found support for something the charter did *not* address: consequences for bishops who had failed to take proper action when they learned of abuse by their priests. In an April 2002 Quinnipiac poll, 64 percent of Catholics agreed that "Catholic bishops who did not report allegations of sexual abuse of young people by priests to public authorities and instead relocated these priests to other churches, should resign from their positions."[9] The charter, however, created no mechanism by which the USCCB could force a bishop to resign, or otherwise discipline him. This was partly because of constraints set by canon law; authority over the bishops is reserved for the pope. In the immediate aftermath of the scandal, the only U.S. bishop to resign was Cardinal Bernard Law, who stepped down as archbishop of Boston in December 2003.

Another issue addressed in the 2003 CARA survey was the possibility that the moral authority of the church had been damaged by the scandal. This was a topic being discussed publicly in the media (and privately among the bishops themselves). In November 2002, the *St. Louis Post-Dispatch* ran an article entitled, "Catholics Hope Policy Will Revive Church's Moral Clout." It discussed this issue and described the hope of some Catholics that the new policies established by the Dallas Charter could reclaim some of the lost trust and respect. Francis Fiorenza, a Catholic Studies Professor at Harvard Divinity School, was quoted: "One of the major tragedies of the recent scandals has been precisely the loss of moral authority at a time when such moral authority is most needed."[10] Fiorenza was referring specifically to the plight of refugees at the U.S.-Mexico border, but his remark would have fit with any number of important social and political issues on which Catholic teaching can offer guidance.

Pastors and bishops tell us that they still experience repercussions of the scandal today. Bishop Larry Kulick of the Diocese of Greensburg, Pennsylvania discusses whether it has hurt the moral authority of the church:

> Definitely yes, and as you know the priests and people of our diocese were deeply affected by the Pennsylvania Attorney General report.[11] I find the most active and engaged Catholics in our diocese are still very supportive. But beyond that, in general the response is, "Don't talk to me about being pro-life. Don't talk to me about the moral integrity of life. Don't talk to me about family life. Look what happened to the children you were supposed to protect." So, when I talk about those moral issues I'll always say, "I know the church has a track record where we have at times failed, but if we just stay silent we can't change things in society."

This is typical of comments in our interviews. It is a virtually unanimous opinion among church leaders on both the "left" and "right" that the scandal has turned Catholics off from listening to the bishops.

The 2003 CARA survey asked, "In your eyes, how much, if at all, has the issue of sexual abuse hurt the credibility of church leaders who speak out on social or political issues?" Thirty-seven percent of all Catholics said the credibility of church leaders had been hurt a "great deal" in their eyes, and 38 percent said "somewhat." Just 26 percent said "only a little" or "not at all." Table 2.1 shows results among three subgroups of Catholics. Weekly Mass attenders were more positive regarding the credibility of their leaders in the wake of the scandal, which is unsurprising given that committed and engaged Catholics typically rate church leadership more positively. Interestingly, those who said they had heard about the Dallas Charter policies did not differ from those who had not. But there was another factor that made a somewhat bigger difference—believing that most church leaders were probably *enforcing* the policies. Of Catholics who thought the bishops were probably enforcing the policies, 34 percent said the scandal had hurt the credibility of leaders in their eyes "to a great extent." This compares to 48 percent of those who believed most leaders were probably *not* enforcing the policies. Thus, if Catholic

TABLE 2.1: Extent to which Catholics say the Abuse Scandal Has Hurt the Credibility of Church Leaders on Social and Political Issues, 2003.

	A Great Deal	Somewhat	Only a Little or Not at All
All Catholics	37%	38%	26%
Catholics by Mass attendance			
Every week	28	42	30
Once or twice a month	38	40	23
A few times a year	42	27	24
Rarely or never	49	28	23
Catholics by whether they have heard of the Dallas Charter policies			
Yes	37	40	23
No	37	37	26
Catholics by whether they think most leaders are probably enforcing the policies[a]			
Yes	34	42	24
No	48	26	26

Source: Authors' analysis of 2003 CARA survey data.
[a] Asked of everyone, regardless if they had heard about the policies.

leaders wish to reassure Catholics about the problem of abuse, one approach might be to focus on the ways in which they are enforcing rules to prevent abuse from occurring in the future.

Unfortunately from the standpoint of the bishops, there is currently little evidence of attitudes having moved in a more positive direction since the 2002–2003 blowup. The 2011 American Catholic Laity Survey repeated the CARA question, asking whether the scandal had hurt respondents' perception of the credibility of church leaders on social and political issues. Time had not healed this wound. In fact, responses were even more negative. The percentage who responded "a great deal" had risen from 37 percent in 2003 to 46 percent in 2011. The percentage saying either "only a little" or "not at all" had fallen to 18 percent. A 2019 Pew poll asked Catholics to rate the job by the bishops as a whole "responding to the recent reports of sexual abuse and misconduct by Catholic priests and bishops." Sixty-seven percent said either "fair" or "poor." This is more negative than responses to the very similar question (noted earlier) about the bishops' handling of the scandal in April 2002.

For further analysis, we looked for survey questions that could shed light on Catholics' views of their leaders' authority both before and after the time when the scandal broke (2002–2003). Polls conducted for CNN in 2001 and late 2003 asked Catholics whether the pope is infallible when he teaches on "matters of morals, such as birth control and abortion."[12] The percentage who said "yes" dropped marginally, from 44 to 39 during this period (see the first column in table 2.2). However, when we look back to previous times the question was asked, 1994 and 1995, this change is very much within the range of what Catholics had said in the past. In other words, the scandal does not appear to have made a notable difference on this attitude. The polls also asked about papal infallibility on "matters of faith, such as the divinity of Christ," though this question was not asked in 2001. Again, there is no evidence of an impact of the scandal; 45 percent of Catholics replied "yes" in both 1994 and 2003. (The percentage actually increased to 59 in 2013). The final panel in table

TABLE 2.2: Catholics' Beliefs about Papal Infallibility and Conscience, Before and After the Scandal.

"Do you believe the pope is infallible when he teaches on . . . Matters of morals, such as birth control and abortion?"

	Yes	No	No Opinion
1994	38%	56%	6%
1995	33	55	12
2001	44	45	11
2003	39	57	4

"Do you believe the pope is infallible when he teaches on . . . Matters of faith, such as the divinity of Christ?"

	Yes	No	No Opinion
1994	45%	44%	11%
1995	50	36	14
2003	45	50	5
2013	59	35	5

"On difficult moral questions, which are you more likely to follow: The teachings of the pope, or your conscience?"

	Pope's Teachings	Your Conscience	Both/ No Opinion
1993	16%	79%	5%
2003	14	83	3
2013	23	72	5

Sources: Published CNN poll data.

2.2 shows results for another question: whether Catholics are more likely to follow the teachings of the pope or their own conscience on difficult moral questions. It comes as no surprise that a majority of Catholics, more than seven in ten, say they follow their own conscience. But again, there is just a minimal difference between 1993 and 2003.

In summary, and perhaps surprisingly, there is little evidence that the sexual abuse scandal in and of itself produced strong or enduring effects on Catholics' deference toward the teaching authority of their leaders. How then should we interpret the finding that, in 2003, many Catholics said the scandal had hurt the credibility of church leaders when speaking on social or moral issues? For some respondents, it may be a statement about priorities—that addressing the abuse problem should take urgent precedent over social and moral pronouncements. Another possibility is that Catholics are expressing their feelings about an underlying hypocrisy that they perceive coming from leaders who did not live up to their own ideals and who set a poor example to the faithful.

Regardless, we speculate that, even if the scandal has not changed Catholics' underlying beliefs about church authority, it has made them more likely either to "shut down" when they hear leaders speak on social issues or to invoke the scandal in reacting to such statements. An example of the latter was conveyed by Father John Burger, a former Regional Director of the Columban order, in pointing to an opinion column from a January 2022 edition of his local newspaper, the *Philadelphia Inquirer*. The column addressed a highly-publicized statement from Pope Francis that young people not wanting children is "a form of selfishness." As Burger puts it, the columnist, who identified herself as a product of Catholic schools, "wasn't shy about dragging in the sexual abuse scandal." That's arguably an understatement; the column excoriated the pope: "Francis' statements smack of the utmost hypocrisy coming from a church leader who heads up an institution that for centuries has overlooked and helped cover up sex abuse by priests as well as nuns against countless children."[13] This type of reference to the scandal seems to indicate that there will be no further discussion on the topic, that the pope's or church's position need not be considered on its merits. As Burger puts it, a reasoned critique of the Pope's comments on couples not having children could have been made without using sexual abuse as a debater's point, but "we're going to be paying for it [the scandal] for a long time."

There is another possibility for the lack of change in Catholics' deference toward papal authority in table 2.2: American Catholics were *already* very inclined to follow their own consciences on many matters of morality. They were already reluctant or unwilling to defer to church leaders on many important teachings. The independent-mindedness of Catholics has been a recurring theme throughout the books in this series. But in the next section we examine in greater depth some of the long-term trends that brought us to the current state of affairs.

The Rise of Moral Individualism: The 1960s and Early 1970s

Two polls of Catholics, conducted in 1963 and 1974 by the National Opinion Research Center (NORC), reveal massive changes during the late 1960s and early 1970s.[14] As shown in the first line of table 2.3, moral approval of the use of artificial contraception for married couples skyrocketed, from 45 to 83 percent. Catholics also expressed increased acceptance of premarital sex for engaged couples, of remarriage after divorce, and of marital sex for the sole purpose of pleasure. At the same time, Catholics' level of agreement that the church has the right to teach Catholics what view they should hold on "means for family limitation," on "immoral books and movies," and on "racial integration" fell. Seventy percent of Catholics agreed in 1963 that "It is 'certainly true' that Jesus directly handed leadership of the church to Peter and popes." By 1974 that had plummeted to 42 percent of Catholics, a decline of 28 percentage points.

People disagree on what caused these attitudinal changes, but social scientists point to various contextual explanations. The first is Vatican II and the transformational changes it implemented in an attempt, as envisioned by Pope John XXIII in convening the Council, to make the church relevant to the modern world. Some argue that in changing long-standing traditions, the Second Vatican Council eroded the perception of church teachings as immutable, notwithstanding the fact that in the long history and tradition of the church, several church teachings had changed prior to Vatican II.[15] The second explanation focuses on debates within Catholicism over church teaching on contraception. Finally, some argue that the sexual revolution, in liberalizing Catholics' attitudes about sexual morality, led to the rejection of the church's

TABLE 2.3: Catholics' Attitudes about Morality and Church Authority, 1963 and 1974.

	1963	1974	Change
Morality			
Approves of . . .			
Artificial contraception for married couples	45%	83%	+38
Premarital sex for engaged couples	12	43	+31
Remarriage after divorce	52	73	+21
Strongly agrees that a married couple may have sex for pleasure alone	29	50	+21
Believes it is "very important" for young people to marry a member of their own religion	56	27	−29
Agrees a family should have as many children as possible	41	18	−23
Church Authority			
Agrees the church has a right to teach what views Catholics should take on . . .			
Proper means for family limitation	54	32	−22
Immoral books and movies	86	60	−26
Racial integration	49	37	−12
It is "certainly true" that Jesus directly handed leadership of the church to Peter and the popes	70	42	−28
Agrees with the doctrine of papal infallibility in certain pronouncements on faith and morals	*	34	

Source: Published results from NORC polls.
* Not asked.

teaching authority on this and other matters. These three explanations are all plausible, and not necessarily mutually exclusive. In fact, we suspect there is some truth to each and review each below.

Vatican II

First, some social scientists argue that Vatican II inadvertently undermined Catholics' respect for church authority.[16] Whether it undermined or simply changed how Catholics came to construe the authority of the church hierarchy and the definitive hold of certain teachings is an open question. The Council document *Gaudium et Spes* elevated the importance of the individual conscience in discerning moral duty:

> In the depths of his conscience, man detects a law which he does not impose upon himself, but which holds him to obedience. Always summoning him to love good and avoid evil, the voice of conscience when necessary speaks to his heart: do this, shun that. For man has in his heart a law written by God; to obey it is the very dignity of man; according to it he will be judged.[17]

This tenet, coupled with several other of Vatican II's exhortations, encouraged Catholics to question church teachings and to take a more discerning approach to their own religious beliefs and identity.[18] A related argument about the Council is that the simple act of creating change itself caused repercussions for Catholics' deference to the church. Vatican II re-framed time-honored teaching and practices that many Catholics believed were immutable. No longer, some critics argued, was the church the bastion of certainty and clarity it had been for hundreds of years.[19] On the other hand, as documented by priest and sociologist Andrew Greeley, reliable survey evidence indicated that most American Catholics liked the Council's most visible changes, including replacement of Latin with English in the liturgy.[20] This fact also coexists with the possibility that, as sociologist and religious sister Patricia Wittberg puts it, Catholics may have reacted to Vatican II by "giving themselves permission to question."[21]

Indeed, Vatican II obliged Catholics to take on the responsibilities of being Catholic in a much more proactive and agential manner than had been the case. In doing so, it shifted the terms of interpretive authority within the church. While the Council reaffirmed the hierarchical structure of the church and the teaching authority of the bishops, it also clearly recognized the interpretive competency of the laity and the importance of lay inquiry and discernment:

> Let the layman not imagine that his pastors are always such experts, that to every problem which arises, however complex, they can readily give him a concrete solution, or even that such is their mission. . . . Often enough, the Christian view of things will itself suggest some specific solution in certain circumstances. Yet, it happens rather frequently, and legitimately so, that with equal sincerity some of the faithful will disagree with others on a given matter. Even against the intentions of their proponents,

however, solutions proposed on one side or another may be easily con-
fused by many people with the gospel message. Hence it is necessary
for people to remember that no one is allowed in the aforementioned
situations to appropriate the Church's authority for his opinion. They
should always try to enlighten one another through honest discussion,
preserving mutual charity and caring above all for the common good. . . .
Let it be recognized that all the faithful, clerical and lay, possess a law-
ful freedom of inquiry and of thought, and the freedom to express their
minds humbly and courageously about those matters in which they enjoy
competence.[22]

Contraception

Irrespective of how one assesses the impact of Vatican II, the debate over
contraception occurring within the church in the years coinciding with
Vatican II and its aftermath is also critical. The debate was driven by
three sets of events. One, the FDA approved the first birth control pill in
1960. Some theologians concluded that using the pill did not violate the
church's prohibition against "artificial" contraception.[23] They reasoned
that, rather than being a traditional barrier method, it worked in concert
with women's natural biology. Second, there was tremendous humani-
tarian concern in the 1960s that the global "population explosion" was
contributing to poverty in developing nations. In April 1963, Catholic
President John F. Kennedy announced that, for the first time, foreign aid
would include assistance for family planning.[24] During his campaign he
had avoided taking a position on the issue, perhaps concerned it would
alienate Catholic supporters.

That same year, Pope John XXIII established a commission to study
the church's position on birth control and make a recommendation.
Pope John died mere months afterward, and was succeeded by Paul
VI. The existence of the commission was not initially publicized and
did not become known until Pope Paul announced it in June 1964.[25]
Later that year, at a Vatican II session, bishops from several nations
called for reassessing the teaching on birth control. They reportedly
received "thunderous applause" from the assembly.[26] One bishop argued that, because so many married Catholics already practiced birth
control, "The authority of the church has been called into question on a

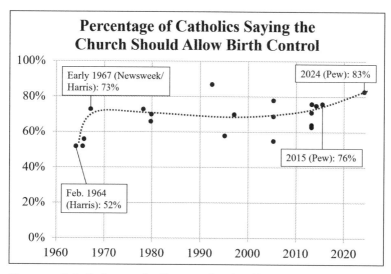

Figure 2.1: Catholic Support for Changing the Church's Position on Birth Control, 1964–2024.

Sources: Published results from various pollsters and the authors' own analyses of publicly-available data sets.

vast scale. . . . The official position of the church on this matter should be revised."[27] The commission's final report was completed in 1966, and it recommended that the pope allow all forms of birth control. Though not intended for the public, it was leaked to the *National Catholic Reporter* in April 1967.

Not coincidentally, in light of the increased public availability of the pill and the opening of discussion about birth control among church officials, the mid-1960s saw a dramatic shift in American Catholics' attitudes toward the teaching on contraception. Figure 2.1 presents results for various media polls asking Catholics if the church should "allow" or "change its rules" on birth control. In a February 1964 Harris poll, 52 percent supported the church doing so. By early 1967, the proportion jumped to 73 percent.[28] Further, many Catholics also anticipated that the church *would* revise its position. A 1965 Gallup poll found that 61 percent of Catholics thought the church would someday allow contraception. Of those, most thought it would happen within five years.

After studying the topic for two years, Pope Paul released the 1968 encyclical *Humanae Vitae*.[29] It reaffirmed the church's existing position, forbidding all forms of artificial contraception. This did nothing to change American Catholics' attitudes on birth control; most had simply made up their mind on the issue. As the trendline in figure 2.1 shows, there has been relatively little change since 1967 in the proportion of Catholics who want the church to allow birth control. Greeley argued it was the encyclical *itself* that caused declining respect for church authority. In his view, the laity did not just ignore the pope. Rather, they saw him as having overstepped the bounds of his authority, and they essentially rebelled. And while some Catholics left the church in the wake of *Humanae Vitae*, many returned within a few years and participated fully in the sacraments while continuing "in good conscience" to use contraception.[30]

A 1971 *Newsweek* poll directly asked Catholics about the encyclical and their views of papal authority, allowing evaluation of this argument. Just 18 percent of the 1971 respondents thought the pope asserted his authority too much.[31] So most Catholics do not seem to have concluded that the encyclical was part of a larger pattern of overreach by the pope. Next, a slightly larger proportion of Catholics (26%) said the encyclical had caused them to question papal authority more. These results provide modest support for a negative effect of the encyclical itself, but perhaps not enough to explain all the declining respect for church teaching previously evident in table 2.3.

The Sexual Revolution

A third, and broader, explanation views the birth control debate as just one aspect of something that was influencing American Catholicism from the outside: the sexual revolution. Many of the large attitudinal shifts in table 2.3 involve sex, contraception, childbearing, and marital life. How much of the change was simply Catholics being caught up in the larger social transformation on sexual mores? To answer this question, we compare attitudes of Catholics with those of other members of the public (sometimes with all non-Catholics, and sometimes with Protestants, depending on what data are available). We examine three issues: birth control, remarriage after divorce, and premarital sex.

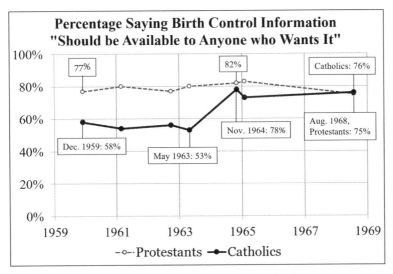

Figure 2.2: Support for Legal Availability of Birth Control Information, 1959–1968.
Sources: Published Gallup results and the authors' analysis of Gallup data sets.

Figure 2.2 presents results of Gallup polls taken from 1959 to 1968 on the issue of legal availability of birth control information. Ideally, we would prefer a question about the morality (rightness or wrongness) of using contraception, but too few such questions were asked of the entire public at that time. In 1959, 77 percent of Protestants and 58 percent of Catholics agreed that "birth control information should be available to anyone who wants it,"[32] a difference of 19 percentage points. This gap stayed roughly the same for the next three years. Then, between May 1963 and November 1964, it narrowed considerably. (It is probably safe to infer that the June 1964 announcement of the papal birth control commission played a big role in this abrupt shift in Catholic opinion.) And by August 1968, a few weeks after the encyclical, it had disappeared completely. Protestants were roughly where they had started (75%) while Catholics had risen to match them (76%). Though not shown in the figure, this question was repeated in 1974 by the General Social Survey (GSS).[33] The responses for Catholics and Protestants were identical: 91 percent. In other words, Catholics "caught up" to Protestants during the 1960s, and then both groups changed in unison between the late 1960s and mid-1970s.

Attitudes about divorce show a pattern somewhat similar to those about birth control information, with Catholics "catching up to" the general public, albeit over a longer period of time. Figure 2.3 shows the percentage of people who approve of remarriage after divorce. Because polling agencies did not repeat their questions often enough, we have drawn on surveys from multiple pollsters (with some variation in question wording). The figure compares Catholics to all other members of the public. In 1952, 69 percent of non-Catholics and 38 percent of Catholics said that "divorced people who remarry" are not "living in sin," a difference of 31 percentage points.[34] When the identical question was asked in 1965, non-Catholic opinion was essentially the same (70%), but Catholics were at 50 percent, a difference of just 20 percentage points. In the following decade, Catholic approval of remarriage rose sharply, in most cases based on questions asking if it is "wrong." There are no data points for non-Catholics in the late 1960s or 1970s. But by 1987 the gap between Catholics and all other members of the public was just 6 percentage points.

It is not surprising that Catholics were initially more disapproving than other Americans of divorce and remarriage. There is a stronger stricture against it in Catholicism than in most Protestant denominations. The same can be said about contraception. But attitudes about the morality of premarital sex present a contrast: evidence suggests that Catholics did not initially differ much from Protestants. The first poll that allows this comparison was taken by Harris in 1965. Seventy-nine percent of Protestants and 83 percent of Catholics said "engaged couples who loved each other should wait for marriage" before having sex. Similarly, in a July 1969 Gallup poll, Protestants and Catholics were about equally likely to say it is "wrong" for people to have sex before marriage (70 and 72% respectively).[35] During the next four years, there was a very dramatic change in public opinion—arguably the single biggest attitudinal change related to the sexual revolution.[36] In 1973, Gallup asked the same question and found that only 53 percent of Protestants and 45 percent of Catholics still thought premarital sex was wrong.[37]

The important point is that, in this case, Catholics' attitudes changed in concert with those of non-Catholics. However, the full picture is more

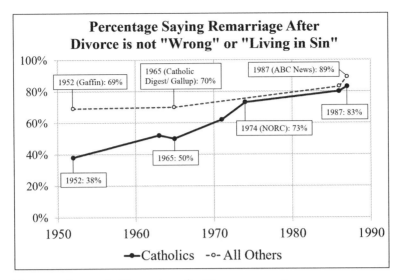

Figure 2.3: Approval of Remarriage after Divorce, 1952–1987.
Sources: Published poll results and the authors' analysis of data sets.

complicated than a simple Catholic-Protestant comparison would suggest. Since at least 1969, Catholics' attitudes about premarital sex have aligned most closely with members of the relatively liberal mainline denominations as opposed to the more traditionalist evangelical denominations. Drawing primarily on data from the General Social Survey, figure 2.4 shows trends across time for Catholics, mainliners, and evangelicals.

Evangelicals were more disapproving of premarital sex to begin with. In 1969, approximately 80 percent of them described it as "wrong." This compares to 74 percent of mainliners and 72 percent of Catholics. And while disapproval fell among all three groups during the early 1970s, the decline was less steep among evangelicals. The attitudes of Catholics and mainliners have stayed strikingly similar to one another, and the gap between these two groups and evangelicals has widened. In 2018, just 16 percent of Catholics and 22 percent of mainliners said premarital sex is "always" or "almost always" wrong. This seems to be a case where Catholics were indeed influenced by external society. But it was probably the preceding attitudinal changes

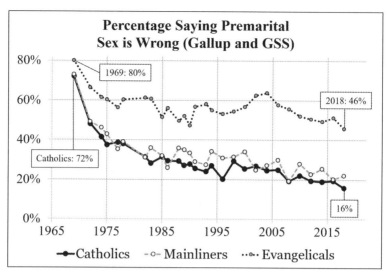

Figure 2.4: Disapproval of Premarital Sex by Religious Tradition, 1969–2018.
Sources: 1969: A Gallup question with binary "wrong/not wrong" response
categories. 1972–2018: General Social Survey [GSS] responses of "always" or
"almost always" wrong. In the early 1970s, these two polls produced very similar
results.

during the 1960s, on issues like contraception and divorce, that set
the stage. Those earlier changes realigned Catholics with a "modern"
or "liberal" outlook on morality. To some extent, they had already re-
jected the more "conservative" outlook that resulted in less extreme
change among evangelicals.

Public opinion on an issue can shift in two primary ways: by people
changing their mind over time, or by what social scientists call "cohort replacement." The latter occurs when younger generations gradually replace older generations. In the case of premarital sex, both
types of change occurred, as illustrated in figure 2.5. Many members
of the pre-Vatican II generation changed their minds on the topic
between 1969 and the early 1980s. They are the ones primarily responsible for the rapid decline in disapproval evident in figure 2.4. After
the 1980s, however, their views on the matter stabilized and did not
change any further. By contrast, members of the Vatican II generation
entered adulthood already very approving of premarital sex. The same

is true for post-Vatican II Catholics and succeeding generations.[38] So the very gradual change that has occurred since the 1980s is due almost entirely to older Catholics passing away and younger Catholics replacing them.

In summary, Catholics' shifting views on contraception and divorce, which began changing by at least the mid-1960s, may have been influenced by secular norms, but probably not by the "sexual revolution" per se. Most non-Catholic Americans were already permissive in those two areas. Attitudinal changes associated with the sexual revolution (e.g., greater acceptance of premarital sex) began somewhat later, at the very end of the 1960s and the early 1970s. And on premarital sex Catholics were indeed almost certainly influenced by larger changes in secular society. Along with 1960s factors unique to Catholicism—that is, Vatican II and the birth control debate—changing sexual mores set the stage for a Catholic moral individualism that has persisted. Later analyses will examine this individualism in greater depth, showing that just a minority of Catholics want church leaders to be the final moral decision makers in areas related to sex and family.

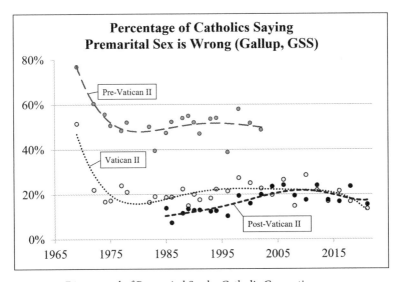

Figure 2.5: Disapproval of Premarital Sex by Catholic Generation.
Sources: Authors' analysis of Gallup (1969) and GSS (1972–2021) data sets.

Moral Decision-Making

If relatively few Catholics automatically defer to their church leaders on moral issues, how do they go about making moral decisions? Our survey asked respondents how frequently they use each of several sources for guidance. Table 2.4 summarizes the results. Among the most common approaches is praying or meditating; three-quarters of Catholics report doing this at least "sometimes" when confronted with a moral decision. Not surprisingly, consulting with loved ones is also a very common approach to moral decision-making; four-fifths (80%) of respondents talk to a close family member at least "sometimes," and about three-quarters (76%) talk to trusted friends at least "sometimes." In contrast, only a quarter of Catholics talk to their local priest at least "sometimes." The remaining items in the table—which all involve consulting various Catholic media resources—are also relatively infrequent ways that our respondents make moral decisions.[39]

Of those Catholics who talk to their priest about moral decisions, most (63%) are weekly Mass attenders, and nearly all others attend at least a few times a year. This finding makes sense, as pre-existing contact and familiarity with one's parish priest is a likely precondition for having the motivation and for feeling comfortable enough to approach him for personal advice. But with fewer Catholics attending Mass weekly, pastors may be losing opportunities to act as trusted confidants and

TABLE 2.4: Frequency with which Catholics Use Various Sources for Moral Decision-Making.

	Always	Sometimes	Rarely or Never
Pray or meditate	40%	36%	24%
Talk to a close family member	37	43	19
Talk to trusted friends	28	48	24
Read the *Catechism of the Catholic Church*	6	20	74
Talk to my local priest	6	19	75
Look at/read Catholic media	5	22	74
Read papal statements or encyclicals	3	15	82
Visit the website of my diocese or the U.S. Catholic bishops	3	10	87

Source: 2017 ACLS.

sources of advice. The various generations are well-represented among those who consult with their local priest—with the exception that there are very few who are members of iGen, perhaps because they have not yet established regular parish involvement.

Thus, the primary way that Catholics draw on their faith when making moral decisions is through personal prayer. Surveys have consistently found that most Catholics pray regularly, the majority every day.[40] Our results show that Catholics' prayer lives are not something abstract but are connected to important issues and choices they face in their lives. Depending on how "religious" one considers the practice of meditation, it is clear that Catholics' moral decision-making is not a purely secular process.

Recent Developments: The 1990s to the Present

In this section, we examine trends in recent decades, focusing on Catholic attitudes that are relevant to their willingness to defer to the hierarchy. First, we explore attitudes toward legal abortion. These attitudes have become closely aligned with party identification, helping to drive partisan polarization among Catholics. Next, we summarize the biggest swing in Catholic opinion since at least the 1970s: growing tolerance of same-sex relationships, a trend that began in the early 1990s. Trends in attitudes about these two issues, along with the sexual abuse scandal, suggest that American Catholics are increasingly reluctant to defer to the teaching authority of the bishops.

Abortion

On February 13, 1973, the U.S. Catholic bishops issued a pastoral message vehemently denouncing the decision made by the Supreme Court three weeks earlier in *Roe v. Wade*.[41] They also called for Catholics to resist, including civil disobedience if necessary: "Catholics must oppose abortion as an immoral act. No one is obliged to obey any civil law that may require abortion." John Deedy, editor of the Catholic magazine *Commonweal*, wondered how effective the bishops would be at rallying Catholics to the cause: "The pastoral message is a test for the bishops in relation to civil authorities. The bishops have laid their full episcopal prestige on the line, and will soon learn how much the gesture counts. Some fear they are in for a disappointment on the ground that much of the bishops' credibility and clout drained away in their dogmatic opposition to birth control and their inability to convince all Catholics of the validity of their points of view. . . . The opposition of the laity, should it come, is likely to display itself in a quiet disregard for the bishops' moral counsel."[42] This was not, of course, the first time the bishops had advocated against legal abortion, nor the first time they had encouraged action from the laity. But as Deedy noted, a difference in this statement was its "hard line" tone, which included an explicit reminder that, in the bishops' words: "In order to emphasize the special evil of abortion, under church law, those who undergo or perform an abortion place themselves in a state of excommunication." How successful were the bishops in convincing lay Catholics of the pro-life position on legal abortion and of the necessity of voting for pro-life politicians?

First, it is worth noting that before *Roe v. Wade*, Catholic opinion had been moving against church teaching on legal abortion. The pattern of change varied, depending on whether abortion should be allowed in "hard" cases (e.g., rape, incest, health of the mother, deformity in the baby) or "soft" cases (e.g., poverty, a married couple already having as many children as they desire, or being single). As examples, figure 2.6 shows trends between 1962 and 1980 in disapproval of abortion in the hard case of health of the mother and the soft case of a family being unable to afford more children. The figure compares White Catholics with White Protestants.[43]

In both cases, White Catholic opposition to abortion was consistently greater than that of White Protestants. For health of the mother, the difference was relatively large in 1962 (36% compared to 9%). But between 1962 and 1968, Catholic opposition declined to 19 percent while that of Protestants stayed relatively constant (8%). This pattern bears some resemblance to what happened for birth control and divorce during the 1960s, with Catholic attitudes becoming less distinct and more similar to those of other Americans. In this case, however, the attitudinal gap between Catholics and Protestants never closed completely. For the case of a family being unable to afford more children, attitudes of Catholics and Protestants shifted together, with the greatest change occurring during the late 1960s and early 1970s. Opposition

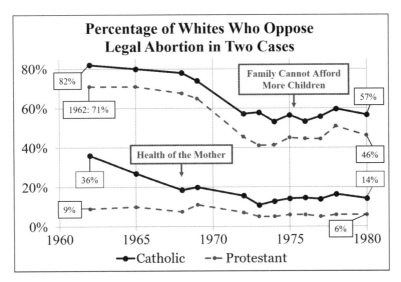

Figure 2.6: Opposition to Abortion among Whites, 1962–1980.
Sources: 1962–1969: Published Gallup figures. 1972–1980: Authors' analysis of GSS data.

among Catholics fell from 78 percent in 1968 to 57 percent in 1972. In this case the pattern is somewhat similar to that for premarital sex: a very strong and sudden change in public opinion during the late 1960s and early 1970s. Again, however, Catholics remained slightly more pro-life, on average, than Protestants.

Since the early 1970s, average Catholic attitudes about abortion have remained relatively stable and unchanging (albeit with random year-to-year fluctuation). Whether coincidence or not, their opinions appear to have solidified and become "locked in" at about the same time as the *Roe* decision. So, a simple answer is that the bishops did not successfully shift Catholics' attitudes in the pro-life direction after the ruling. But it is conceivable that they stopped the ongoing trend in the opposite direction. That said, abortion attitudes for the entire public have also been relatively constant since the time of *Roe*.

A Pew Research Center survey conducted in March 2022 illustrates one reason it is challenging to move Catholics' opinion toward banning abortion: a tension between abortion as a moral and a legal issue.[44] Pew asked people what they "personally think" about the morality of abortion. Among Catholics, 16 percent said it is "morally wrong in all cases." At the other end of the spectrum, 22 percent said either "morally acceptable in all cases" or "not a moral issue" at all. Most Catholics fell somewhere in the middle, including 38 percent who said it is "morally wrong in most cases" and 24 percent who said "morally acceptable in most cases." In separate questions the survey asked about the legality of abortion. Ten percent said abortion should be *illegal* in all cases, no exceptions; 13 percent said legal in all cases, no exceptions. Again, most Catholics fell in the middle, with 32 percent saying *illegal* in most cases and 43 percent saying legal in most. But our primary interest lies in the way attitudes on these separate questions intersect. Twenty-two percent of Catholics believe abortion is morally wrong in at least some cases and should be illegal in all those cases. And as mentioned earlier, another 22 percent say abortion is never morally wrong or is not a moral issue at all. But a majority of Catholics (54 percent) say *there are at least some situations where abortion is morally wrong but nevertheless should remain legal.* Even when Catholics are aligned with the church's ethical outlook on abortion, it is a further step to convince them of legal prohibition.

Nevertheless, it is worth keeping in mind that many Catholics do remain open to the church's moral vision. Pew asked respondents how the following statement reflects their views: "Human life begins at conception, so a fetus is a person with rights." Among Catholics, 44 percent said it describes their views "very" or "extremely" well and another 20 percent said "somewhat" well (with the remainder choosing either "not too well" or "not at all"). This indicates that 64 percent of Catholics are favorably inclined, at least somewhat, toward the fundamental belief about unborn human life that undergirds the church's position on this issue. Additionally, just 17 percent of Catholics describe abortion as "not a moral issue." By way of comparison, 48 percent of Catholics describe contraception as "not a moral issue."[45]

If there is a way that the bishops may have been successful in their advocacy, it is in shaping the voting choices of Catholics who were already inclined toward the pro-life position. During the 1980s and 1990s, Catholics on both sides of the abortion divide gradually started voting in a way that reflected their attitudes on this issue. Using data from the American National Election Studies, figure 2.7 shows the percentage of Catholics who voted Democrat in each presidential election since 1970.

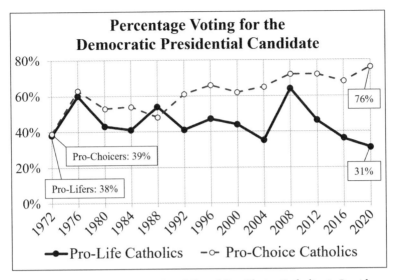

Figure 2.7: Divergence Between Pro-Life and Pro-Choice Catholics in Presidential Voting, 1972–2020.
Source: Authors' analysis of National Election Studies data (percentage of the vote for major candidates).

Separate data points compare pro-life Catholics (defined in this analysis as those who think abortion should never be permitted or permitted only in cases of health or rape/incest) and pro-choice Catholics (those who think it should always be permitted).[46] For sake of simplicity, the figure omits a middle category of those who think there should be some additional restrictions on abortion.

There was essentially no difference in how these two groups voted in 1972. Thirty-eight percent of pro-lifers voted for the Democrat (George McGovern), as did 39 percent of pro-choicers. This was before *Roe v. Wade*, and abortion rights were not yet strongly associated with the Democratic Party. McGovern campaigned on the position that the issue was best decided at the state level, and his running mate Sargent Shriver was a pro-life Catholic.[47] The two groups again voted very similarly in 1976, but in 1980 a small gap of 10 percentage points opened. In his campaign, Ronald Reagan strongly denounced the *Roe v. Wade* decision, and he received an endorsement from the National Right to Life Committee, originally a Catholic organization.[48] By 1984, the pro-life position was

clearly associated with the Republican Party and the pro-choice position with the Democratic Party; both parties included strongly-worded
planks about the issue in their respective platforms. In a well-publicized
1984 statement, Cardinal O'Connor of New York said he could not see
"how a Catholic in good conscience can vote for a candidate who explicitly supports abortion."[49] O'Connor later criticized Democratic
vice-presidential candidate Geraldine Ferraro, a pro-choice Catholic,
for giving the impression that "the Catholic teaching on abortion is not
monolithic, that you can be a good Catholic and believe in abortion."[50]

In 1992 the voting gap on abortion began to expand in earnest. Sixty-
one percent of pro-choice Catholics voted for Clinton, compared to 41
percent of pro-lifers, a difference of 20 percentage points. The gap has
gradually widened since then, with the notable exception of 2008, an
election in which many voters focused on the economy due to the reces-
sion. The 2020 election was the most polarized of all. Seventy-six percent of pro-choice Catholics voted for Biden. Just 31 percent of pro-life
Catholics did so.

A potential side effect of this type of polarization among Catholics,
where agreement with church teaching becomes increasingly associated
with partisan identity, is that members of one party may reject the idea
that church leaders have any authority to speak on political issues at all.
Indirect evidence suggests this might be happening. In a 2014 Pew poll,
half (51%) of Catholic Democrats agreed that "churches and other religious organizations are too involved with politics." Just one-third (34%)
of Catholic Republicans agreed. We cannot be certain, but it appears that
this partisan difference did not exist several decades ago. In the early
and mid-1980s, amid a growing prominence of the religious right, several pollsters asked about the proper role of religious leaders in speaking
out on politics (though no questions used the same wording as Pew).
In a 1980 NBC News/Associated Press poll, Catholic Republicans and
Democrats were equally likely to agree that, "Churches and members
of the clergy should be involved in politics, like backing a candidate for
public office." And in a 1986 ABC News/Washington Post poll, they were
equally likely to agree that "Religious leaders should stay out of politics
entirely, even if they feel strongly about certain political issues."

This is not to suggest that only Democrats are susceptible to skepticism of church leadership. Perusing large Catholic social media accounts

and blogs quickly reveals a deep polarization over Pope Francis among members of the church's "thinking class." In particular, conservative elites tend to be very critical of what they see as the pontiff's departure from tradition, his unwillingness to take harder stances against cultural liberalism, and his openness to listening to dissenting voices in the synod process. The Pew Research Center has shown that a somewhat parallel polarization over Pope Francis has emerged among the general Catholic populace, albeit to a much smaller extent.[51] In the early years of his papacy, Catholic Democrats and Catholic Republicans were equally likely to say that they had a favorable view of Francis. In January 2014, 89 percent of Democrats and 89 percent of Republicans were favorable toward the pope. But gradually, over the next several years, a small divide in opinions appeared as Republicans became a little less warm toward him. In January 2018, 89 percent of Democrats and 79 percent of Republicans held a favorable view of Francis, a difference of 10 percentage points. In January 2020, it was 87 and 71 percent, respectively (a difference of 16 percentage points). And in the most recent survey of January 2021, it was 92 versus 72 percent (20 percentage points). Still, we emphasize that a majority of Catholic Republicans do remain positive toward the pope, and it seems quite unlikely that he will fall into negative favorability with them.

Abortion and Communion

In January 2004, Catholic politician John Kerry campaigned in Missouri while running for the Democratic presidential nomination. Archbishop Burke of the St. Louis archdiocese told the press that he would not give Kerry the Eucharist if, hypothetically, Kerry attempted to receive it from him. Because of Kerry's support for abortion rights, Burke said he would simply give Kerry a blessing.[52] Previously, it was not unusual for bishops to state that pro-choice politicians should not present themselves for communion. But it had been rare for bishops to actively deny them communion, and Burke became the most prominent to advocate doing so.

Three months later, Francis Arinze, a Nigerian Cardinal who headed the Vatican office on worship and the sacraments, was asked about the communion issue by reporters.[53] He replied that pro-choice politicians were "not fit" to receive the Eucharist and therefore should not take it.

He added, "If they should not receive, then they should not be given." Though the Cardinal did not mention Kerry by name, this latter statement seemingly signaled Vatican support for Burke's stance. Archbishop Sean O'Malley of Boston, Kerry's home diocese, stopped short of saying he would deny anyone the Eucharist. But O'Malley rather vehemently declared that politicians at odds with the church "shouldn't dare come to communion."[54]

During the following few months, several pollsters asked Catholics whether they favored withholding communion from pro-choice politicians. The far left-hand side of figure 2.8 shows results for three polls. Only a minority of all Catholics supported the idea, but not surprisingly, there was a partisan divide. An average of 30 percent of Republicans and 16 percent of Democrats supported withholding communion. In Spring 2005, a *Washington Post* poll asked about the issue again. This time 45 percent of Republicans supported withholding communion, an increase of 15 percentage points over the previous year. The issue faded from the press after 2004, but continued to simmer within Catholic circles. It received renewed media attention in 2021 when the U.S. bishops met to approve a document on the Eucharist—with extra fuel on the fire due to a pro-choice Catholic occupying the White House.[55] Two recent polls in 2021 and 2022 (see the right-hand side of figure 2.8) confirm that the 2005 jump in Republican support for withholding communion was no aberration. As of 2022, 47 percent of Republicans continued to support it. Some Catholic Republicans have apparently been persuaded that this approach is an appropriate way to handle dissident politicians. It is a rare instance of statements by church leaders having an observable impact on the attitudes of Catholics. But because it has only affected attitudes of Republican Catholics, it may further contribute to partisan polarization.

Finally, a new development in the abortion debate occurred in 2022. In Spring 2022, the U.S. Supreme Court overturned the 1973 *Roe v. Wade* decision, giving the pro-life cause a new victory. A draft of the ruling was leaked in early May, and a few days later the Associated Press polled Americans about the issue.[56] Results among Catholics were exactly what one would expect based on the discussion above: a large partisan divide. Fifty-two percent of Catholic Republicans favored overturning *Roe*. In comparison, just 14 percent of Catholic Democrats favored overturning it.

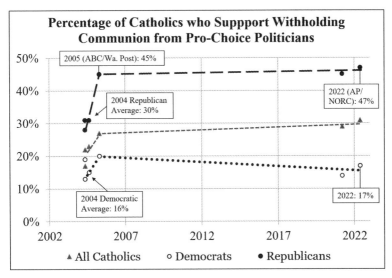

Figure 2.8: Catholic Support for Withholding Communion, 2004–2022.
Source: Authors' analysis of various poll data sets.

Same-Sex Relationships: Growing Acceptance

Since the American Catholic Laity Surveys began, there has been a new and massive change in the American public's attitudes about sexual morality. Throughout the 1970s and 1980s, a large majority of Americans disapproved of same-sex relations.[57] Abruptly, in the early 1990s, disapproval dropped. This was the start of a trend that, sometimes gradually and sometimes quickly, has continued to the present. Catholics were swept along in this sea change of public opinion. Drawing on data from the General Social Survey, figure 2.9 shows the proportion of Catholics, mainliners, and evangelicals saying that "sexual relations between two adults of the same sex" is "always wrong." In just five years, from 1991 to 1996, the percentage of Catholics saying same-sex relations are always wrong fell from 72 to 47 percent. After something of a lull in the late 1990s and early 2000s, the decline continued; as of 2018, just 21 percent still saw it as always wrong. And as with changes in attitudes toward premarital sex, Catholics' views have tracked very closely with those of mainline Protestants through the entire timeframe in the figure (1980

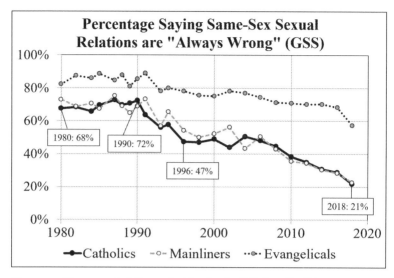

Figure 2.9: Disapproval of Gay or Lesbian Sex by Religious Tradition, 1980–2018.
Source: Authors' analysis of GSS data.

to 2018). This appears to be another example of Catholics taking cues from more "accepting" aspects of secular culture and disregarding their church's teachings.

Neither church leaders nor even most journalists seemed to take note of this shift in public opinion until well after the fact. In the 1990s, the U.S. bishops did occasionally reaffirm church teaching on same-sex relationships, but most public debate at the time revolved around proposed anti-discrimination laws to protect gay and lesbian people in employment and housing. And on that front, individual bishops took varied positions.[58] But the attitudinal shift set the stage for Catholics' later openness toward a legal change on which the bishops would become very outspoken, as will be discussed in a later chapter.

Implications

This chapter has reviewed changes in Catholics' deference to the teaching authority of the church. The most dramatic occurred during the 1960s and early 1970s. Since then, growing permissiveness on behaviors such as premarital sex or same-sex relations probably reflects larger cultural influences—not dynamics specific to Catholicism. Two interviewees described the changes since the 1960s in their own words, each with their own understanding of authority in church life. Linda Ruf, CEO of the JPII Life Center, touches on issues of authority in discussing why many Catholics are resistant to the church's pro-life message:

> I think prior to 1960, the church stated the rules, taught catechism, and people didn't ask questions. They generally trusted that the priest knew more than they did and obeyed or tried to obey. After 1960, the precepts of Vatican II were not fully understood. Some of the rules changed, churches and priests got more casual. In an effort to "reach the people," I think something holy was lost. Some of the "wonder and awe" of the Mass and the Eucharist was lost. There is inconsistency in the teachings of the church and its leaders now. There are Catholic schools, universities, priests, and Catholic parents who openly contradict church teachings with their actions and words. No wonder young people are confused and left to their own devices. The "cafeteria Catholic" model went unchecked. Truth is only truth if you want it to be and it fits into your life according to you. Permissive teachings about contraception, divorce, premarital sex, abortion, and homosexuality were at first tolerated, then tacitly approved, then applauded by many.

In Ruf's view, much of the responsibility for lax adherence to church teaching falls on Catholic leaders for not being firm in promulgating those teachings. She faults the bishops for failing to speak with a unified voice, causing confusion among Catholics. But she does not let the laity off the hook. She emphasizes the need for Catholics to stand against a secularized American culture that is hostile toward traditional morality—and for them to disregard those who would view Catholic teaching as judgmental or intolerant.

Robert McCarty is a former leader of the Catholic Mobilizing Network, an anti-capital punishment advocacy group. He has also conducted sociological research for church organizations, and he shares his view of the laity's relationship with church leadership:

> The traditional model of authority is vertical and top-down. The church is structured much like a pyramid with the pope at the top, then the bishops

and the priests, with the faithful as the base of the pyramid. In that model, the people relied on ecclesial leaders to interpret and to be the keepers of religion for them, and they would tell us what we need to believe and to do. The acceptance of this top-down model of authority has disappeared in our church, perhaps accelerated by the clergy abuse crisis. . . . The vertical model is being replaced by a more horizontal understanding of shared leadership. And Pope Francis is reinforcing this shift with his emphasis on synodality. That's a horizontal model of leadership because it trusts the Spirit working in the people. People are no longer waiting for the clerical caste to mediate the Spirit.

From McCarty's perspective, it remains unrealistic to turn back the clock to an era when Catholics automatically internalized and followed the teachings of their leaders. But he takes a somewhat hopeful view about the present situation as one where everyday Catholics—rather than simply turning their backs on the church and its leaders—take on a meaningful, shared role in discerning the Spirit and charting a course for the church.

Thus, Catholic leaders on both the "right" and "left" recognize that Catholics are not immediately deferring to church leaders the way they once did. This does not necessarily mean our interviewees do not want the Vatican or bishops to proclaim Catholic teaching with a strong voice. As might be expected, however, they tend to differ on which teachings should receive emphasis. For example, Ruf wishes that priests and bishops would take a stronger and more unified stand on the protection of unborn life: "Some bishops are very clear [on abortion], and some are not. It's the inconsistency that confuses people. I don't think any pastor can speak too much about the need to protect our most vulnerable. Pope Francis has said that abortion is wrong, but many of his words are taken out of context [by some liberals,] which causes confusion. 'Who am I to judge?' is his famous and often-repeated quote that was taken out of context and has been a source of confusion for many." For Ruf, a problem with current division in the church is that the hierarchy does not speak with one voice. Another is that the issue of abortion is not always prioritized; she is critical of those on the left who downplay the centrality of abortion in Catholic social teaching.

A contrast is seen in comments shared by Joan Neal, a lay woman and deputy executive director of NETWORK, a Catholic social justice lobby founded by religious sisters in 1972. Neal describes her belief that the American bishops have not been sufficiently forceful in promoting the church's social teachings. Her disappointment in the bishops in their relative silence on gun violence was instrumental in bringing her to NETWORK and is an ongoing source of frustration:

> When the Sandy Hook school shooting happened, I was concerned because the bishops weren't saying anything about it. They hadn't come out and forcefully condemned gun violence. They hadn't really provided any guidance for people in parishes, certainly not in my parish. . . . The USCCB, as well as individual bishops, have written several pastoral letters, and some of them are pretty good. But they have not really put their whole teaching authority behind them. There's a 1971 pastoral letter from the World Synod of Bishops, called "Justice in the World." In that letter, the bishops said, and this is a quote: "Action on behalf of justice and participation in the transformation of the world fully appear to us as a constitutive dimension of the preaching of the gospel, or in other words, of the church's mission for the redemption of the human race and its liberation from every oppressive situation." That could not be clearer. The tradition of Catholic social teaching is a part of our faith and is the responsibility of every Catholic. But the USCCB and our American Catholic officials have not pushed their letters down through the system to the pews and educational institutions. They could have, for instance, done something as simple as printed copies of their letters and provided them to every person in every diocese and archdiocese in the country.

For Neal, the destruction of young, innocent lives by guns is viscerally wrenching in a way that is similar to that felt by anti-abortion activists in reaction to the loss of unborn lives. Like many in the church who work for social justice on a number of fronts, she wishes the bishops would emphasize Catholic social teaching's large breadth of issues.

The question of whether communion should be withheld from pro-choice Catholic politicians elicited a variety of opinions from interviewees. To some extent, their reactions reflected the left-right divide that is evident among everyday Catholics. Cassie Guardiola, a pro-life activist

at the JPII Life Center, says of pro-choice politicians: "Such public officials receiving communion poses scandal to other Catholics and further
enables the culture of 'cafeteria Catholicism.' Abortion is a grave matter,
and compromising your faith by publicly endorsing this practice for political gain has significant repercussions on the minds and hearts of the
faithful." This was a rather straightforward issue for Guardiola and other
pro-life activists we spoke with. Abortion is literally a matter of life and
death, and it is necessary to make clear that pro-choice politicians are in
defiance of their own church on the matter.

Robert McCarty brings up the issue of communion while discussing tensions that arise from Catholicism's somewhat unique array of
political stances, in this case, opposition to both abortion and the
death penalty:

> When I worked for the Catholic Mobilizing Network, we often went
> to the pro-life march in Washington, D.C. with banners about ending
> the death penalty. I was surprised at being challenged by other Catho-
> lics who did not make the connection between being pro-life and anti-
> capital punishment. Comments like, "What are you doing here? Those
> people [convicted killers] deserve to die. Babies don't," were fairly com-
> mon. Thankfully, Pope Francis and our bishops have been more forceful
> and public in their pro-life stance from conception to natural death . . .
> however, this issue, too, has become politicized. I haven't heard any bish-
> ops suggest that those leaders who support the death penalty should be
> denied communion. The bishops did not do themselves any favors with
> the communion wars over the past year in response to pro-choice Catho-
> lic politicians. But because of my work with CMN, it did challenge me
> personally to be consistent in how I understand the relationship between
> receiving communion and one's public stances that are counter to church
> teachings. I can't be selective, nor should the church.

McCarty, who is pro-life on abortion, has landed on the belief that if
communion is to be withheld from those who dissent on one of the
church's life teachings, then it should also be withheld from those who
dissent on other life issues—or it should not be withheld from anyone.
He mentions by name a few Catholic politicians whose participation in
executions appalls him, but he is also introspective and feels the need

to apply his own principles in an even-handed manner. McCarty also expresses concern that withholding communion, when limited to the single issue of abortion, risks the church becoming too "associated with the Republican party" in the eyes of everyday Catholics. From this perspective, the broader and perhaps more restrained statement in the U.S. bishops' 2001 document on the Eucharist may be a good approach: "Lay people who exercise some form of public authority have a special responsibility to form their consciences in accord with the Church's faith and the moral law, and to serve the human family by upholding human life and dignity."[59]

Another interviewee, who requested confidentiality here, harshly criticizes bishops who withhold communion from pro-choice politicians:

> Pope Francis told the bishops not to continue the practice of withholding communion over the abortion issue. Jesus never turned away sinners. He ate and drank with them. It is absolutely *unconscionable* that the bishops would politicize the Eucharist in this way. The issue of abortion is so complex. There are many shades of gray. The bishops have not taken time to educate themselves about how this issue interacts with women's health care. If they did, they would come to less radical positions and would be more circumspect about speaking out on abortion in a way that degrades women. . . . We have bishops politicizing the Eucharist, but we also have bishops and priests publicly supporting [conservative] politicians who are morally corrupt, whose lives are known to everyone to be outside the moral framework of our faith.

Relatively few Catholic leaders speak so bluntly in public, but these comments probably align with the feelings of many everyday Catholic Democrats regarding the church's abortion stance. Another noteworthy aspect of these comments is that they appear to mention the same remarks from Pope Francis briefly referenced above by Linda Ruf. Speaking to reporters in 2021, Francis called abortion "homicide."[60] He also emphasized that the decision on whether to withhold communion should be made pastorally: "What should a shepherd do? Be a shepherd and not going around condemning or not condemning. They must be a shepherd with God's style. And God's style is closeness, compassion and tenderness." Francis declined to comment specifically on the controversy over communion in the United States. He also stopped short of instructing bishops and priests that they must administer the Eucharist to everyone presenting themselves.

With lay Catholics today being so independently-minded, how should church leaders try to persuade them? We spoke with several people about this question, and received a number of differing perspectives. But if there is one unifying theme, it is for church leaders to start by *meeting people where they are*, the ethos reiterated time and again by Pope Francis. Bishop Daniel Flores has been on the USCCB's Committee on Doctrine for several years, and in late 2021 became its chair. He emphasizes the importance of drawing upon affective expressions of faith already present among the people and connecting those to church teaching. He begins by describing his diocese: "Brownsville is at the very southern tip of Texas, very close to Mexico, very poor. It's largely bilingual, bicultural. We probably have the youngest demographic of any diocese in the country. I think the average age here is twenty-seven." Flores goes on to explain how he tries to meet the laity where they are when introducing a theological concept like the "real presence" of Christ in the Eucharist:

> We, the theologically trained, have a certain language, which is very good and has been chiseled. But we can never overlook the fact that sometimes the faithful have a simpler language, which is also part of the tradition, but it's a language more of the heart. Let me give you an example. This is a diocese that has a fairly strong local sense of popular devotion. The people may or may not be able to tell you what "transubstantiation" is. But they show you something important by how they respond when they walk into a church or when the Blessed Sacrament is taken out for adoration. There is a responsiveness that is instinctive in some ways. You've got to build on that, and you've got to start explaining *why* we do that.

Flores explains that he takes a parallel approach when speaking to the people of his diocese about the church's political stances. He begins with the issues that are important in their lives and their local area and branches out to connect those with other teachings. And he emphasizes, above all, the importance of linking teachings on social issues to Jesus rather than dry doctrine:

As a bishop, when I preach, I'm not speaking to a national group. I'm speaking to *my people*, and usually I'm addressing topics the people are facing. Down here we face, every day, the reality of immigration from Central America. We have a respite center in downtown McAllen for Central American immigrants, the largest run by the Catholic Church. So, I address the teaching of the church with regard to welcoming immigrants. I talk about it in basic Gospel terms, which I think is the most important aspect of how a bishop teaches and how the church teaches. You have to connect it to Jesus, otherwise it just sounds like "what the pope or bishop says." In the end, that's not really the issue. The church's teaching should be a very fairly transparent connection to what Jesus says in the gospel. The people of God instinctively sense when, "Yes, this is something Jesus would ask us to do." . . . Immigration is a life issue. I explain that this ties to the life of the unborn child, and the death penalty.

The well-being of Latin American immigrants and refugees is an issue that is visible and highly relevant in the day-to-day life of Bishop Flores's people. He ties it to the teachings of Jesus but goes further, using it as a springboard to address other social issues, ones that may seem unrelated on the surface but are intimately connected in the context of a Catholic life-affirming ethic.

Frank Donio is a Pallottine priest and founding director of the Catholic Apostolate Center, a ministry dedicated to evangelization. He also teaches part-time at the Catholic University of America. Father Donio discusses his approach to talking about church teachings, particularly with young people like college students:

If there's not a relationship with us, the people who are ministers of the church, there's not an opportunity to discern together, and sometimes people are intimidated to approach us. So, what I have advocated in my teaching and pastoral work is *accompanying* people. When we accompany, we're able to *be where people are*. . . . There are always going to be particular matters in people's lives that may not align with the teachings of the church, and it's at these times that they'll make important moral decisions. Among the university students I teach, the issues that are raised most often are around LGBTQ+ people, in terms of lifestyle and orientation, and in terms of sexual morality. That's the one area students can't understand, especially because of their relationships with people. "This is my friend, the person who's in my life, and is LGBTQ." I try to help people understand where church teaching is emanating from, because often they're just looking at the discrete issue that is in their life. They're not necessarily looking at the larger picture. So, if somebody brings up something about church teaching, usually there's a story behind that. And I try to get to the story and hear what their life reality is.

Donio describes his approach as "pastoral." It is a personal interaction between a priest and a lay person, in this case a college student. His remarks provide a reminder that Catholics first encounter the church's teachings as young people, often in their religious education, sometimes in homilies. Young adult Catholics are in a stage of life when they are typically thinking about their faith and whether to accept it. Many of them say they want to learn what the church teaches on various issues—but also that they ultimately wish to make up their own minds.[61] If there is any good time to reach Catholics, this is probably it. And it seems reasonable that understanding their existing viewpoint and the experiences that undergird it, as Donio tries to do, is important.

Cassie Guardiola likewise emphasizes the importance of meeting young people where they are when speaking to groups who may not be sympathetic to the pro-life position on abortion:

Audiences, like those at Catholic colleges and in young adult ministries, have been fifty-fifty on the pro-life issue. Their level of receptivity heavily depends on your ability to meet them where they're at. When you empathize with their concerns and seek common ground, you're more likely to get through to them. I always like to speak their language and choose words that are commonly used in progressive, pro-choice messaging. I communicate our message in a way that will resonate with them. For example, "Abortion is an act of injustice against a vulnerable, marginalized group of people. It's a form of discrimination against those smaller, younger, and differently-abled than us." I frame abortion as a human rights abuse rather than a religious issue. Even if they don't convert from pro-choice to pro-life, they are at least able to warm up to a new perspective.

There may not be a political or social issue more contentious or emotional than abortion. One of the (perhaps counterintuitive) insights of Guardiola's approach on this fraught topic is that using explicitly religious justifications will turn some people off. The inadvertent alignment of Catholicism with conservative Protestantism on abortion has probably exacerbated the wariness of more liberal Catholics toward an overtly religious defense of unborn life. A secular "social justice" vocabulary and framing may better resonate with young, liberal Catholics.

We began this chapter by raising the question of whether the clergy sexual abuse scandal diminished Catholics' willingness to listen to the moral and social teachings of their leaders. The scandal probably did not reorient Catholics' general approach to church authority—they were already quite individualistic and inclined to make up their own minds on various moral issues, as we will see again in chapter 5. But the scandal has likely given some Catholics an easy justification for completely tuning out their leaders. There is also lingering anger about the handling of sexual abuse cases, which probably hurts the extent to which some Catholics view the U.S. bishops as morally credible.

Bishop Kulick of the Greensburg Diocese describes his approach to addressing the scandal with his people. It focuses on informing them about the procedures that were put in place under the Dallas Charter and about his insistence that the diocese follow them scrupulously. He notes that the Catholics who are most active in their parishes are often already familiar with the church's policies because of the child protection training required for volunteers. But many other Catholics in his diocese remain unaware:

> Many times, what I have done in small groups is to hold an in-depth discussion where I share the church's process for the protection of children and vulnerable adults. You can't necessarily do this in a homily, but I think it is very beneficial for people to hear of the church's efforts. Not in a defensive manner, but I share that procedural map of how allegations are handled. For instance, in some cases I've had a priest removed from active ministry within two to three *hours* of an allegation. We report the allegation to ChildLine [the state hotline for reporting child abuse] and turn it over to the respective district attorney in the four counties of our diocese in under twenty-four hours. I try to

communicate with that level of specificity on things. I understand the reaction of Catholics who feel nothing has changed with the church's response to abuse. But it's frustrating to me because when you're on the inside, and you see firsthand what is being done and how the bishops are doing their best, you know things have changed for the better. I *know* the time, I *know* the energy, I *know* the processes we've worked so hard to put in place. It's hard to get that information out.

Our analysis of CARA survey data from 2003 implies that this may indeed be an effective approach. Catholics were less likely to view the scandal as having hurt the credibility of their leaders if they believed the policies of the Dallas Charter were being followed.

Michael McDonnell discusses recent abuse cases in which he and SNAP were assisting victims who had come forward. Asked whether dioceses had correctly followed procedures in those cases—by immediately removing priests from ministry and turning their cases over to diocesan review boards—he replies flatly, "Yeah, they're doing that," as if he isn't particularly impressed. Like Bishop Kulick, he talks at length about how bishops communicate with the laity and public about the sexual abuse problem, but he focuses on very different things. He criticizes official church statements released when a specific allegation is made: "In the statements that bishops have made within the last six or so months when an allegation has come out or a priest is removed from ministry, there is very little talk about the victim. Very few dioceses will even offer a prayer for all those involved. Church officials immediately say, right off the bat, 'This allegation does not mean guilt.'"

McDonnell is one of the few people we spoke with who seems unimpressed with Pope Francis. He feels the synod is a distraction from work that church leaders ought to be doing on the sexual abuse problem. He is also highly critical of the Vatican's reluctance to deal seriously with bishops who have failed to protect children. He slams the 2019 code of procedures[62] established by Pope Francis for addressing sexual abuse, calling it "an absolute joke." These procedures aim to hold bishops and priests to a similar level of accountability. But McDonnell complains that subsequent investigations by the Vatican have led to few bishops being seriously disciplined, let alone removed from ministry or defrocked. What could restore the trust of the Catholic laity, in McDonnell's opinion?

"A ton of church officials losing their positions and mass resignations of bishops here in the U.S. I would love to see that."

McDonnell admits this will not actually happen, but his comments touch on two points consistent with survey data. First, the fact that few bishops have been removed from ministry probably continues to depress American Catholics' confidence that there has been proper introspection and accountability among church leaders. As we saw previously, polls taken in 2002 and 2003 showed that a large majority of Catholics expected the resignations or removals of bishops who moved abusive priests from one assignment to another. Second, church leaders would do well to state their sympathy and offer prayers for victims of sexual abuse. A 2019 Pew survey asked people whether, in the past few months, they had heard clergy or religious leaders at their place of worship "speak out in support of victims of sexual harassment, assault, or abuse."[63] We analyzed the results for Catholics who attend church at least a few times a year. Those who have recently heard a parish leader—presumably a priest in most cases—speak out for victims are substantially more likely to give their own bishop a positive rating for his response to the sexual abuse issue.[64] Obviously we cannot be sure there is a causal relationship here and not just a correlation. But it seems plausible that hearing one's pastor speak for sexual abuse victims sends a signal that the issue is being dealt with seriously and pastorally at the local, diocesan level. This finding, as with the admonition of our interviewees to meet people where they are, suggests that one way to be more authoritative is to be more pastoral.

3

Race

In July 2022, Pope Francis took a "penitential pilgrimage" to Canada to publicly apologize for the church's role in the history of abuse and forced assimilation—what some have termed "cultural genocide"—of Indigenous Peoples in that country. In his apology, the pope said he was "deeply sorry" for the ways in which "many Christians supported the colonizing mentality of the powers that oppressed the Indigenous peoples." He asked for forgiveness "for the ways in which many members of the church and of religious communities cooperated . . . in projects of cultural destruction and forced assimilation promoted by the governments of that time, which culminated in the system of residential schools."[1]

A similar history of the church's participation in the cultural genocide of Native Americans through boarding schools unfolded in the United States. This became abundantly clear in our interview with Maka Black Elk, a Lakota Catholic who serves as the director for truth and healing at Red Cloud Indian School on the Pine Ridge Reservation in South Dakota. During our interview, Black Elk described how Indigenous Peoples' relationship with Catholicism in the United States has been both a source of pain and trauma as well as a wellspring of joy and empowerment. To illustrate this, he shared a story about his recent experience facilitating a listening session among former boarding students of the Red Cloud Indian School:

> We had a gathering of boarders who went to school here in the 1950s, and one of them started talking. She laid bare her experiences, her negative experiences with heavy expression of how terrible it was and why it was so oppressive. . . . And then suddenly, she switched gears, and couldn't help herself but to start talking about her love for what she learned here, and her love of learning Latin, because the Jesuits taught the kids Latin, and how that inspired her to become a writer, and that's what she's done

for the majority of her life. She found her power in writing. And this was just after lambasting the place, right? Then just spending this deep amount of time just appreciating it also. And I thought to myself that I was just witnessing this dichotomy of deep loathing for this place and a deep love for it. That's so reflective of the challenging nature of this history and of people's individual experiences. That's where the nuances are hard to explain. It's hard to get at the deep nuance that these schools were both incredibly bad and full of good. And as time went on, as the decades passed, they were more and more good.

As our interview with Maka Black Elk reveals, the history of the church's work among the Lakota people of South Dakota is a history of contradictions. In some historical moments, such as during the mission's founding and then again in recent decades, Jesuit priests and Franciscan sisters tried to preserve and honor the cultural traditions and languages of the Indigenous People. At other moments, however, they failed miserably. As Black Elk explained, during the saddest chapters of this history, Catholic missionaries cooperated with the U.S. government's colonization and forced assimilation of Indigenous Peoples through an extensive system of over 300 boarding schools. During this time, Catholic and other Christian missionaries who ran these schools separated Lakota children from their parents, changed their names, required them to speak only English, and prohibited them from speaking the Lakota language or wearing traditional Lakota dress.[2] In some cases, children were sent to boarding schools hundreds, if not thousands, of miles from their families, and some children would never see their families again.

This experience with Catholicism—one that involves a combination of pain and empowerment—is shared by other Catholic communities of color. They experienced pain and trauma when White Catholics minimized, denigrated, or suppressed their distinct cultures and contributions in order to prioritize or standardize European cultural traditions. They experienced empowerment and hope when their communities were able to find within Catholicism unique ways to express their memories and hopes about God's presence and action in their lives. Many interviewees acknowledged this, and spoke of the need for the church to own its complicity in systems of oppression to advance reconciliation, and to honor the distinct cultures and contributions of Catholics of color.

This chapter describes the distinct beliefs and practices of Catholics of color in the United States. It does so by using our 2017 American Catholic Laity Survey to compare responses across four different racial and ethnic subgroups. After describing the distinct beliefs and practices among these subgroups, we turn our attention to the themes that emerged among our interviewees, who were asked how the church could more effectively minister to Catholics of color and ensure their full and active participation in the church. Before embarking on these objectives, we set the stage by describing some of the historical experiences of communities of color within the U.S. church as well as their growing presence among the U.S. Catholic population.

Distinct Historical Experiences of Catholics of Color

Communities of color have faced various forms of prejudice, discrimination, and racism during the church's history. Mexican Americans, for instance, having established their own network of parishes throughout the Southwest and California when they were part of Mexico, can rightly be considered "the largest and oldest ethnic group in the American Catholic Church."[3] Despite their historic and autonomous presence in these regions, after their territories were seized by the U.S. government following the Mexican-American War of 1846–48, their parishes were gradually absorbed into the U.S. church, which at that time was dominated by Irish-American bishops and priests. In some cases, Mexican-American Catholics found their new, predominantly Irish church leaders "to be condescending and insufficiently supportive of Mexican Catholic traditions such as devotion to the Virgin of Guadalupe," leading them to form their own, independent lay groups for devotional practices, religious processions, and familial celebrations.[4] Even after Vatican II, when priests began celebrating Mass in the vernacular, many Hispanic Catholics found themselves in parishes whose Irish-American clergy spoke little or no Spanish outside of reading the Mass in Spanish. Hispanics have been—and continue to be—underrepresented in leadership positions in the church, and some, as described by our interviewees, experience prejudice and anti-immigrant sentiments to this day.[5]

Black Catholics have also experienced discrimination in the church. Historically, this entailed denial of full access to parish life, segregated seating and communion lines in churches, and denial of the receipt of some sacraments, including ordination to the priesthood.[6] Some Catholics and Catholic religious orders owned slaves well after Pope Gregory XVI's condemnation of slavery in 1839, and many church leaders and clergy in the South sided with the Confederacy during the Civil War.[7] As African Americans migrated to the urban North in the decades after World War I, they observed that some Catholic parishes became "rallying points for bigotry."[8] Native Americans, as we have seen, suffered a campaign of forced assimilation through the boarding school system in the nineteenth and twentieth centuries, and Asian Americans have been victims of stereotypes, in the church as in society, as perpetual foreigners and model minorities.[9]

This is not to say that the Catholic Church, through its parishes and schools, has not also been a source of hope and empowerment for these same communities. It has. Catholics of color have benefitted in numerous ways from Catholicism's commitment to solidarity with and among marginalized groups , and various immigrant communities have derived a variety of social, psychological, and spiritual resources from Catholic parishes and schools to assist their adaptation to a new society.[10] Black Catholics, too, have found in their churches resources for education, social services, social action, and evangelization.[11]

This historical context provides an important foundation for understanding the distinct identities of Catholics of color, as their historical experiences within the church have become part of their collective memory. It is through the lenses of these experiences that we can also appreciate the need for church leaders today to speak clearly on contemporary issues, such as immigration, anti-immigrant sentiments, White nationalism, White privilege, and systemic racism.

The Changing Racial and Ethnic Composition of American Catholics

As we saw in the introduction, American Catholics are more racially and ethnically diverse today than ever before. In 2017, White, non-Hispanic

Catholics are 56 percent of respondents (from 86% in 1987), and Hispanics are 35 percent (from 10% in 1987). Black, non-Hispanic Catholics still make up only 3 percent of respondents, but all others (including Asians, multi-ethnics, and those of some other race or ethnicity) now make up 6 percent of respondents (1% in 1987).[12]

This increasing racial and ethnic diversity is largely due to the passage of the Immigration and Nationality Act of 1965, which eliminated the decades-old national quota system designed to favor immigrants from northern and western Europe. This new policy, together with U.S. economic incentives, fueled the entry of new waves of immigrants from Catholic-dense countries and regions such as Mexico, Central and South America, and parts of Africa and South Asia. Their arrival on U.S. shores and at U.S. borders has not only ensured the vitality of American Catholicism, but made it more culturally, linguistically, and ethnically diverse than at any period in its history.[13] Hispanic immigrants make up the largest portion of these new immigrant streams, leading some analysts to predict that Hispanics will make up as many as half of all American Catholics by mid-century.[14] In fact, a similar ethnic distribution can already be seen among the youngest generation of Catholics, as we noted in the Introduction.

Distinct Understandings and Expressions of Faith

Social scientists have long observed differences across racial and ethnic groups in their understandings and expressions of faith and their participation and attachment to faith communities.[15] These cultural distinctions stem partly from distinct experiences of exclusion and oppression, which can lead communities of color to view their faith communities as a "special kind of home."[16] One of the interviewees, Tara Segal, who works as director of university ministry at Dominican University, a Hispanic-serving institution, states it this way: "We each come to our faith through this lens of culture. And as universal as the Catholic Church is . . . we still navigate our faith through this really particular experience of culture." A recent study by Pew confirms this.[17] Pew finds that Black Catholics are more likely than either White or Hispanic Catholics to say "it is essential for churches to" do each of the following: "help the needy with bills, housing, or food"; "offer a sense of racial affirmation or pride"; "teach practical job and life skills"; and "offer sermons that address political topics, such as immigration and race relations." Compared to White and Hispanics Catholics, Black Catholics are also more likely to believe that opposing racism and sexism are essential to what it means to be a faithful Christian.

Using data from our 2017 survey, we can examine differences among Catholics by comparing responses across four subgroups: White, Hispanic, Black, and "Other, Non-Hispanic" (hereafter "Other") Catholics; this final category is inclusive of Asian, Native Hawaiian, Pacific Islander, and Native American/Alaskan Native populations. Unfortunately, our survey did not have a separate category for Asians as a group, but relying on estimates provided by the Center for Applied Research in the Apostolate at Georgetown University (CARA), we estimate that this Other group is approximately 80 percent Asian or Pacific Islander (API) and approximately 20 percent Native American.[18] Because the category "Mixed, Non-Hispanic" represented less than one percent of our sample, they are excluded from our analyses. Using these categories for comparisons, we discover that, although Catholics of different races and ethnicities share many beliefs and attitudes in common, the most pronounced differences are in their beliefs about what is essential to being Catholic, beliefs about what is required to be a good Catholic, and beliefs about and engagement in the sacraments and parish life. It is important to note that the Black and Other subgroups are too small to draw robust comparisons, but we include these categories for exploratory purposes given the dearth of data on Black, API, and Native American Catholics.

Beliefs and Practices Essential to Being Catholic

Our 2017 survey asked respondents what things they consider essential to their vision of what it means to be Catholic. As table 3.1 illustrates, a large majority of all Catholics (almost 75%), regardless of race or ethnicity, agree that belief in Jesus's resurrection from the dead is essential to the faith. Except for Black Catholics (43%), a majority of Catholics also claim the necessity of having a pope as essential to being Catholic. Although 50 percent or more of Catholics believe that devotion to Mary the Mother of God is essential to the faith, Hispanic Catholics (65%) stand out in their adherence to this belief.

TABLE 3.1: Percent of Catholics Reporting Items as "Essential" to the Faith.

	White, Non-Hispanic	Hispanic	Black, Non-Hispanic	Other, Non-Hispanic
Belief in Jesus's resurrection from the dead	74%	74%	73%	74%
Necessity of having a pope	57	54	43	59
Devotion to Mary the mother of God	54	65	50	55
Charitable efforts toward helping the poor	47	51	58	48
Engaging in daily prayer	44	54	50	51
Obligation to attend Mass once a week	32	45	28	43
Participation in devotions such as eucharistic adoration or praying the rosary	30	48	43	40
Private confession to a priest	28	42	25	17
A celibate male clergy	20	32	13	27

Source: 2017 ACLS.

Hispanic Catholics also stand out in that, in comparison to the other groups, they assign greater importance to participating in more private and traditional devotional practices, particularly Marian devotions. Hispanic Catholics are more likely than most, if not all, other racial and ethnic groups to report that having a devotion to Mary the Mother of God (65%), attending Mass once a week (45%), participating in devotions such as eucharistic adoration or praying the rosary (48%), and going to private confession to a priest (42%) are essential to what it means to be Catholic. Hispanic Catholics (54%) are also more likely than White Catholics (44%) to regard engaging in daily prayer as essential to the faith.

That Hispanic Catholics are more devoted to personal piety and more theologically conservative are among the major takeaways from our analyses. However, other differences evident in table 3.1 are also worth highlighting. For instance, while approximately half of Catholics believe that engaging in charitable efforts toward helping the poor is essential to what it means to be Catholic, Black Catholics are the most likely to believe this, a finding consistent with Pew's research.[19] Black Catholics (43%) are also more similar to Hispanic Catholics (48%) than to White

Catholics (30%) in their belief that participation in devotions such as eucharistic adoration and praying the rosary are essential to the faith, a finding consistent with previous studies that show that Black Catholics exhibit higher engagement in private devotional practices than do their White counterparts.[20]

Where do White, non-Hispanic Catholics stand out, relative to the other racial and ethnic groups? As table 3.1 illustrates, White Catholics (30%) are the least likely to report that participating in devotions such as eucharistic adoration or praying the rosary is essential to what it means to be Catholic, and along with Black Catholics, they are among the least likely to report that having a celibate male clergy (20%) or attending Mass once a week (32%) is essential. If there are any ways in which Other Catholics stand out regarding these elements of Catholicism, it is with respect to their belief about the importance of confessing sins privately to a priest. Only 17 percent of Other Catholics believe that confessing sins to a priest is essential to what it means to be Catholic.

What It Takes to Be a Good Catholic

Our 2017 survey also asked respondents if they think someone can be a good Catholic *without* performing certain actions or affirming certain beliefs. The overall pattern is consistent with some of the observations made above. White and Black Catholics (85% and 84%, respectively) are the most likely to report that one can be a good Catholic without going to Mass every Sunday, and on many of the items measuring respondents' theological views, Hispanic and Other Catholics evince a more conservative theological orientation.

As table 3.2 reports, Hispanic and Other Catholics are the least likely to believe that someone can be a good Catholic without going to Mass every Sunday (72% and 70%, respectively). They are also the least likely to believe that someone can be a good Catholic without obeying the church hierarchy on various issues of sexual morality. Specifically, Hispanic and Other Catholics (75% and 70%, respectively) are less likely than either White or Black Catholics (88% and 95%, respectively) to believe that someone can be a good Catholic without obeying the church hierarchy's opposition to artificial contraception. Hispanic (71%), Black (74%), and Other Catholics (56%) are less likely than White Catholics

TABLE 3.2: Perceptions of What It Takes to Be a "Good Catholic."

Percentage of Catholics Saying One Can be a "Good Catholic" *Without . . .*

	White, Non-Hispanic	Hispanic	Black, Non-Hispanic	Other, Non-Hispanic
Going to Mass every Sunday	85%	72%	84%	70%
Obeying the church hierarchy's opposition to artificial contraception	88	75	95	70
Their marriage being approved by the Catholic Church	83	71	74	56
Obeying the church hierarchy's opposition to same-sex relationships	79	67	71	71
Obeying the church hierarchy's opposition to abortion	66	61	76	54
Donating time or money to help the poor	66	58	54	67
Believing that Jesus physically rose from the dead	34	33	26	44

Source: 2017 ACLS.

(83%) to believe that one can be a good Catholic without having their marriage approved by the Catholic Church. Hispanic Catholics (67%) are the least likely to believe that someone can be a good Catholic without obeying the church hierarchy's opposition to same-sex relationships, although Black and Other Catholics are more similar to Hispanic Catholics in this regard than they are to White Catholics. Other Catholics are the least likely to believe that someone can be a good Catholic without obeying the church hierarchy's opposition to abortion (54%).

Where are White and Black Catholics most distinctive in comparison to the other racial and ethnic categories? White and Black Catholics (approximately 85%) are the most likely to believe that someone can be a good Catholic without going to Mass every Sunday. Black Catholics are the most likely to believe that someone can be a good Catholic without obeying the church hierarchy's opposition to artificial contraception (95%) or to abortion (76%). Black Catholics, along with Hispanic Catholics, are the least likely to believe someone can be a good Catholic without donating time or money to help the poor (54%) or believing that Jesus physically rose from the dead (26%). White Catholics are the most likely to say that someone can be a good Catholic without obeying the church hierarchy's opposition to gay or lesbian sexual relationships (79%) or without having their marriage approved by the Catholic Church (83%).

In sum, the general pattern presented in table 3.2 is one in which Hispanic Catholics, and in some cases Other Catholics, distinguish themselves for being more conservative on issues of sexual morality and more deferential toward the institutional church and Catholic tradition. These findings are consistent with previous waves of our survey.[21] White and Black Catholics, on the other hand, tend to be more liberal on these issues.

Beliefs about, and Engagement in, the Sacraments and Parish Life

In addition to exhibiting several distinct beliefs with respect to what it means to be Catholic and what is required to be a good Catholic, everyday Catholics of different races and ethnicities show distinct patterns of involvement in the church's sacramental and parish life. Before we examine the data in this area, it is helpful to understand one of the reforms called for by Vatican II: the inculturation of the liturgy.

Although Vatican II's 1965 document *Gaudium et Spes* (the Pastoral Constitution on the Church in the Modern World) acknowledged that "Man comes to a true and full humanity only through culture," the Catholic Church presented a fuller understanding of the relationship between faith and culture in its 1988 document *Faith and Inculturation*.[22] Recognizing that faith "takes root and blossoms" in culture, this document called ministers to engage in the process of inculturation, which it defined as "the incarnation of the Gospel in native cultures and also the introduction of these cultures into the life of the Church."[23] It encouraged an appreciation of "popular piety" in which people "express their religious sentiment in . . . festival, pilgrimage, dance and song." It supported efforts to inculturate the liturgy by incorporating into the liturgy various cultural elements—language, music, symbols, art, and imagery—that reflect the culture of the local population. These reforms helped stimulate a movement of inculturation, whose advocates created culturally specific worship aids, like the African-American Catholic hymnal, *Lead Me, Guide Me*;[24] developed ministry training programs to teach church personnel the customs, traditions, and languages of diverse populations; and supported the emergence of various "contextual theologies," like Black theology and Hispanic theology.[25] By the end of the 1980s, dioceses were establishing offices to address the specific needs of various racial and ethnic populations (e.g., Offices of Black Ministry), and laity and clergy had formed various associations based on race or ethnicity (e.g., the National Black Catholic Congress).[26]

Although our 2017 survey did not ask respondents whether the parishes and Masses they attend inculturated the liturgy, some of the interviewees we spoke with talked about the importance of inculturation, as we will see in the next section. What the survey does enable us to examine is whether and how different racial and ethnic groups view, and engage in, the sacraments and life of their parishes.

As table 3.3 shows, although a large majority of all Catholics agree that the sacraments of the church are essential to their relationship with God, Hispanic and Other Catholics are slightly more likely to agree with this statement than are White Catholics. For most racial groups, about half of Catholics believe that parishes are too big and impersonal. Interestingly, Black Catholics are much less likely than their counterparts to describe their parishes as "too big and impersonal," suggesting that Black Catholics are more likely to find a special kind of home in their parishes. Large majorities of all Catholics believe that their parish priest does a good job, with White Catholics being slightly more likely to agree with this statement than Other Catholics.

Table 3.3 also reports whether respondents believe that it is important that younger generations of their family grow up as Catholics. Hispanic Catholics (81%) and Other Catholics (84%) are the most likely to say that it is important that younger generations grow up as Catholic, and Black Catholics (53%) are the least likely, with White Catholics (71%) falling in between. Perhaps one reason why Black Catholics are the least likely to believe it is important for younger generations to grow up as Catholic is that, because only seven percent of African Americans are Catholic, they are more likely to have either a personal background or

TABLE 3.3: Catholics' Attitudes about Sacraments and Parish Life.

Percentage Reporting They "Somewhat Agree" or "Strongly Agree"

	White, Non-Hispanic	Hispanic	Black, Non-Hispanic	Other, Non-Hispanic
The sacraments of the Church are essential to my relationship with God.	73%	81%	75%	82%
Catholic parishes are too big and impersonal.	40	51	20	49
On the whole, parish priests do a good job.	90	86	85	82
It is important to me that younger generations of my family grow up as Catholics.	71	81	53	84

Source: 2017 ACLS.

other family members, friends, and acquaintances who are in a Protestant congregation.

Our survey asked a series of questions about parish membership, frequency of Mass attendance, involvement in parish activities, financial giving, and participation in interfaith activities. As table 3.4 shows, although a majority of all Catholics in our survey report being registered at a Catholic parish, Other Catholics are the most likely to report being registered (69%), while Hispanic (55%) and Black (55%) Catholics are the least likely. Other Catholics are also the most likely to attend Mass two to three times a month or more (58%), to contribute financially to their parish "occasionally" or "regularly" (72%), and to participate in interfaith activities (45%). Except in terms of parish registration, Hispanic Catholics are the next most highly involved, with 44 percent of Hispanic Catholics attending Mass two to three times a month or more, 63 percent contributing financially to their parish "occasionally" or "regularly," and 37 percent participating in interfaith activities.

The 2011 National Black Catholics Survey[27] and the Pew Research Center's recent study of "Black Catholics in America" reveal that the vast majority of Black Catholics do not attend predominantly Black parishes.[28] This fact alone has important implications for the religious experiences of Black Catholics, because attendance at predominantly Black parishes has been shown to diminish exposure to racial intolerance and

TABLE 3.4: Catholics' Engagement in Parish Life and Interfaith Activities.

	White, Non-Hispanic	Hispanic	Black, Non-Hispanic	Other, Non-Hispanic
Percentage who report being registered at a Catholic parish	62%	55%	55%	69%
Percentage who report attending Mass 2-3 times a month or more	34	44	22	58
Percentage who report engaging "occasionally" or "regularly" in . . .				
Giving financial contributions to their parish	55	63	58	72
Parish life beyond attending Mass	35	43	39	43
Interfaith or ecumenical gatherings	26	37	35	45

Source: 2017 ACLS.

to enhance overall levels of religious engagement and parish satisfaction among Black Catholics.[29]

Distinct Expectations for the Church's Advocacy around Public Policy Issues

Catholics of color are more likely to agree with the U.S. Catholic bishops' stances on key policy issues that affect them. Specifically, data from our survey show that between 80 and 90 percent of Catholics of color agree with the bishops' advocacy to make the immigration process easier for families, or to provide government-funded health care, compared to only six in ten White Catholics who support these initiatives. The gap between Catholics of color and White Catholics is also evident in their levels of support for the bishops' opposition to the death penalty, with Black Catholics exhibiting the highest level of support.[30] These differences often translate into different expectations among Catholics of color for church leaders at all levels to advocate for and act on these sorts of social justice issues. Such expectations are reflected in what our interviewees claim is important for ensuring the full and active participation of Catholics of color. It is to these themes that we now turn.

Catholic Leaders' Insights and Concerns

We asked interviewees what the U.S. church could do to ensure the full and active participation of Catholics of color in the life of the church and to show solidarity on issues of racism and immigration. Recurring themes include: more effectively ministering to Catholics of color, inculturating liturgies and programs, and acknowledging and addressing racism and the marginalization of immigrants within the church and in society.

Effectively Ministering to Catholics of Color

Interviewees identify several ways that the church might improve its ability to minister effectively to Catholics of color. The first effective ministry practice that interviewees lift up focuses on ensuring that ministers at all levels are properly trained to work with diverse populations. This includes requiring those preparing for, or already engaged in, ministry to Catholics of color to take courses, attend workshops, and have immersion experiences designed to expand their ability to communicate in various languages and to understand and appreciate the unique cultures and experiences of the various communities they serve.[31] Dr. C. Vanessa White, an African-American associate professor of spirituality and ministry at the Catholic Theological Union in Chicago and past convener of the Black Catholic Theological Symposium, explains, "It's not enough to learn the Catholic faith to know what it means to be a Catholic minister. You also need to be mindful of the fact that our Catholic tradition is rooted in various cultural contexts." Ministers need to know the way the faith is rooted in the various communities in which they minister.

Intercultural inclusion starts with being linguistically inclusive, but interviewees argue it must never end there.[32] It also entails learning and appreciating the diverse cultural traditions of the communities that comprise the church, and abandoning one's own cultural preconceptions. For instance, Maka Black Elk, himself a Native American, describes how some Native American parishes have been disrupted when clergy who lack cultural competence or sensitivity are assigned to lead them. He says that in some cases untrained or insensitive clergy "come in, see that Native communities have incorporated some of their own cultural traditions in the Mass, and become incensed and say no to the inclusion of these traditions." He finds this regrettable, and attributes it to a lack of cultural competence and sensitivity that is rooted in "a White supremacist cultural paradigm about our faith." According to Black Elk, for clergy and other pastoral ministers to be genuinely receptive of—and ultimately to value—the distinct cultures of the people they serve requires that they abandon their own preconceptions, usually Eurocentric preconceptions, about the church and its liturgies. It requires pastoral ministers to familiarize themselves with the language and cultural traditions of the communities they serve so they can effectively inculturate the liturgy by incorporating culturally distinctive language, music, symbols, art, and imagery.

Some of the interviewees believe ministers could more easily let go of their Eurocentric preconceptions about the church if their theological education and training "decentered whiteness" and raised awareness of cultural pluralism within the Catholic Church. For Father Linh Hoang, O.F.M., a Vietnamese-born Franciscan friar and associate professor of religious studies at Siena College, decentering whiteness in theological education entails raising awareness of the long history that Catholicism has had in various countries around the world, not just European countries. To illustrate his point, he describes how some ministers in the United States think that "Asian Americans and other recent immigrants" are newcomers to Catholicism. "There's this assumption that if you're Asian American that you are either practicing Buddhism or Hinduism," which, he says, fails to recognize that "many Asian Americans are already Christians and may have been practicing Catholicism for generations." The stereotype of being "forever foreign" can happen not just in secular American society, but within their own church.

According to Dr. Ansel Augustine, director of the Office of Black Catholic Ministries for the Archdiocese of New Orleans and a faculty member at Loyola University New Orleans, decentering whiteness means challenging Eurocentric preconceptions of what it means to be authentically Catholic. In the course of our interview, Augustine reflects on times when he, as an African-American Catholic, or his parish, as a predominantly African-American congregation in New Orleans, have had their Catholic identities challenged. He describes occasions when, for instance, visitors to his parish wondered whether "our worship style—with the Afrocentric art, the kente cloth, the gospel music—was authentically Catholic." These kinds of challenges to authenticity of the Catholicism of predominantly African-American parishes or African inculturated liturgies, Augustine maintains, falsely hold up Eurocentric Catholicism "as a model of what is ideal" and devalue the universality of the Catholic faith.

Dr. Stephanie Russell, vice president for mission integration at the Association of Jesuit Colleges and Universities, also believes that the American Catholic Church needs to decenter whiteness, but she expresses it in a slightly different way. She says that every time she hears people in the church speaking about immigrants "joining us," they fail to grasp the fact that "they"—the immigrants—are actually "us":

> I don't know that we, at a very basic human level, understand that the advent of immigrants in our communities . . . organically changes the identity of those communities. So, we will have the Spanish Mass or a Cinco de Mayo celebration, but I don't know that we have done a great job of gluing and integrating the identity of new members into the D.N.A. of who a given parish community is. . . . I don't think generally we've come to understand that the shift in the makeup of the American church, and where its new members are coming from, changes the historically Anglo, especially the Anglo middle class, church in the United States.

As conveyed in this quote, Russell believes that church ministers and everyday Catholics still exhibit a sense that immigrants "are joining us," rather than recognizing that the very base of our church has changed. Immigrant Catholics are remaking the church on U.S. shores into the universal, culturally pluralistic, immigrant community it has always been.

Another effective ministry practice lifted up by the interviewees focuses on ensuring that ministers at all levels—from the parish to the top leadership of the church—reflect and represent the communities they serve. Father Robert Boxie, an African-American Catholic chaplain at Howard University in Washington, D.C., speaks about his own prior experiences on the pastoral staff of St. Joseph's parish, a predominantly Black parish in Largo, Maryland. When Father Boxie first joined the pastoral staff there, he and the other priests and lay ministers were all African Americans, yet the parish was experiencing an influx of African immigrants from Nigeria and other countries in Africa. Recognizing that none of the parish's leaders were African, Father Boxie and the other ministers called upon some of the African immigrants to join their leadership team so that, in his words, "the leaders would be more reflective of the community." Having leaders who are reflective of the community entails more than simply having ministers of the same race or skin color; it entails having ministers of the same cultural and linguistic backgrounds. Dr. C. Vanessa White also acknowledges this, speaking about the difficulties that often arise when African immigrant priests are assigned to serve as ministers at predominantly African-American parishes. She states that church leaders need to be "attentive to the fact that just because you have brown skin or darker complexion doesn't mean you are all alike. Even within the continent of Africa, there's diversity there between different tribes and different communities." As this statement conveys, it is a significant mistake to conflate race or skin color with culture. To avoid making these potentially harmful assumptions, the church needs to ensure that ministers are either from the cultural communities they serve, or are trained sufficiently to understand and appreciate the cultures of those to whom they minister.

Having ministers who reflect and represent the communities they serve extends beyond the parish to other levels of church administration. Several interviewees speak of the need to have Catholics of color represented at all levels of decision-making and leadership. Dr. Stephanie Russell, for instance, states that "we don't have, as a general rule, leaders of color in our American church. And what is it that has kept them from entering positions of leadership? . . . The nature of racism generally is that it privileges one group over another. So, what is it about the selection process? Are we really doing some deep listening to leaders of color or people who would have been leaders of color, and seeing whether that will teach us something as a community?" Here, Russell is encouraging church leaders to not only listen and learn from the experiences of people of color within the church, but also to consider the numerous ways that they, perhaps unknowingly, encourage Catholics of particular backgrounds to pursue leadership while systematically discouraging others, such as Black Catholics, from doing the same.

The final effective ministry practice that our interviewees highlight focuses on providing ministers with the encouragement and resources needed to teach all Catholics to respect the distinct cultures within the church. According to Maka Black Elk, it was during the early period of Christianity—the time of the first apostles—that "the church decided that it was a universal church, that people didn't have to conform to one culture in order to become followers of Christ." Indeed, the church traces its history of respecting distinct cultures and languages back to the early church, when Peter the Apostle defended Greek converts to Christianity by arguing that the Greeks did not need to become culturally Jewish in order to become Christians.[33]

Several of the interviewees suggest that one of the primary ways that ministers can raise awareness of, and respect for, distinct cultures is to lead by example by honoring and embracing distinct cultural traditions in liturgies, devotional practices, and faith formation programs that take place in homes, parishes, schools, and universities. This ties into the next general theme that emerged from our interviews, when we asked about what the U.S. Catholic Church could do to ensure the full and active participation of Catholics of color in the life of the church—the inculturation of liturgies and programs.

Inculturating Liturgies and Programs

Inculturating liturgies and programs not only raises awareness among everyday Catholics, particularly White Catholics, of the diverse cultures within the universal church, but doing so also serves to solidify the faith, commitment, and feelings of inclusion of Catholics of color. The interviewees speak about the benefits and challenges of inculturation among the communities they serve.

Discussing the benefits of inculturation among Asian-American Catholic communities, Father Lin Hoang, O.F.M, describes the importance of the veneration of ancestors at home altars among some Asian-American communities. According to Hoang, these practices, while not dominant, "are still acceptable, and should be respected and embraced" because for many Asian communities "keeping the memories of those who have passed before is extremely important." Many Asian Americans, he claims, "believe it is their responsibility" to do this. Focusing on the African and African-American experience, Father Robert Boxie describes some of ways predominantly Black parishes can incorporate distinct cultural traditions into their liturgies. Reflecting on his experiences in ministry at a predominantly Black parish with a growing African immigrant community, Boxie states:

> We have incorporated a number of things at St. Joseph that were requested by the African community, and some of them have been absolutely beautiful. For instance, a large tradition in some African countries . . . is what they call a Harvest Thanksgiving, and it's one of the most beautiful, moving Masses I've ever been to in my entire life. At the Harvest Thanksgiving back home, folks would bring animals and food and plants as gifts to show thanksgiving for what God had done during the prior year. So, we modified it at St. Joseph, because we can't really have live donkeys and cows walking around inside the church. So, people bring monetary offerings, they bring canned goods and food items for the food pantry, things like that. Everyone's in their incredibly beautiful African garb and headdresses. It's absolutely beautiful when each family processes down the aisle with their gifts, showing how God has blessed them through the past year. It is a long Mass, but it's totally worth it . . . because people are singing and dancing, families' names are announced. . . . It's just beautiful.

Maka Black Elk, a descendant of the famous Nicholas Black Elk, expresses a similarly positive evaluation of the level of inculturation apparent in the Catholic parishes on the Pine Ridge Reservation today. As he describes, "We incorporate our cedar into Mass incense burnings, we incorporate drum and song, we incorporate [the Lakota] language into our services. Certainly we could do more, but inculturation should come from the indigenous communities themselves." He also describes how, at one Lakota Catholic parish, the Mass starts "with a four-direction song where they acknowledge all of their directions—above and below and the whole of creation—and that's a beautiful way to start the Mass."

The church leaders who work in schools or university campus ministry programs similarly describe how understanding and incorporating the cultural traditions of their students is essential to the success of their programs. According to Tara Segal, for instance, because Dominican University is largely a commuter campus, she and her staff initially faced challenges getting their predominantly Hispanic student body to participate in Masses and campus ministry activities on campus. This lack of involvement, she reasons, was understandable, because among some Hispanic ethnic groups the family is extremely important, and students would rather join their families for Mass in their home parishes than come to campus for Mass. Recognizing this, Segal and her staff decided to invite students' families to their events, and the response was transformative.[34]

Inculturating liturgies and programs—while recognized by church leaders as important for strengthening the faith, commitment, and active participation of Catholics of color—is not without its challenges. Several of the interviewees, in relating their own experiences of inculturation, describe difficulties created when they or other ministers lump various ethnic groups into pan-ethnicities or racial groups. For instance, Archbishop John Wester states that when he served in the dioceses of San Francisco, Salt Lake City, and now Santa Fe, there would be such a variety of cultures that "You just can't say Latino, because you've got people from Colombia, Mexico, Peru, all the different cultures there. I think there is a sensitivity to that more and more." Father Linh Hoang shares the same perspective by relating a story from the history of the church's outreach to Chinese Americans in San Francisco. He says:

> In the 19th century, when Bishop Joseph Alemany [the first archbishop of San Francisco] saw the growing number of Chinese Catholics, he asked for a native Chinese priest to come and minister. But what he failed to do is recognize the distinct linguistic and cultural traditions of the Chinese Americans in his diocese. The Chinese Americans in his diocese were Mandarin-speaking Chinese, and he brought in a Cantonese-speaking priest to minister to them. So, there are these differences in language and culture that are important to recognize.

These observations highlight that, in any effort at inculturation, care needs to be taken to understand the cultural diversity among groups that our society might lump together on the basis of some other trait, such as race or pan-ethnic identity.

The second challenge of inculturating liturgies and programs is doing so in spaces shared by two or more racial or ethnic groups when one of them is more dominant, either in terms of numbers or influence, within the parish.[35] But there are a number of other ways in which being a minority in a parish presents challenges. Describing the challenges faced by Black Catholics in predominantly White or multicultural parishes, Father Robert Boxie states that "a lot of times the issues that are important to Black Catholics are not being talked about. And certain ways of worshiping, certain ways of doing things, are just not welcomed. When that happens, this is honestly when people start to leave." To illustrate his point, he uses the example of the mass shooting that occurred at the Tops supermarket in Buffalo in which ten Black people were killed and three others injured: "[T]hat this was probably on the minds of every Black person in America, and if something isn't said about that at church, then people will ask if they are living in the same reality. Like, 'What's going on?'" The point that Boxie is making is that it is important for ministers to speak about issues that are of concern to the various communities within their parishes.

Our interviewees acknowledge a third challenge in trying to inculturate liturgies and programs: trying to bring people of different racial or ethnic groups together in shared multicultural liturgies. Archbishop John Wester says that "My goal, my hope, would be that someday, all of our English speakers and Spanish speakers would be equally at home in a bilingual Mass where all the Catholics could say the Our Father in English and Spanish, they could do the Confiteor [Penitential Act], the Gloria, the creed, and the music in both English and Spanish." This idealized vision of a bicultural liturgy would be hard enough to enact; one can only imagine how difficult it would be to orchestrate a truly multicultural liturgy for several cultural groups.

Several of the interviewees speak about their challenges and joys in planning and celebrating multicultural liturgies. As Tara Segal describes her experience of planning multicultural liturgies at Dominican University, "It's an adventure, and we mess up, and we figure it out as we go. This past weekend was the first time we offered simultaneous interpretation. . . . We had headsets, and our families all had headsets. . . . My favorite part . . . was during the communal prayers, during the creed, and the Our Father, you heard multiple languages at the same time. It was just really, really cool because each person is speaking in their own language using their own headset." When Segal refers to the planning of multicultural liturgies as "an adventure," which "we mess up, and figure it out as we go," she displays a willingness to step into the unknown, courageously trusting that something better—something more inclusive and integrated—is possible in the church's ritual life.

Acknowledging and Addressing Racism and the Marginalization of Immigrants

Interviewees also spoke about the importance of acknowledging and addressing racism and the marginalization of immigrants in both the church and society. In fact, they cite this as one of the leading ways to ensure the full and active participation of Catholics of color in the life of the church, and to show solidarity. When asked how they thought this could best be accomplished, they highlight a few distinct strategies the church should employ: 1) acknowledge that racism is a reality in both the church and in society, historically and presently, and that it exists at both the individual and institutional levels; 2) more clearly and publicly identify contemporary manifestations of racism and condemn them as sinful, regardless of whether these sins are personal or social[36] in nature; 3) show support for, and help raise awareness of, anti-racist and immigrant rights causes; and 4) encourage people to be open to encountering and accompanying "the other" through "crossing over."[37]

The first strategy that these Catholic leaders identify for acknowledging and addressing racism is for members of the church to recognize that racism is a reality in both the church and in society, historically and presently, and that it exists at both the individual and institutional levels. In focusing first on the individual level, Dr. C. Vanessa White states, "I think one of the major challenges is the fact that Catholic leaders were socialized here in the United States of America. And by virtue of being socialized here in the United States, you have biases, stereotypes, and racism embedded in your spirit and your soul. And so one challenge is just recognizing that, recognizing that this has shaped you." It is important for church leaders, and all Catholic laity, to simply acknowledge their own personal biases.

Equally important to our interviewees is for the church to acknowledge the institutional dimension of racism, including how the church, both historically and today, has practiced and participated in institutionalized racism. Dr. Stephanie Russell says that the first step in addressing the sin of racism is for members of the church to acknowledge the history of its own involvement and complicity in this sin. "I think as in any justice issue, but maybe particularly with respect to racial justice, that we will not have much credibility as a church until we are willing to address our own history." That history, as we saw earlier in this chapter, has included, for some Catholics of color, serious ecclesial exclusion. The interviewees recognize that Catholics need to tell this story and, in the company of their Catholic brothers and sisters, express their sorrow and ask for forgiveness, just as Pope Francis did in his recent trip to Canada.

Some of the interviewees recognize that it is not an easy task for everyday Catholics or for their parish ministers to acknowledge the church's complicity in institutionalized racism. They describe how it is often difficult for Catholics who love their church and regard it as their home to criticize it. As Tara Segal states, "To say that this church, that's the foundation of who we are and teaches us how to love and do all of these good things in our lives, has also perpetuated acts of racism," can be a real challenge. "People hate talking about issues of conflict in the church, despite the fact that we have Jesus as our model." However, the goal of these conversations is being able to own responsibility and to create a path toward reconciliation.

Maka Black Elk reports having similar difficulties talking about the history of racism in the church, but from a different perspective—one that recognizes the general public and the media as interlocutors. For him, the challenge is talking about the nuances of the church's history on Indian reservations, which included aspects that were both negative and positive, "without sounding defensive," or coming across as trying to be apologetic for the church or for the individuals who ran the boarding schools. He certainly acknowledges the painful past, such as the suppression of the indigenous languages and cultures, the separation of children from their families, and so forth, but he says "the actual history is more nuanced. It is not the black-and-white story the media wants to make this into—a story of Native peoples versus White peoples, Native peoples versus the White government and the White Catholic Church."[38] Like Tara Segal, he recognizes the importance of taking responsibility for a racist past and charting a path toward reconciliation, but he said this should entail acknowledging what he sees as two truths of Native Americans' experiences—that the boarding schools were "sites of oppression, of cultural genocide, and of abuse, and that they were also sites of cross-cultural relationship building, of cultural resilience and growth." Part of acknowledging the truth of a painful past, he believes, is to also recognize the nuances of the history.

The second strategy that Catholic leaders identify for acknowledging and addressing racism is to more clearly and publicly identify contemporary manifestations of racism and condemn them as sinful, regardless of whether these sins are personal or social in nature. The interviewees believe that it is important for leaders and ministers, especially, to name and condemn racism, including systemic racism, whenever it is apparent in society.

Although the Catholic Church's teachings condemning racism are clear and unambiguous, some interviewees say that the church could do more to get this message out, especially since to do otherwise may result in the church losing credibility, members, or both. As we saw earlier, Black Catholics expect their church leaders to speak out about racial and social justice. Catholics of color overwhelmingly support their bishops' advocacy of immigration reform, comprehensive health care, and an end to the death penalty. According to Father Robert Boxie, although these issues are "high in the minds of Black Catholics," "they hardly ever hear homilies about them." Their likely response, he claims, is to say, "This place isn't speaking to the things that are important to me. So why should I stay here? I'm going to a place that speaks to where I am." To put it bluntly, it is easy to talk the talk. Boxie and other interviewees want Catholic leaders to walk the walk.

According to our interviewees, just as the church needs to be more vocal about issues that affect the Black Catholic community, it similarly needs to be more vocal about issues that affect the Hispanic community. Dr. Stephanie Russell, who previously served on the board of Jesuit Refugee Services, makes this point in reference to issues surrounding immigration:

> I believe that we as a church have been relatively silent on the needs of immigrants in the United States. . . . What is it that we are doing in terms of the formation in our parishes? . . . What is it that we are imbuing them

with in terms of a heart for justice that orients itself towards the needs of immigrants? . . . And this goes, I think, to the U.S. bishops' advocacy for migrants and refugees, which has been consistent and has been stated as part of a consistent ethic of life. But I think this could be so much stronger, so much stronger. And lives are in the balance.

Clearly, Russell believes that the church can and should do more, especially at the parish level, to awaken concern among native-born Catholics to the plight of immigrants in our country. She sees the needs of immigrants as part of a consistent ethic of life and believes that church leaders could do more to frame immigrant rights in this way.

One of the challenges faced by some church leaders in effectively communicating the church's anti-racist teachings is the reticence of some pastors to address issues they fear will make their parishioners uncomfortable. Archbishop John Wester acknowledged this hesitation among some of his clergy in Santa Fe, and he hopes to find ways to help clergy overcome it. "In these, and in other, areas of Catholic social teaching," he said, "they're very reticent, they just don't want to upset their base, or they know people won't agree. . . . That's when I've had bishops come to talk to our priests about not being afraid to teach Catholic social teaching from the pulpit." Interviewees want to see more courage among the clergy to bring the faith to hot-button issues.

Archbishop Wester's concerns relate to a point made by Maka Black Elk. He believes that one of the reasons the church needs to be more vocal in speaking about social issues from a theological perspective is that American Catholics, like many other Americans, often let their views on these matters be influenced by their political affiliations rather than by their faith. He states that "politics tends to be the thing that drives people's views on racial justice in this country, not our theological views. I think that's something that we need to be more vocal about. And I think the church needs to take a stronger stance in terms of what we believe theologically." Clearly, Maka Black Elk believes, like many of the highly committed Catholics in our survey, that Catholics' views on social issues should be more informed by their theological understandings than by their political orientations or party affiliations. As we report in our chapter on citizenship, Catholics who are more highly committed to their faith are more likely to see things from a theological, rather than a political, perspective.

A third strategy that emerged for acknowledging and addressing racism is to show support for, and help raise awareness of, anti-racist and immigrant rights causes. Several interviewees believed that one of the best ways the church can communicate its commitment to its anti-racist teachings is to show its support for such causes as Black Lives Matter and the Dreamers Movement. Dr. Stephanie Russell states:

> There's been this wave of fear about the Black Lives Matter movement. One of the critiques of the Black Lives Matter movement outside the Catholic community is that it doesn't emanate out of the church, in the way the civil rights movement of the sixties and early seventies did, that it doesn't exercise a spiritual or religious language in quite the same way. So, there's that critique. But on the other side of the equation, in terms of the Catholic community, there's this narrative that grew up in some corners, that it's anti-Catholic, that it's somehow a danger to the Catholic community, and I think that's very unfortunate. I think that we as a Catholic community have missed a tremendous opportunity to learn from and support the Black Lives Matter movement with our presence, with our sense of solidarity, with our ability to engage as listeners. That doesn't mean that people have to agree with every movement or every practical choice that the BLM movement makes, but to not be in solidarity with the principal voice for the healing of the racial wound of this country, its original sin, is to me unthinkable. The church partners with all kinds of groups where there are overlapping areas of concern and need, and this is the central issue of the United States in terms of our credibility as people of faith, in my estimation.

Father Robert Boxie adds to this, comparing the Black Lives Matter movement with anti-abortion efforts, "The simple statement 'Black lives matter' is a pro-life statement, especially because we know from our history, from the beginning of our nation, that Black lives haven't mattered. They've been considered less than, and so the statement 'Black lives matter' is a pro-life statement, just like here in Washington every year, we have a rally, a march on the mall basically saying 'unborn lives matter.'" By drawing a parallel between how both Black lives and unborn lives have been treated in American society, Boxie points out that Black Lives Matter is promoting a pro-life message in the same way that anti-abortion activists do. In a sense, Father Boxie is saying that the cause of Black Lives Matter and the cause of anti-abortion activists fall under the same pro-life umbrella, or what many ethicists refer to as the "consistent life ethic," popularized by the late Catholic prelate Joseph Cardinal Bernardin.

Both Russell and Boxie recognize that it is important for the church to show support for anti-racist causes. They believe that it is possible to engage with organizations that advance social movements without necessarily endorsing every practical or tactical choice made by their leaders. For Russell, this engagement entails engaging first as listeners, and then in a way "that is prayerful" and rests on "the tradition of non-violence of Doctor King, and Gandhi, and Dorothy Day." Both see this type of engagement as carrying out the call that Pope Francis has made to all Catholics—to listen and to humbly accompany.

A final strategy that interviewees identify for addressing racism is to encourage people to be open to encountering and accompanying "the other" through "crossing over." Pope Francis has modeled this approach, not only by asking for forgiveness for past wrongs, but also by encouraging people to be open to encountering and accompanying people with whom we may not typically interact. Interviewees believe that this level of encounter requires learning about communities with which they are unfamiliar, and then taking the extra steps of encountering them—by sharing spaces, stories, activities, and ritual experiences—to build relationships of respect and mutual understanding. A fundamental benefit of reaching out to "the other" is simply to raise our awareness of the diversity of the church, to humanize the stranger, and to lessen prejudices.

Raising awareness of the diversity of the church is a theme that ran throughout our interviews. Historical theologian Father Linh Hoang speaks about the importance of raising awareness among American Catholics of their own history as immigrants. "Historically, Catholics were immigrants, and the early immigrant groups—the Irish, the Italians, the Germans—were all persecuted and stigmatized. . . . So just remembering that might be a first step." According to Father Hoang, church leaders can foster a more welcoming church today by showing that the Catholic experience in the United States has historically been one of immigration and aiding those who have newly arrived.

Although raising awareness is, for interviewees, an important first step, the ministry of accompaniment requires encounter, or crossing over, in order to truly know the other person, community, or culture. Dr. Ansel Augustine states: "We need to be in each other's spaces. Whenever there's a diocesan event, it's always the people of color who have to go to the suburbs or to the archdiocesan chancery. When are people coming to our spaces? When are people coming into our genuine worship experiences so they understand why we do the things we do the way we do? When are people having those conversations where the White people might be the minority in the room?" He believes it would be good to do this on a regular basis so we can really get to know one another. As he explains, "The issue of proximity, where I'm in your space, your sacred space, not just church sacred space, but sacred spaces in homes, communities, schools, wherever those sacred spaces are in our communities." Only then, he contends, can someone truly "understand our communities, and understand how, even though we are different, we're still all made in the image and likeness of God and deserve that dignity, and that our culture, our lifestyles, are just as valuable as anyone else's." Becoming guests and hosts to one another— mutuality—is a key part of encounter.

Dr. Stephanie Russell reflects on her own experience of encountering and accompanying "the other" when she and her husband moved to the Pine Ridge Reservation in the 1980s. As she explains, "By living among the Lakota people, in the context of the Lakota community, my own faith was changed in a more significant way than almost anything else in my life with the exception of parenthood." She describes the funeral rituals among the Lakota people and how they awakened in her a profound understanding of what it means to be a eucharistic community, in ways that she had never experienced in White Catholic communities. During the funeral rituals of Lakota Catholics, everyone present receives a "giveaway" from the family, some object that belonged to the deceased— e.g., a quilt or a pair of socks—that would now be shared with another member of the community. As she explains:

> The whole experience of this is that no one is singular. Everyone is a part of a community. It's like the African *ubuntu* experience, meaning "I am because we are"—you cannot pull apart the thread of the rope of the

community and have any of the twine be as strong as the whole rope is together. And that's what we are supposed to live by being in a eucharistic community as Catholics; no one is alone. My wellbeing is tied up in your wellbeing; if you are suffering, I am suffering. And so, when I say that the only thing that came close to this experience for me is motherhood, it is because a mother is only as happy as her least happy child— that we are tied up in our children in a visceral and permanent way that does not allow us ever to be separated from them. That's what I saw on the reservation—that we are tied up in each other in a visceral way that does not allow us ever to be separated from each other. And that's what eucharistic communities should be about. So, if they're suffering in Latin America, if there are children who are separated from their parents, if there are children who are going without food, that visceral connection, that eucharistic connection echoes what I learned on the reservation, what I learned as a mother, what should tie me to the rest of God's people.

What Russell is conveying here is that Catholics have something to learn from, and to teach to, one another, if they engage in the practice of encounter. In this instance, the ritual experiences of the Lakota people, their witness, their example, powerfully communicate what Catholics traditionally conceive of as the eucharistic community, and they do so in ways that Russell had not previously experienced. In short, intercultural encounters can sometimes teach central concepts of Catholicism that otherwise remain hidden.

Immersion experiences, intercultural conversations, and storytelling can be important ways to encounter "the other," especially when those include sharing experiences of marginalization. Tara Segal believes that one model for intercultural storytelling is a model used by "Journeying Together," an initiative of the United States Conference of Catholic Bishops' Committee on Cultural Diversity in the Church. Through her experience in this program, Segal believes that the act of sharing and listening to stories itself raises awareness of how other people perceive and understand their experiences. The value of storytelling in small group encounters has been confirmed by a variety of social scientists who study group interactions in both religious and nonreligious spaces.[39]

A few interviewees also emphasize the importance of shared ritual experiences. Certainly, as Dr. Russell conveyed earlier, participating in the ritual experiences of another community can powerfully raise awareness of what it means to be a eucharistic community. According to other interviewees, the power of shared ritual in solidifying what it means to be a eucharistic community is especially evident when participating in collective ritual experiences after incidents of racism or hate that cause national trauma.

Implications

It is clear from our findings that, because Catholicism has been both a source of pain and a source of joy, both in their lifetimes and historically, Catholics of color navigate tension between their Catholic identity and their racial or ethnic identity. Perhaps nothing communicates this more clearly than the stories of the former students of the Red Cloud Indian School in Pine Ridge, South Dakota, who experienced moments of both profound anguish and abundant affirmation in their interactions with Catholicism. A few interviewees acknowledged this paradoxical relationship of tension, and a couple described how this relationship explains why some Catholics of color may be uncomfortable or hesitant to talk about both experiences. Only after a period of healing and reconciliation might it be possible for them to sit with both of these clearly oppositional realities. Church leaders and ministers can assist with these processes of healing and reconciliation by acknowledging the church's history of complicity in the sin of racism, asking for forgiveness, and initiating reparation.

One of the most pressing issues identified by interviewees is the need for the church to "decenter whiteness," by which they mean that church at all levels—leaders, ministers, and everyday Catholics—should let go of their Eurocentric preconceptions and expectations, both for society and for Catholicism, and more fully embrace and celebrate the cultural pluralism of the United States and the U.S. Catholic Church. This is essential not only for the church to thrive as it lives out what it means to be a universal church, but also for the church to respond most effectively to the various pastoral needs of an increasingly diverse U.S. Catholic population.

This project of decentering whiteness and more fully embracing the cultural diversity of the church will undoubtedly be met with some resistance, as it already has in some quarters. Some of our interviewees allude to tensions that have surfaced within the church over use of the expression "Black lives matter," for instance, noting the controversy that has stemmed from the use of this simple expression, which some people regard as too closely associated with the identity politics that fuels America's culture wars. The USCCB has helped address this resistance by publishing on its website a series of articles that present various perspectives on the movement for Black lives as a way to promote "further reflection and dialogue on the important matter of racial justice."[40] These articles highlight the fact that the statement "Black lives matter" is not contrary to the belief that all lives have dignity, and point out that supporting an organization like Black Lives Matter does not necessarily mean endorsing all aspects of the movement.

In so many ways, the 1960s marked an important time of change in both the church and society that laid the foundation for today's calls for decentering whiteness. One of the influential liturgical changes ushered in by Vatican II was the development of different contextual theologies (e.g., Black theology, Latino theology) and the infusion of the liturgy with cultural elements and musical styles indigenous to particular groups. Since that time, advocates of the movement of inculturation have created scores of new culturally distinct songs and hymns, and developed cultural training programs to teach church personnel the customs, traditions, and languages of the diverse populations that make up the U.S. Catholic Church. As a result, Vatican II marks an important milestone for reshaping the church's congregational and liturgical life to be more expressive of the distinct cultural experiences of Catholics of varying races, ethnicities, and cultures.

The other critical events that transformed American society during this time were the civil rights movement and, as noted earlier, the Immigration and Nationality Act (1965). The civil rights movement raised the consciousness of American Catholics about the need for racial justice and helped fuel the movement of inculturation in the church. The Immigration and Nationality Act transformed the demographic landscape of American Catholicism by unleashing a new pattern of immigration characterized by a greater linguistic and cultural diversity than seen before in American history. These new immigrants included people from various parts of the world, especially from Central and South America, where Catholicism is strong, as well as from Africa and Asia. Hence, their arrival on U.S. shores helped maintain Catholicism's ranking as the single largest religious denomination in America. Of the major demographic shifts described in the introduction, the shift in the church's racial and ethnic composition has had profound significance.

The American Catholic Church today is more diverse racially, ethnically, and linguistically than it has ever been in the past. This trend is unlikely to be reversed. Differential fertility patterns between White Catholics and Catholics of color, combined with continuing waves of new immigrants, ensure that these changes will have an enduring impact on the composition and character of American Catholicism, even if not all these Catholics and their children remain Catholic as they settle into American life. One implication of this is that we no longer think of the typical U.S. Catholic as a White, middle-class, middle-aged suburbanite. The typical U.S. Catholic is increasingly a younger Hispanic Catholic, who is often of lower socioeconomic status than other American Catholics.[41]

Because the U.S. Catholic Church has been fundamentally reshaped by these major events of the 1960s, no single racial, ethnic, or cultural group can claim that its way of understanding or expressing Catholicism is "authentically Catholic" or distinctly "American Catholic." There is no "authentic" American Catholicism in terms of cultural or linguistic expressions. As Stephanie Russell expressed, American Catholics should not speak about any Catholic immigrant groups as needing to "join us," as if there was a particular, distinctly American cultural expression of Catholicism that immigrant groups need to "assimilate into." The American Catholic Church, just as in the past, continues to be an immigrant church in the sense that, aside from Native American Catholics, few can trace their ancestry on this continent back more than a couple of centuries. While new immigrant groups, like many of their predecessors, will pass through stages of integration into American society, there is no "melting pot" into which they *need* to assimilate. As a result, church leaders, ministers, and the laity as a whole can be confident in embracing the recommendations and strategies offered by our respondents. They can be confident in embracing a culturally pluralistic form of Catholicism that decenters whiteness and fully embraces the rich texture of races, ethnicities, languages, and cultures that now defines the U.S. Catholic Church.

One concrete way that everyday Catholics can participate in this endeavor is to step outside of whatever boxes and boundaries they erect that prevent them from encountering others who, though different, are part of the same human family. We will return to this theme of encountering "the other" in both the next chapter on citizenship and in the conclusion.

One dimension of diversity in the church that is worth exploring in greater detail is the socioeconomic diversity evident among U.S. Catholics, especially since socioeconomic status is so closely associated with race, ethnicity, and immigrant status in the American context. In a forthcoming book, sociologist Lisa Keister uses data from the General Social Survey and the Panel Study of Income Dynamics to present a socioeconomic portrait of American Catholics relative to other religious groups—both in terms of objective measures, such as education, work, income, and wealth, and subjective measures, such as their sense of class position and financial well-being.[42] Our 2017 American Catholic Laity Survey did not include the same number and variety of measures, especially with respect to Catholics' wealth, inheritance, and subjective sense of class position and financial well-being. For this reason, instead of presenting analyses of the socioeconomic status of U.S. Catholics, we refer readers to Keister's work. Among the primary findings of Keister's analysis is that, while White Catholics have largely achieved socioeconomic parity with White mainline Protestants in the United States, as of 2021 Hispanic Catholics (and Hispanic Protestants) lag behind White Catholics (and white mainline Protestants) in educational attainment, full-time employment, dual earner marriages, income, wealth, and homeownership. Some of these patterns, Keister finds, are partially explained by Hispanics' increased likelihood of being immigrants. As a consequence, the church's outreach to Hispanic Catholics and those who are immigrants should be sensitive to their unique socioeconomic circumstances that shape who they are and their prospects for current and future well-being.

4

Citizenship

On January 20, 2021, Jesuit priest Leo O'Donovan comes forward to give the invocation at Joseph Biden's inauguration. O'Donovan, who served as president of Georgetown University from 1989 to 2001, is a longtime friend of Biden, and presided at the funeral Mass of his son Beau, who died in May of 2015. O'Donovan is wearing clerical dress and, just before he begins, he turns to face Biden and affectionately places his fist over his heart, to which Biden offers a sincere bow. Just before O'Donovan begins, Biden blesses himself with the sign of the cross.

The invocation opens with themes of both contrition and hope. It recognizes that we have failed to live up to our country's ideals, that we have not brought "equality, inclusion and freedom for all." Yet, more is possible. We can be more caring, "especially to the least fortunate among us" and be a beacon of light for the world. What will bring us there, contends O'Donovan, is a generous love. This love is "American patriotism, born not of power and privilege but of care for the common good." O'Donovan recalls the words of Pope Francis, that it is important that we "dream together." The invocation closes with a hope for the reconciliation of Americans and for a restoration of peace, justice, and joy.

The ceremony continues, with the color guard, anthem, and pledge. Lady Gaga, a Catholic, approaches the balcony and through a golden microphone sings "The Star-Spangled Banner." Shortly thereafter, Jennifer Lopez, raised Catholic, sings "This Land is Your Land," adding a line in Spanish from the nation's pledge, "Una nación, bajo Dios, indivisible, con libertad y justicia para todos!"

Biden and Chief Justice John Roberts meet at the lectern. This is the first time in U.S. history that a Catholic Chief Justice will swear in a Catholic president. Jill Biden holds the family's 1893 Bible, and her husband rests his hand upon it as he becomes the nation's 46th president and second Catholic president. Biden's address, like O'Donovan's invocation, begins by recognizing challenges while holding onto hope, and likens this moment to a crucible. Some of America's challenges are the coronavirus, systemic racism, climate change, and extremism. And the only solution, Biden proposes, is unity. Unity is the hope and the answer to these ills. He suggests that Americans need to start listening to each other and work together. We do not need to agree, but we do need to respect each other, and when we dissent, dissent peacefully. "Disagreement must not lead to disunion." He promises to be as good a president for his supporters as he will for those who did not support him. Drawing upon St. Augustine, Biden says that a people is defined by the common objects of their love. He proposes for Americans that these are opportunity, security, liberty, dignity, respect, honor, "and, yes, the truth." We need to fight the lies. We need to end the "uncivil war" that pits Americans against one another. We can do this by "opening our souls" and showing "tolerance and humility." He rallies, "We will lead not merely by the example of our power but by the power of our example." He invites Americans to write a story "of hope, not fear, of unity, not division, of light, not darkness, of decency and dignity, of love and of healing, of greatness and of goodness." Healing is the major theme of both the invocation and the address; healing through love in the former and healing through unity in the latter.

After Garth Brooks' moving rendition of "Amazing Grace," National Youth Poet Laureate Amanda Gorman approaches the lectern. She is 22 years old, a Harvard sociology graduate, and Catholic. Her poem, "The Hill We Climb," begins by acknowledging the shared pain in our world. Gorman identifies the work we need to do, the work that our nation's ideals point us to. Her poem recognizes the divisions in our country, and yet our hopes for unity that remain. In a rhythmic cadence, she makes scriptural references to visions of abundance and peace. The poem continues with references to both our nation's frailties and our strengths, as well as a litany of how the various regions of the nation will rise from our contemporary suffering. The poem concludes by circling back to the opening lines, but with a shift from pain to hope-filled conviction.

Rev. Dr. Sylvester Beaman, pastor of an African Methodist Episcopal church and longtime friend of Biden, leads the final prayer. He prays for the Bidens and Vice President Kamala Harris and her husband, and offers a reflection on humanity, especially our wounds and our need for justice and reconciliation. With that, the color guard retires and the president, vice president, and honored guests depart to the sound of "The Stars and Stripes Forever."

This high moment of civil religion proposed a way forward from the intensified polarization of the presidential campaign and occurred just two weeks after the unprecedented violent insurrection at the Capitol. Sociologist Robert Bellah uses the phrase "civil religion" to describe the ethical principles, symbols and rituals that exist beyond the nation itself, are evoked during significant political moments and public events, and against which the nation measures itself.[1] A civil religion has sacred days of joyful celebration (e.g., the Fourth of July) and solemn remembrance (e.g., Veterans' Day), prophets and martyrs (e.g., Abraham Lincoln, Martin Luther King), and values and ceremonies (e.g., inaugurations) that mark a collective people. Biden's inauguration provides a window into a specifically American Catholic iteration of civil religion. With this denominationally-specific articulation, observers can glimpse the ways Catholic thought mingles with American public life through ideas like the common good, resurrection, sacrifice, and reconciliation. It also articulates some of the concerns and aspirations that our interviewees have when considering how American public life might be more intentionally shaped by Catholic ideas, such as the dignity of the human person and a concern for the common good.

Catholics have undergone significant shifts in their voting patterns since World War II. For instance, two-thirds of White, non-Hispanic Catholics identified as Democrats in 1952, and one-fourth were Republicans.[2] With the exception of their rallying around Catholic nominee John F. Kennedy in 1960 and Lyndon B. Johnson in 1964, White Catholics gradually moved to the Republican party until 1988, when party identification stabilized at similar proportions of Republicans and Democrats. But even with this increased Republican identification, White Catholics remain 8 to 12 points more liberal than White Protestants today.[3] Further, the U.S. Catholic population is more racially diverse than ever before, and Catholics of color tend to vote Democratic. Looking at AP VoteCast's 2020 election data, 57 percent of White Catholics voted for Trump while 67 percent of Hispanic Catholics voted for Biden.[4] Given these shifts in party affiliation and the increasing racial and ethnic diversity of Catholics, an in-depth exploration of Catholic political commitments is in order.

According to Catholic teaching, Catholics are obligated to bring their faith to public life.[5] Although Catholics have historically engaged civil society through a variety of Catholic organizations, today's Catholics are more involved as individuals.[6] Other works document the behaviors and commitments of highly-engaged Catholics; it is likewise important to know how these individuals compare with everyday Catholics. Our survey reveals the areas in which Catholics are more and less active in their parishes as well as in civil society.

This chapter begins with an overview of the survey findings to explore the relationship between everyday Catholics' political affiliation and other demographic characteristics, like race and gender. Next, we examine their civic beliefs and engagement. Interviewees also weigh in on what public engagement might look like if it were more informed by Catholic teaching. Finally, because polarization is a concern among many interviewees and the American public at large, we explore interviewees' observations about the challenges the U.S. church faces and their ideas for bringing about healing and reconciliation.

Party Identification and Its Relationship to Demographic Characteristics

The vast majority (96%) of respondents identify as either Democratic, Republican, or independent or no party (hereafter referred to simply as "Independent"). As shown in table 4.1, 44 percent of Catholics identify as Democratic, 28 percent identify as Republican, and 23 percent identify as Independent. Only small percentages identify as Libertarian (2.5%), and the remainder identify in roughly equal numbers with the Green Party, Tea Party, or "other." And while Catholics lean Democratic, contrary to what this might indicate, they also lean conservative. Fourteen percent say they are very conservative politically, 26 percent are moderately conservative, 32 percent moderate, 19 percent moderately liberal, and 10 percent very liberal. This demonstrates that Catholics as a bloc are somewhat of a "mixed bag" when it comes to political identity. The following analyses focus on the 96 percent of respondents who identify as Democratic, Republican or Independent.

Before exploring the political attitudes and practices of U.S. Catholics, it is helpful to see the ways their political partisanship correlates with

TABLE 4.1: Party Affiliation by Demographic Characteristics.

	Republican	Democratic	Independent
Total	28%	44%	23%
Race and Ethnicity			
White, non-Hispanic	41	34	21
Hispanic	11	57	27
Black, non-Hispanic	0	85	15
Other, non-Hispanic	20	42	36
Gender			
Male	32	43	20
Female	25	45	26
Annual Household Income			
Under $25,000	19	52	23
$25,000–$74,999	23	50	23
$75,000–$149,999	33	38	23
$150,000–$199,999	38	39	18
$200,000 or over	43	31	19
Generation			
Pre-Vatican II	41	46	12
Vatican II	36	43	18
Post-Vatican II	30	43	24
Millennial	18	46	30
iGen	22	44	24
Region			
Northeast	29	43	23
Midwest	38	38	21
South	31	46	20
West	18	47	29

Source: 2017 ACLS.
Rows do not add to 100% due to a few respondents who identify with third parties.

other demographic factors. In doing this, we can understand the ways political differences might be expressions of and are intertwined with ethnic, regional, or other variables. To examine racial variation, we compare non-Hispanic White (hereafter White), Hispanic, non-Hispanic Black (hereafter Black), and those identifying as some other category (hereafter

Other) Catholics. White Catholics are more likely to be Republican (41%) than are Hispanic (11%) or Black Catholics (0%). Hispanic Catholics (57%) and Black Catholics (85%) are more likely to be Democrats than are White Catholics (34%). Catholics classified as Other are more likely than other racial and ethnic groups to be Independent. Whereas 36 percent of Other Catholics identify as Independent, smaller percentages of White (21%), Hispanic (27%) and Black (16%) Catholics do so.

With men and women showing little variation in political party affiliation, it does not appear that gender has much effect on party identification among Catholics. Roughly the same percentage of men (43%) as women (45%) identify as Democratic, and only slightly more men (32%) than women identify as Republican (25%). Household income appears to have a relationship with political party affiliation among Catholics. For instance, respondents in the lowest income bracket, those making less than $25,000 per year, are much more likely to identify as Democratic (52%) and much less likely to identify as Republican (19%) than are those in other income brackets. The general, although not consistent, pattern is that as Catholics' income increases, so too does their Republican party affiliation. The highest-earning Catholics are most likely to identify as Republican, with 38 percent of Catholics earning $150,000–$199,999 per year and 43 percent of those earning $200,000 or more identifying as Republican. There is no meaningful difference by income for identifying as Independent.

Generation also affects party affiliation, with some caveats. Older Catholics are more likely to identify as Republican and less likely to identify as Independent than their younger counterparts. However, a similar proportion of Catholics from each generation identifies as Democratic, roughly 44 percent. Region has a strong effect on party affiliation among U.S. Catholics. Larger percentages of Catholics in the South, Northeast, and West identify as Democrat; very few, less than one in five, in the West identify as Republican, and this is the region with the highest proportion of Independents (29%). Republicans and Democrats claim equal proportions of Catholics—38 percent—in the Midwest. As the foregoing demonstrates, when we discuss party differences among Catholics, we are also implicitly discussing differences in race, income, generation, and region. Political party affiliation is less associated with gender.

Political Attitudes and Civic Engagement

Catholics in the United States navigate a complicated political landscape if they hope to bring their faith and politics together. Catholic teachings on political issues do not collectively fall into the red/blue binary of U.S. politics. For example, official Catholic teaching reflects the Republican platform on issues such as abortion and same-sex marriage, but is more aligned with Democrats on issues like poverty and climate change. Cardinal Robert McElroy of the Diocese of San Diego highlighted this in his interview, "Our partisan system bifurcates Catholic social teaching. That's the core problem we face. . . . We witness to the unity of Catholic social teaching and to the breadth of it. And there are very few political candidates who reflect even most of that. That's the problem. It's not that Catholics are somehow uncertain of what their faith tells them to do. It's that they're being put in a conflictual situation where no matter what they do politically, they're leaving behind important elements of their faith." Unlike many other religious groups in the United States that have diverged into more conservative and liberal branches, Catholicism remains a single religious body that does not easily fit either party's platform.

Political Attitudes

Examining the influence of the bishops, most Catholics (55%) claim that they consider what the U.S. bishops have to say about politics and public policy, but ultimately make up their own mind. Fewer than one in ten (9%) show significant deference by responding that they try to follow the bishops' guidance and instructions on political and public policy matters. A large minority (36%) claim that the bishops' views are irrelevant to their thinking about politics and public policy. When asked to reflect on these data, John Carr—founder of the Initiative on Catholic Social Thought and Public Life at Georgetown University and former director of the Department of Justice, Peace, and Human Development at the USCCB—has an important insight:

> About two-thirds [combining the 9% and 55% groups] of Catholics try to follow the bishops' guidance or consider what they have to say, but make

up their own mind. Actually, that's a good description of what *Faithful Citizenship* says.[7] The role of the church in public life is to form consciences. So, if in fact they use what the church teaches to form their conscience and make their own judgment, that's encouraging, frankly, and reflects a pretty healthy approach. So, the bishops' views are relevant. . . . And the fact that [Catholics] ultimately make up their mind is very American and very Catholic.

Carr's analysis of these findings is that most Catholics are actually following the church's teaching on religiously-informed citizenship. And, going even further, he claims that when Catholics part ways with their bishop and vote in a way that goes against official church teaching, their engagement and discernment—even with eventual disagreement—demonstrates a mature faith that fundamentally aligns with Catholic teaching on citizenship. Engagement with what the church teaches—rather than obedience—reflects Pope Francis's sentiments in *Amoris Laetitia*, "We [the church] have been called to form consciences, not to replace them."[8]

Regardless of the extent to which Catholics intentionally use bishops' statements to come to their positions, when asked about their agreement with the bishops' stances on three particular issues—universal health coverage, making the immigration process easier for families, and the death penalty—Catholics tend to agree with them (figure 4.1). Over 70 percent of respondents agree with the bishops' support of expanding government-funded health insurance and helping families immigrate. Fewer Catholics, though still a majority, agree with the bishops' opposition to the death penalty (52%).

Interviewees were very encouraged by the findings for these three issues. Bishop Mario Dorsonville-Rodríguez, chair of the USCCB Committee on Migration, was quite pleased with the strong support among Catholics for this sort of immigration reform, yet still was quick to identify an obstacle to further acceptance of migrants: "I really think we need to clear up the misunderstanding that the immigrant or the refugee came to take from us. This is not accurate. The refugee or the immigrant came to walk, work, and live with us. In so many ways, migrants define this country." Given his role, he is well-acquainted with anti-immigrant arguments and eager to clear up any

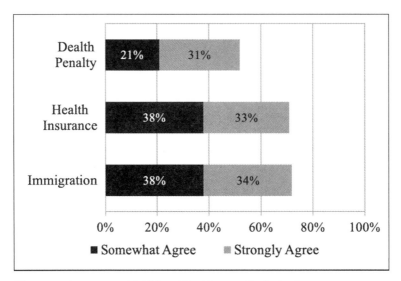

Figure 4.1: Agreement with Bishops' Positions on Particular Issues.
Source: 2017 ACLS.

misconceptions, later also discussing the taxes that many migrants also pay. Joan Rosenhauer, lead staff for the USCCB's 2007 statement *Faithful Citizenship* as well as executive director at Jesuit Refugee Services, an international organization that serves and advocates for refugees, clarifies that leaders need to give everyday Catholics tools from their tradition to think through an issue:

> But what I'm talking about is preaching about the *values*. It's not telling people that you must support a certain immigration policy. It's telling people that when you make your decision about your position on immigration policy, you have to think about what it means that we're called to welcome the stranger, that we have a preferential option for the poor, that we care about global solidarity. Catholics have to be reminded that these values have to play a key role in our decision making, and then we make our decisions. It's part of forming our consciences, being aware of our values and principles and then making our decisions in public life.

Rosenhauer brings up a crucial point for those who care about the role of Catholicism in American public life: Catholics need religious tools, ideas, and well-formed consciences if they are expected to engage issues in a distinctly Catholic way. And equipped with these tools, deeply-engaged Catholics might disagree on a particular migration policy, but then their differences should be about the most effective means for supporting migrants and refugees, not about whether they are worthy of support. Also implicit in her statement is a consideration; even with these encouraging numbers, it is important for leaders to discover whether Catholics are using tools from their tradition to think through migration. If they are only arriving at their position because of ideas in secular society, this shows that Catholics "happen" to agree with church teaching, not that they are thinking through the issue using resources from their tradition.

Although 48 percent of Catholics support the death penalty, some leaders take a positive read on this, noting there has been a decrease in support over time and that Catholics are less likely to support the death penalty than those of other faiths. Comparison with our 1999 data confirms a decrease, as 70 percent of our sample at that time supported "stronger enforcement of the death penalty for people who commit murder." This dropped to 55 percent by 2005. This earlier wording is different from our 2017 question, which asks about agreement with the American bishops' opposition to the death penalty. Our results also align with other data sources showing a decrease in support of the death penalty among all Americans, which dropped from 78 percent in 1996 to 60 percent in 2021.[9] Yet Catholics stand out on this issue. Using Pew data, we find Catholics are less supportive of the death penalty than some religious groups. White evangelical Protestants (75%) and White non-evangelical Protestants (73%) express more favorability toward the death penalty than White (56%) or Hispanic (61%) Catholics; Black Protestants show the lowest levels of support (50%).[10] In addition to race and ethnicity, these findings show that religion itself also makes a difference.

Turning to their voting patterns, 76 percent of our respondents report having voted in the 2016 presidential election. Forty-eight percent of these voters cast their ballot for Hillary Clinton and 43 percent voted for Donald Trump; the remainder voted for Jill Stein (1%), Gary Johnson (4%), or "another candidate" (4%).[11] When asked what role religious beliefs played in their choice, just 10 percent of respondents say they voted for their candidate because of their own religious beliefs. Even fewer

Catholics voted for their candidate because their bishop or pastor recommended that candidate (<1%) or because of the candidate's religious beliefs (4%). A large majority of Catholics in our sample, 86 percent, say *their religious beliefs played no role in their decision*. Even in the 2020 election, when Biden offered an opportunity for Catholics to vote for a fellow Catholic, they were no more likely to favor him than Protestant Christians were. Fifty-eight percent of Catholics voted for Biden, compared to 63 percent of Protestants and 56 percent of those identifying as "Christian" only.[12] Even with non-partisan documents from the USCCB (e.g., *Faithful Citizenship*) encouraging Catholics to allow their religious beliefs to inform their public lives, few American Catholics do this in any intentional way.

Bishop John Stowe of the Diocese of Lexington identifies the disunity of the bishops and the focus of the press as part of the reason Catholics are less able to bring their religious and political beliefs together, "The first thing that comes to mind is that the bishops don't speak with a single voice. And because there is evident division in the episcopacy of the United States about the prominence that the abortion issue should have over all other political issues, I think that is played up very much in the press. And I think that many Catholics just equate the bishops' entire position on politics with abortion and maybe opposition to same-sex marriage. I don't know how seriously they take teachings on the environment,[13] teachings on the poor, teachings on migration." This division among the episcopacy on the prominence of the abortion issue was demonstrated quite visibly when Archbishop Salvatore Cordileone of San Francisco banned Speaker of the House Nancy Pelosi from receiving the Eucharist within his archdiocese in May of 2022.[14] One year prior to this, San Diego Cardinal (then Bishop) Robert McElroy wrote that, because of its sacred nature, the Eucharist "must never be instrumentalized for a political end, no matter how important."[15] Linda Ruf, CEO of the JPII Life Center, an organization that offers prenatal care and engages in pro-life advocacy, agrees, however, with Archbishop Cordileone's approach: "I think it is the duty of every pastor in the case of public scandal to make every effort to correct his parishioner and in the cases where there is obstinacy and no effort to correct—to ask the public figure to refrain from presenting themselves for Communion until such correction can be made. I believe this should be a personal request. . . . Where even more harm comes is when communion is denied by one bishop and then given by another. I think the onus must be on the individual [lay Catholic]." Clearly the bishops and other Catholics see this issue very differently. Bishop Stowe's comment also underscores a concern that, unless everyday Catholics know about Catholic resources like *Faithful Citizenship*, they will hear through secular media that the Catholic Church endorses one or two Republican-friendly issues, but they will be less likely to hear about other more Democratic-friendly issues. *Faithful Citizenship* and other church resources may help left-leaning Catholics better connect their faith commitment to their politics. Given what we learned of everyday Catholics' thoughts on withholding communion earlier, although media coverage itself is ultimately out of the bishops' hands, being mindful of the optics of what they say and do as well as speaking with a more unified voice are prudent considerations. As the foregoing demonstrates, everyday Catholics are a "mixed bag," which makes understanding the motivations and values animating their political beliefs complicated, but it also points to the complexities contained within Catholic teaching and the ethics espoused.

Civic Engagement

Turning to their participation in civil society, Catholics—like Americans generally—are not especially engaged in American civic life. According to the 2008 General Social Survey, 15 percent of Americans participated in a community service or civic association monthly or more; Catholics are slightly under this, at 12 percent. Our data show that small majorities report that they give financial contributions to their parish and other Catholic organizations and causes "regularly" or "occasionally," with smaller minorities reporting that they volunteer in their community, are involved in their parish beyond Mass attendance, do voluntary work with poor or vulnerable communities, or are engaged in interfaith or ecumenical gatherings with this frequency (figure 4.2). The most common response across all activities is "not at all," while "regularly" is the least common, underscoring the real dearth of strong commitment to the parish or public good.

For the first time in our various survey waves, we asked Catholics about their perception of whether Catholicism is growing or waning

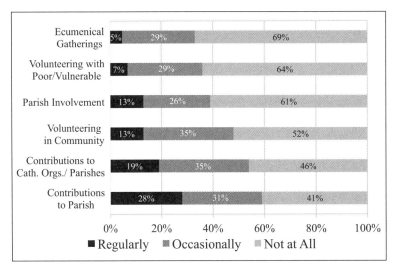

Figure 4.2: Frequency of Civic Engagement.
Source: 2017 ACLS.

in its influence on American life, as well as whether this is a good or bad thing. The responses to this second question are reflected in table 4.2 below. Fifty-one percent of respondents say that Catholicism is losing its influence on American life, followed by 39 percent who say that its influence is about the same, and 9 percent who believe it is increasing in its influence (these data are not shown in the table). The lion's share of those who say that religion is losing its influence (88%) also say that this is a bad thing. For those who do not see any significant change, nearly three-quarters (70%) say this is a good thing. For the few who see Catholicism's influence rising, nearly nine in ten (88%) say this is a good thing.[16] In sum, few Catholics believe that Catholicism's influence is growing, most say it is shrinking, and among those who believe Catholicism's influence has changed, the large majority desire a society that is more influenced by Catholicism.

Predictably, interviewees would love for Catholicism to have more of an impact on American public life. Four themes from Catholic social thought that ran through many interviews were solidarity, the common good, interpretive lens, and encounter. As articulated by the *Catechism of the Catholic Church*, solidarity means "'friendship' or 'social charity,' [and] is a direct demand of human and Christian brotherhood."[17]

TABLE 4.2: Perceived Influence of Catholicism on American Life.

	A Good Thing	A Bad Thing
Among those who say Catholicism is increasing its influence, is this . . .	88%	13%
Among those who say Catholicism's influence is about the same as always, is this . . .	70	30
Among those who say Catholicism is losing its influence, is this . . .	12	88

Source: 2017 ACLS.

Solidarity includes the just distribution of goods, a connection between socio-economic groups and nations, and an encouragement of Catholics to spread spiritual goods.[18] In short, solidarity connects persons and communities to one another and makes a peaceful, just, and moral society possible. The common good refers to the social nature of the human person and the recognition that each person's good is connected to the common good.[19] The common good consists of three "essential elements": respect for the particularity of each person, social well-being and development of the group, and peace understood as a stable and just social order.[20] As the *Catechism* emphasizes, "The common good is always oriented towards the progress of persons. . . . This order is founded on truth, built up in justice, and animated by love."[21] As these definitions demonstrate, solidarity and the common good are two Catholic ideas that lend themselves well to the building of a better society.

Interpretive lenses are shorthand ways that a person or group may understand or otherwise ascribe moral meaning to reality.[22] For instance, when thinking about people migrating to the United States from low-income countries, some people will see them as dangerous or opportunistic, and others will interpret their migration as seeking a better life while they contribute to American society. These people see the same reality (migrating persons), but they interpret that reality through very different lenses. Although interpretive lenses may vary considerably, one may offer a more accurate interpretation of reality. The interviewees interpret the world through the lens of their faith and want to invite others to share in a more compassionate, just, and richly Catholic interpretive lens in approaching political and civic life. As will be shown below, these three themes of solidarity, common good, and interpretive lens are connected, with one often intertwining with another and together culminating in a fourth theme of encounter. Encountering one another has been a hallmark of Francis's papacy, with his morning meditation "For a Culture of Encounter" reading, "[N]ot just seeing, but looking; not just hearing, but listening; not just passing people by, but stopping with them; not just saying 'what a shame, poor people!' but allowing yourself to be moved with compassion; and then to draw near, to touch and to say: 'Do not weep' and to give at least a drop of life.'"[23] Encounter connects people in a deeply human way.

Michelle Dunne, executive director of Franciscan Action Network—an organization working to shape public policy in the realms of peace, poverty, climate change, and human rights—believes the charisms of the Franciscan tradition offer solidarity and a better interpretive lens for contemporary society:

> I think the two things that Saint Francis is most known for is putting himself on an equal plane with all people, explicitly rejecting privilege and hierarchy. That leads us to always be in solidarity with people who have been marginalized or impoverished or excluded in some way. And then the other really big thing with Saint Francis is kinship with all creation. This means not seeing humans as being above the rest of God's creation, but one with it, and therefore a good deal of care for creation and care for the earth. So those are the two really big things. And then these translate into activity on a lot of different issues, be it issues related to climate, economic equity, healthcare equity, various issues relating to human dignity, and the dignity of human life, and consistent ethic of life.

Dunne hopes that the Franciscan tradition, especially in its values of equality, inclusion, and care for creation, can be a prophetic witness that offers a solution to many social problems.

John Carr uses understandings of solidarity and the common good when discussing how a Catholic voter might look different from voters not animated by these principles: "The question, 'Am I better off than I was four years ago?' That's not the question. Instead the questions are, 'Are the poor better off? Are the unborn protected? Are immigrants welcome? Is human dignity being lifted up?'" Rather than thinking about self-interest narrowly, Carr suggests questions that are rooted in

Catholicism and focus on poverty, vulnerability, and the dignity of the human person. With this interpretive lens, the interest of others also becomes the interest of oneself.

Dr. Stephen Schneck, recently retired, enjoyed a lengthy career at the intersection of politics and Catholicism, from founding the Institute for Policy Research & Catholic Studies at Catholic University of America to serving on the White House Advisory Council for Faith-Based and Neighborhood Partnerships under President Obama. Schneck connects solidarity and the common good as he underscores their importance for a healthier society and expanded interpretive lens:

> Citizenship for us Catholics should really revolve around our recognition that the common good should be primary. And our private interests—whether those private interests are partisan or business interests and so forth—that those things should be secondary. The common good should come first. And we should recognize that because of the primacy of the common good, our citizenship should be based primarily on solidarity—the solidarity that we feel among ourselves as part of a community with an almost corporate sense of community. And American individualism and American competitiveness and so forth, make that hard. But ideally that's what our citizenship should be.

That our own personal good is tied up in the collective good and the solidarity that this calls us to is harder to see from a more individualist and competitive perspective. Dan Misleh, founder of the Catholic Climate Covenant—an organization that educates, advocates, and provides resources involving climate concerns—sees a special role for Catholic politicians to think about issues in light of the common good: "Catholic politicians have a special obligation to think about what's good for everybody, not just for me, not just for my constituents, not just for my party, but what's good for humankind. And I think if Catholic politicians get back to the common good, I think that could go a long way." Catholics, Schneck and Misleh contend, can shape the American public's interpretive lens by more deliberately drawing on frames that employ notions of solidarity and the common good.

Kerry Robinson, president of Catholic Charities USA, which engages in policy advocacy and offers material assistance to those affected by poverty, reflects on the importance of a mature faith in propelling one to the common good: "I do believe that one's faith—if it is a mature, adult faith—informs all that one does. It's not something you just add on, but it really does ground you into a certain understanding of responsibility to the common good—to one another, to our common home—out of a love of being loved by God." A mature faith—that is, a faith that is foundational to a person rather than an afterthought—comes from being loved by God and points believers toward other persons and society as a whole. Having a deep faith, in short, shapes a person's interpretive lens.

Bishop John Stowe of the Diocese of Lexington is grateful to Hispanic and other immigrant Catholics for bringing alternative interpretive lenses from their home cultures that benefit American culture more broadly: "The Hispanic community and some of our immigrant communities come from a more sacred world or a world where religion is more a part of everyday life than just what they do on Sunday. And we [in the United States] have bought into so much individualism and separation of church and state to the point that religion has become a completely private affair." The individualism of American life and especially the privatization of religion dampens what could be a more compelling and relational faith-based response to civil society.

These three themes, for the leaders, point to encounter. Solidarity ties us to others. The common good links our personal fate and happiness to that of the community. Transformations in our interpretive lenses can help us see reality in ways that we were blind to previously. Encounter is a common method these leaders propose to help form Catholics and society to have greater solidarity and focus on the common good, and a more Christ-centered interpretive framework. In an encounter, people's lives connect. People's hearts are opened to new ways of understanding their reality (interpretive lens) and this gives them greater affinity for others (solidarity) and an increased motivation to create a just and merciful society (the common good). Shifts in interpretation and a realization of solidarity and the common good are not, according to our interviewees, going to come about simply by explaining to people what is wrong with their world. Instead, people need to discover this on a more affective level, which is facilitated by encountering another person who is personally affected by a given issue.[24]

Highlighting the importance of a personal encounter in transforming someone's thinking on an issue, Johnny Zokovitch, executive director of Pax Christi USA, an organization that promotes peace and nonviolence, notes, "It's when those parishes come to have some personal involvement with a person who's been affected by a policy, that you start to see people change. They start to embrace the person. It's no longer an ambiguous, nameless, faceless issue that's out there, but it's Alejandro or it's Maria. It's their real life that's impacted." As we develop the beginnings of a friendship with a human person, we open the door to compassion and a concern that the society we share treats them justly.

Echoing this is Bishop Stowe: "I think on the immigration case, I think the strategy that has been employed for some time now, but just takes a lot of time to sink in, is to put a human face on stories of migrants and refugees. It's one thing to have a position on the category of migrants. It's another thing to engage with migrant families or at least to know their stories. I think that helps when it becomes real and not just a matter of statistics." In moving from "just a matter of statistics" to encounter, we humanize a previously abstract social problem. Further, both Stowe and Zokovitch use the word "real." Encounter brings a problem that was once "out there" into a person's reality in a vivid and urgent way. Pope Francis's encouragement of encounter could be an important step in more vividly bringing solidarity, the common good, and a more Catholic interpretive lens to American Catholics.

Polarization

Polarization, whether among Catholics or the American public broadly, is a topic that is quite visible in the media. Pew data show that our country's polarization is getting worse. In 1994, 64 percent of Republicans were more conservative than the median Democrat and 70 percent of Democrats were more liberal than the median Republican.[25] Twenty years later in 2014, this gap had widened enormously, with 92 percent of Republicans more conservative than the median Democrat and 94 percent of Democrats more liberal than the median Republican. And it is not that we simply see things differently. We are more likely to see political opponents as enemies; this same 2014 Pew study found that more than one-quarter (27%) of Democrats "see the Republican party as a threat to the nation's well-being" and over one-third (36%) of Republicans say the same of Democrats. At a time when we are witnessing increasing public approval for interracial and same-sex marriage, people are less likely to approve of inter-party marriage. When Gallup asked Americans in 1958 if they had a daughter of marriageable age, what would they like the political identity of the groom to be, 18 percent responded Democrat, 10 percent Republican, and 72 percent did not care. When political scientist Lynn Vavreck asked this question in 2016 (which also included "son" in the question), she found that 28 percent preferred a Democrat, 27 percent said Republican, and only 45 percent did not care.[26]

Political polarization is probably more frequently experienced within Catholicism than within most Protestant denominations. This is because many other Christian denominations have, in effect, sorted themselves into politically liberal, moderate, and progressive subgroups. For instance, among Missouri Synod Lutherans, 59 percent identify as or lean Republican, while 27 percent identify as or lean Democratic.[27] However, the more moderate Evangelical Lutheran Church in America is more evenly split, with 43 percent Republican or lean Republican and 47 percent Democratic or lean Democratic. Even more extreme is the Baptist tradition, with the conservative Southern Baptist Convention (64% Republicans/lean and 26% Democrats/lean), the moderate American Baptist Churches USA (41% and 42%), and the progressive National Baptist Convention (5% and 85%). In 2023, a related split occurred within the United Methodist Church due to intradenominational debates over same-sex marriage, with many congregations voting to leave the denomination. This demonstrates that many Protestant denominations afford members both theological and political homes, somewhat buffering members from polarization within their ecclesial contexts. Catholics—as members of a single denomination—might be able to sort according to the general political orientation of a parish, but do not have the ability to choose a parish that will offer a different teaching on any specific social issue. That is, although pro-death penalty or pro-choice Catholics may be able to find a parish that does not offer preaching on or engage in political efforts to end capital punishment or abortion, they will not find a place to worship that claims that capital punishment or procuring an abortion align with official Catholic teaching. The political diversity among Catholics, coupled with Catholicism's respect for interpretive diversity, means that Catholicism in the United States holds together both conservative and liberal strands of opinion, and this, in turn, can lead to an experience of polarization, especially at the national level. Not surprisingly, given the increased political polarization both among Catholics and across the American public, polarization is a topic that surfaced readily among our interviewees.

Yet, even amid the data on American polarization, the experiences of our interviewees, and our own data demonstrating that Catholics lean Democratic (44% Democratic, compared to 28% Republican and 23% Independent) even while they lean conservative (40% are very or moderately conservative, compared to 32% moderate and 29% moderately or very liberal), we contend that there is more to the story than the polarization narrative offers. Although our interview questions asked specifically about "polarization," a careful read of the survey findings and our interview transcripts reveals a more nuanced story. If polarization is understood as the *opposition* of groups, then yes, a majority of our survey respondents would probably fall into the larger American pattern of polarization; they will have strong partisan consistency in their desire to have a softer border or to build a wall, to abolish capital punishment or make the appeals process harder, and to loosen or restrict abortion access. However, this does not describe our interviewees or the high-commitment[28] Catholics in our study. These Catholics are those for whom Catholicism is a more entwined part of their identity. For them, the narrative is less one of polarization and more a story of "contested Catholicism." It is not about one church position—like opposing physician assisted suicide—being right, and another church position—like mitigating climate change—being wrong.[29] Instead it is about priority. As Cardinal McElroy observes, "The problem among Catholics is not so much that they disagree on the substance of the issues, although there is disagreement. Rather the question is the focus and the priority." Which issue, among the many issues, most deserves our attention, prayer, and resources given this particular moment in history? This prioritization is found among our interviewees, as well. For instance, Linda Ruf, whose career has planted her firmly in anti-abortion pro-life work, ranks abortion at the top of her priorities: "Equating the evil of abortion with the evil of other social justice issues also causes confusion. Without the right to life, no other rights matter." It is not that she disagrees with church teachings on other issues; rather, in her view, other rights are simply irrelevant if one is not alive to exercise them. This sort of conflict of priorities is not polarization (as opposition), but it causes Catholic teaching as it is applied to public life to remain a contested space, and this conflict can still be a difficult experience at both the institutional and the personal level. This section will explore the conflict—whether as polarization or as contestation—that currently characterizes U.S. Catholicism.

A Serious Problem

Interviewees readily see polarization in society and are very concerned with the ways this deleteriously affects U.S. Catholicism as well as American democracy broadly. Their concerns take a few forms. First, as previously mentioned, interviewees recognize that neither party promotes the full breadth of Catholic teaching. Second, interviewees have experienced this rise in polarization within their work, with Johnny Zokovitch reflecting on this increased tension:

> I've been involved in Pax Christi since the early '90s, and I found it easier to engage people who didn't know anything about Pax Christi USA or the progressive political wing of the Catholic Church. There was greater curiosity and openness, or a greater middle ground of people who could participate in terms of curiosity or without this deeper entrenchment. Folks hold their beliefs about other people's opinions all the more strongly. There's a caricature that is harder to overcome in being able to engage people. The boundaries aren't permeable. There's not a generosity of openness towards positions that might be different, or you might be unfamiliar with. It's much more reactionary.

With increasing polarization, it is becoming more difficult for Catholics to have conversations with others whose political home is not aligned with official Catholic teaching on the particular issue.

This increasing polarization, as difficult as it makes the work of these interviewees, tends to evoke empathy from them. John Carr observes of politicians, "If you were a Republican who supported immigration, if you were a Republican who opposed the death penalty, you'd be in trouble with your party. If you were a Democrat who defended the lives of unborn children, if you were a Democrat who was vigorous in defending religious freedom in some respects, you would have trouble getting approval from the Democratic Party. So, it's a tough time to be a consistent Catholic." These leaders see the ways that things have changed—with party lines becoming more ossified—and understand the plight not just of their predominantly Catholic audiences, but also politicians themselves. The leaders also recall times when the partisan boundaries were more porous. They recognize that for all but a few rare exceptions, politicians have to adhere to their party's platform; to part ways would be political suicide. Illustrating this, Catholic politician Daniel Lipinski, a former member of the House of Representatives from Illinois, published an article about his election defeat after sixteen years of service, attributing it to his stance as a pro-life Democrat.[30]

A third concern of the interviewees is that these rigid partisan boundaries are not simply affecting politicians, but everyday American citizens, including Catholics. This binary is ending conversations rather than beginning them. Instead of Jürgen Habermas' hope that democracies would have thriving public spheres with a plurality of opinions and engaging dialogues, we have strict codes determining party loyalty or betrayal.[31] Again, Catholic teaching does not fall neatly into partisan categories, and so church leaders want Catholics to break out of this binary thinking. Yet few are doing so. As Stephen Schneck observes, "It's much, much easier to just go along with the polarization and say, 'Okay, I'm a progressive. And so I'm for everything that progressives are for.' That's so easy to do. And it's so hard to say, 'I'm a Catholic, and therefore I don't really fit into either the progressive or the conservative ideologies.' It is so very hard in the United States to do that." Right now, it is easy to see where the partisan line is drawn and to place oneself on either side. It is much harder to think outside the box, questioning the merit of the line and the moral grounding of the issues that fall on both sides.

Yet, these leaders contend that this is precisely what Catholics need to do. Ken Johnson-Mondragón, Director of Pastoral Engagement at the California Catholic Conference, which is the official voice of the Catholic Church in California as teaching intersects with public policy, identifies dialogue as an important tool in ending Catholic polarization: "We need to listen in the sacred space of a prayerful encounter with one another and with scripture. I think those kinds of experiences of encounter and dialogue really help to break down the prejudices and stereotypes that exist out there about people who think differently from myself. And the church is doing some of that, but there's certainly room for more." Just as humanizing an issue can change people's thinking, dialogue humanizes people with opposing viewpoints, opening the possibility for empathy even amid disagreement.

Moving from Partisan Thinking to Catholic Thinking

If the gravity and endemic nature of polarization is the first theme interviewees identified when discussing polarization, the second theme is a fruit of it: Interviewees believe that most Catholics see political issues with a partisan lens and only secondarily—if at all—through a lens of faith. A review of Pew data from recent years seems to confirm this on several issues.[32] There is no meaningful difference between Catholic Republicans and Republicans generally with their stance on abortion, and little to no difference comparing Catholic Republicans and Democrats to their respective parties nationally on climate change, the United States-Mexico border wall, and whether government monies for the poor do more harm or good for recipients. But the exceptions are telling. Catholic Democrats (64%) are less likely than Democrats nationally (76%) to say that abortion should be legal in all or most cases.[33] And Catholic Republicans (67%) are less likely than Republicans nationally (77%) to favor capital punishment for murder.[34] Thus Catholics in each party experience a "centering" effect from their religion when it comes to one of two issues central to Catholicism's view of the dignity of life (abortion and capital punishment). Nevertheless, it appears that the vast majority of Catholics of all stripes consider most issues from a political lens and are not strongly affected by Catholic teachings.

Due to this "politics-before-faith" approach of most American Catholics, many interviewees who work to promote Catholic teaching in public life have experienced challenges. Susie Tierney, executive director of JustFaith Ministries, describes the ways this has caused problems for Catholics who are not familiar with church teaching on peace and justice issues: "I will get calls from people who are not necessarily supportive of our work and they will have an issue with how we frame something in a particular program. And they immediately start using very political language to talk about it. So, their politics are informing their faith. . . . If a person is using this political language, I'm already having a disconnect because we don't write our programs from a political perspective." These interviewees begin with Catholic teaching, making it hard to enter into meaningful discussion with people who ground their positions in a partisan framework.

Some interviewees offer solutions as to how we might encourage Catholics to put their faith before their party affiliation when thinking through political issues. Many bemoan the inadequate formation that Catholics receive over their lifetimes. In thinking about how to bring their faith to public life, Joan Rosenhauer wanted leaders—from priests to lay ministers—to help Catholics consider issues using foundational religious principles: "We need our leaders, in preaching and in other formation settings and religious education programs, to encourage people to constantly consider, for example: 'How does the dignity of every human person impact my thinking about this issue? How does our teaching about the preferential option for the poor impact my thinking on this issue? How does our commitment to global solidarity impact my thinking on this issue?' As a Catholic, that's what I have to ask myself, not, 'Where is the Republican party or where is the Democratic party on these issues?'" Rosenhauer argues that Catholics would be able to bring their faith to public life not by insisting on pre-fabricated Catholic or political answers, but by asking religiously-informed questions that would help guide their conscience in a variety of contexts. This would anchor them in the more lasting values of their faith rather than the rhetoric or priorities of a party at any given moment.

Interviewees recognized the reality of the politics-before-faith approach taken by many Catholics even as they aspired for Catholics to put their faith first. Some suggest the church could offer more compelling theological formation for Catholics so that they might bring their faith to public life. But even with stronger formation, interviewees did not think this would be the end of Catholic division, with Kerry Robinson suggesting, "Catholics might end up just as politically divided, however, because we sometimes disagree on what we hold as most important." Even with excellent formation, priorities among individual

Catholics will still differ. That Robinson does not think that a stronger formation for Catholics would lead to uniformity in political thinking is important to note. This potential for political diversity among even well-formed Catholics challenges the assertion of a predetermined prioritization of socio-political issues within the body of Catholic teaching. It also points to the critical importance of dialogue.

Dialogue

When discussing polarization, the third salient theme is the importance of dialogue in the long, but fruitful, road of healing the wounds and removing the obstacles that leaders believe now mark Catholicism. And although the interviewees tend to be hopeful and to have experienced small-scale successes in bridge-building across political divides, they also acknowledged that healing this fissure would be very difficult or that many people were simply not open to dialogue. Interviewees feel that many are missing the goodwill or sense of connection or shared fate that needs to be in place *before* dialogue can begin. This is because dialogue is not simply talking about an issue. According to interviewees, dialogue is about people exchanging perspectives, considering others' experiences and reflecting on them in light of their own experiences. Before the actual discussion of topics, dialogue depends on a sense of relational connection with the other. The dialogue itself requires humility about one's perspective and a genuine curiosity about the other. Dialogue allows participants to come to a greater understanding of themselves and one another. There may or may not be greater agreement at the conclusion of a dialogue, but greater agreement is not the goal; understanding is. In dialogue, everyone wins. Dialogue rests on a desire to truly *encounter* the other. Bishop Mario Dorsonville-Rodríguez shared some of his own experiences with those closed to dialogue, "Most of the time I find myself talking to people who are not listening to me. Rather than a dialogue, they're thinking about how they're going to argue with my concerns." When people are only listening for the sake of strengthening their rebuttal, that is not dialogue, that is debate. In debate, participants are only speaking and listening in the hopes of changing the other's mind. Rather than everyone winning, in a debate there is one winner and one loser. Debate was not a solution any interviewee pointed to in healing polarization among Catholics or in the nation as a whole.

Dialogue means telling stories, which builds relationships, opens hearts, and sometimes even changes minds. While this might strike some as a bit too affective or idealistic, stories need to be taken seriously.[35] Sociologists have documented that stories and experiences can change people and the way they think about certain issues. Christian Smith demonstrates that stories and experiences motivated many to become involved in the Central American Peace Movement of the 1980s.[36] Jerome Baggett found that those affiliated with Habitat for Humanity used stories to put a human face on social problems.[37] Bin Xu discovered the ways parents who lost children in the Sichuan earthquake of 2008 used their grief and the particularities of their children to mobilize against their government's neglect.[38] Maureen Day's work shows the transformations of professional, middle-class Americans when they have immersion experiences with those living in poverty.[39] Stories can expand interpretive lenses and engender new feelings and commitments.

And even while the interviewees recognize the very real challenges in creating a space and fostering a disposition for dialogue, they also voiced a tremendous hope. Stephen Schneck opined that "One of the areas that I think is ripe for Catholic engagement is the issue of polarization itself . . . there's a place for us to awaken Catholics to recognize that we have a way out of this trap." The polarization story is a familiar one, but it is not the only story. Rather than simply being an obstacle, political diversity among Catholics means that the Catholic Church can serve as a neutral space in which dialogue can happen and similarities can surface. Catholics are affected by polarization, but interviewees amplify their unity, like gathering around one table in shared worship. There can be unity even amid difference. There are, interviewees contend, unique tools and alternative stories in Catholicism's "cultural repertoire" that justify and facilitate gathering for dialogue.[40] Catholicism has institutional resources to help adherents think differently about political and politicized issues; the dialogue motivated by the two-year Synod on the Family (2014–2015)—which sought to encounter and engage with the diversity of Catholics' marital arrangements and families with a view toward devising more pastorally attuned practices—is a case in point.[41]

An important role for Catholics in a polarized context is first of all to dialogue within their own party; rather than exacerbating this divide, they can help their party to see things in a new way. John Carr is one proponent of this approach, "We need Catholic Republicans and Catholic Democrats. . . . Journalist E.J. Dionne said it used to be that Catholic Republicans restrained the individualism in their party—markets and immigration and things like that—and Catholic Democrats restrained the individualism in their party around choice and lifestyle. It's become much harder to do that. It has become, 'Are you on the team, or aren't you?'" Individualism was a social ill cited by many interviewees. Catholicism, with a focus on the common good notwithstanding individual rights, can provide a richer understanding of the issues for American political discourse that might ultimately help moderate some of the more extreme partisan positions.

Steven Krueger, president of Catholic Democrats, an organization that reaches out to both Catholics and Democrats, discusses the ways that his organization has tried to help Democrats think differently about abortion:

> What makes us Catholic and what separates us from the Democratic party ideology is that we have vigilantly advanced the worldview that abortion is a moral issue and have separated the issue of morality and the issue of legality. And the reason why that's important is that the Democratic party has moved generally to the left. And as further left progressive voices have risen, the rhetoric around a lot of issues has changed across the board. We haven't questioned the church's teaching on the morality of abortion. Although we have asked some uncomfortable questions and taken a different approach as to the legality of it as a matter of prudential judgment in a pluralistic society that will not accept the elimination of *Roe v. Wade*.

Krueger's assessment shows that Catholic Democrats who seek to think as both Catholics and Democrats have much to say on abortion. First, there is a critique that the Democratic party has become morally nonchalant with regard to abortion, conflating legal access with moral approval. Second, there is the broader "health of the democracy" concern, acknowledging that Americans have very complex thinking on abortion.[42] Krueger continues, "We've highlighted the fact that abortions decrease more under Democratic presidential administrations. That data was clear before Trump was president. And the CDC abortion data for his presidency shows that the number of abortions actually went up under Trump. They've never gone up before. They've always gone down." To embrace both party and faith necessitates considering several audiences, offering new perspectives, and providing multiple opportunities for engagement.

In addition to moderating their own parties, showing the ways that different issues are connected to one another affords the possibility for parties to work together. As Catholics and other Americans consider the ways that issues on each side of the political divide are actually connected, they can begin to build interparty coalitions. Bishop John Stowe demonstrates the ways abortion is connected to a variety of social safety net concerns:

> We don't have a consistent approach from Catholics by and large, and especially from the bishops, in saying that when we have the safety nets, when we have parental leave, maternal leave, paternal leave, when we have tax credits for children, when we have adequate healthcare for pre-natal care, when we have adequate nutrition programs, childcare for working mothers, when a two-income household is almost a necessity for most people, if we don't make those connections as also being part of the pastoral care and what our political engagement should involve, then it is a narrow focus on the abortion issue. By the same token, as Pope Francis says, how do you claim to reverence life in the womb, but allow kids to be in cages on the border, or put somebody to death on death row, or any of the other anti-life positions that can be taken by the same people who call themselves pro-life?

Connecting issues that polarization has torn apart is part of the hard work for Catholic leaders that could illuminate a common cause that both parties could support.

And this bridge-building is not simply idealistic thinking; it has actually begun. The three dioceses of Washington state began an initiative that brought abortion and safety net concerns together in committing to support life from conception to age five.[43] They offer a variety of material and relational support for families, including diapers and clothes, baby showers, parent support groups, children's play groups, parent companions (who offer "unconditional relationship" to the parent), and connections to additional community resources. When Cardinal McElroy went to one of their events, he saw "people working together in a very robust way." This type of effort can bring Republicans and Democrats together in an affectively positive and politically productive way. This nonpartisan approach to the abortion issue is also seen within Catholicism at the national level with the USCCB's Walking with Moms in Need initiative.[44] Efforts like these break out of partisan lenses and are more deeply grounded in Catholic teaching on the issue. The idea of seeing issues as fundamentally interconnected life issues core to human dignity has a long history within Catholicism and is captured in a few different phrases, such as promoting a "culture of life," the "seamless garment of life," and a "consistent ethic of life." Interviewees believe that this broad concern for life and flourishing—from the unborn to the environment to capital punishment to immigration—might help American Catholics out of the political binary.

In addition to influencing their respective parties, interviewees also wanted Catholics to heal the polarization that separates Catholic Democrats and Republicans. Steven Krueger bemoans the absence of a Republican counterpart to his organization, "One of my regrets and, actually, one of my hopes is that there would be an organization called Catholic Republicans so that we could engage with them in public forums." Far from being threatened by ideological competition, Krueger wants there to be a space for politically-engaged Catholics to dialogue about issues.

Our survey findings reveal that high-commitment Catholics are much more likely to view an issue from a faith perspective rather than from a partisan perspective. Our three questions that ask about the bishops' positions on supporting government-funded health insurance, facilitating the immigration process for families, and opposing the death penalty—all Democratic-friendly issues—find a clear difference between Republican and Democratic Catholics (figure 4.3). However, we also see greater agreement with the bishops the higher the level of Catholic commitment. This results in the majority of high-commitment Catholic Republicans—and more than two-thirds on the migration question—agreeing with the bishops on these Democratically-aligned

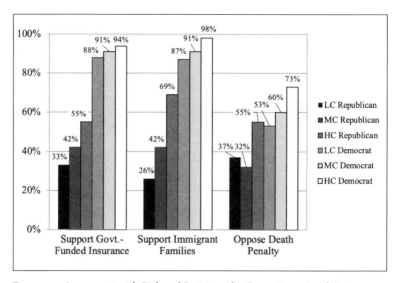

Figure 4.3: Agreement with Bishops' Positions, by Commitment and Party. *Source:* 2017 ACLS.

issues. This indicates that high-commitment Republican Catholics are much more likely to lean into the official teaching on a "blue" issue than their low-commitment counterparts. In other words, high-commitment Catholics are much more likely to defect from their party when the position conflicts with the teachings of their faith. This is also seen among progressive Catholics in other studies, with many disagreeing with their party on the abortion issue.[45]

Our survey also asked about several activities that might prevent a person from being considered a good Catholic. Three of these questions have clear political implications: abortion (Republican aligned), same-sex relations (Republican) and giving time or money to the poor (while not specifying tax policies, this can arguably be seen as Democratically aligned). The high-commitment Catholics, regardless of the political lean that the question implied, are much more likely than low- and medium-commitment Catholics to distance themselves from their party when their party's position goes against church teaching (figure 4.4). Further, while there is a political gap in attitudes about giving time and money to help the poor among low- and moderately-committed Catholics, this gap disappears among highly-committed Catholics.

These demonstrate the importance of faith in shaping political commitments on a variety of issues. Catholicism creates areas of consensus among strong Catholics regardless of political affiliation. Most Catholics' interpretive lens puts politics before faith, but this is reversed for those with high commitment.

To put these findings into a practical context, Ken Johnson-Mondragón did not see much resistance from Catholics when the California Catholic Conference was advocating against Proposition 1, a 2022 California ballot measure that would have amended the state's constitution to expressly guarantee the right to abortion. Because a tight budget did not allow for a mass media campaign, much of the organization's advocacy against the measure happened at the parish level (among Catholics for whom commitment is higher according to our operational definition), especially through homilies. They wanted their messaging to be clear and to not fall into red-blue binary of either the woman's right to choose or the fetus's right to life, "Our concern is twofold. It's for the woman and also for the child. That was the message that was delivered, and I think it was well-received in California even while the proposition

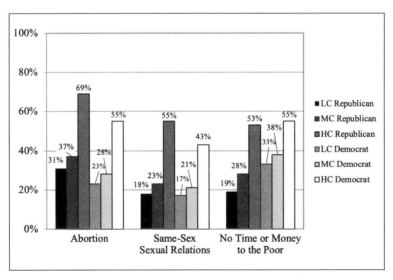

Figure 4.4: Attitude/Practice and Cannot Be a Good Catholic, by Commitment and Party.
Source: 2017 ACLS.

passed fairly comfortably." By crafting a non-partisan message around a very charged topic, his organization believes this affected the way Catholics voted, "And we saw movement . . . the voting differences from county to county paralleled the degree of engagement that we saw from diocese to diocese." The more a diocese tried to get this message to the pews, the more successful they were in affecting the final vote count (even though the proposition ultimately passed with two-thirds of the vote). High-commitment Catholics are open to hearing Catholic teaching on an issue even when it goes against their party's position.

This aligns with the importance of the quality preaching desired by leaders, as outlined earlier. Yohan Garcia, Catholic Social Teaching Education Manager at the USCCB Department of Justice, Peace and Human Development, insists that public-minded preaching is critical in helping get Catholics out of a polarized mindset and helping them do more nuanced and faith-based political thinking, "One of the things we always say is that there has to be more church teaching coming from the pulpit. So if the pastors don't help Catholics form their consciences, then they're going to go with what they hear outside of the church, the norm." Garcia claims that the norm, as polarization, can be effectively countered by church leaders teaching Catholics in the pews *how* to think using the tools of their faith; the Sunday Mass offers a logical forum for this. Catholic polarization is a pressing problem for the interviewees, but they also see in these challenges immense possibilities for becoming a stronger church and society.

Implications

Politics and political differences are not standalone categories when considering the characteristics of today's American Catholics. Catholic Democrats, Republicans, and Independents differ not only in political beliefs but also in region, race, and more. Further, these differences can also appear at the parish level, with people attending parishes that reinforce their own notions of Catholicism and, often, political values.[46] More homogenous parishes mean that parishes will act more as echo chambers than as diverse communities where dialogue can take place.

Race is a demographic factor that is associated with much political difference among Catholics, as it is among non-Catholics, as well.[47] As table 4.1 illustrates, White Catholics tend to most ally with Republicans, followed by those we classified as Other, then Hispanic Catholics, with Black Catholics heavily Democratic.[48] A risk Catholics face when race is so closely connected to political differences is that political divides can exacerbate racial divides. Parish leaders need to be very aware of the impacts that policy and conversation around issues (e.g., "Black lives matter" and "All lives matter") can have on the relational health of a parish.

When considering what a Catholic impact on the United States might look like, solidarity, the common good, and interpretive lens are recurring themes that share much in common with Pope Francis's hope for encounter. Like dialogue, encounter creates a space where our hearts are open to people's stories, stories that might be new to the listener. If done intentionally, creating opportunities for encounter among Catholics and other Americans may prove to be an effective way to shape political and civil society. Parishes, dioceses, and other groups interested in faith formation may want to incorporate stories into homilies, letters, and resources as well as create opportunities for Catholics to encounter real human persons who are affected by the issues at hand.

Given both the story on polarization and the complex results on the role of church teaching in the political beliefs and choices of the faithful, leaders should consider these findings carefully. First, parishes should be attentive to the ways they fall into the red/blue binary in their own discussion of political issues and community outreach. Do they offer opportunities—like town halls, panels, or other discussion-based forums—to learn *what* Catholicism teaches on political issues as well as *why* the Catholic Church takes that position? This latter "why" is especially important and brings us to the second point. As the data show, few Catholics make church teaching primary in their own political discernment. Many Mass-attending Catholics may know *what* the church teaches, but may not understand the *why*. They may (mistakenly) think that the church is against abortion because it favors large families. Or they may (mistakenly) think that the church argues for a preferential option for the poor because poverty and scarcity in themselves are holy. By knowing not just the *what*, but also the *why*, Catholics can engage in deeper discernment and more informed dialogue. They would be better able to consider an issue using Catholic principles, even if their final position does not align with the hierarchy's position. But, in coming to know more about Catholic social thought they would increase their fluency in Catholic concepts and imagination.

Although 10 percent of Catholics identify as "very liberal" and 14 percent as "very conservative," this leaves three-fourths of Catholics somewhere in the middle. Yet, the experience of many Catholics (and observers) is one of political polarization.[49] The data indicate that true polarization might be rarer among highly-committed Catholics. While there are notable exceptions, the more committed to Catholicism any Catholic is, the more they think about social issues through a lens of faith, rather than a partisan lens, which brings highly-committed Catholics of all parties together. But whether centrists or extremists, how their Catholicism shapes their political engagement is complicated. Yes, nearly two-thirds of Catholics consider the bishops' teachings when forming their own political opinions. But no, only 14 percent say that their religious beliefs played some role in determining how they voted in 2016.

Wanting to heal polarization in the church and nation is a resounding theme among interviewees. If "healing polarization" means coming to agreement on political commitments and a resolution of policy disagreements, this seems unlikely, given the political diversity of American Catholics. But if healing polarization refers to a willingness to recognize the varying priorities of individual Catholics, to agree to a universal value of life and other core Catholic principles, to discover spaces for common ground as Republican and Democratic Catholics that their parties have missed, to push back on assumptions within their own party, to commit to investing resources in upholding the dignity of all, and a desire to work together—a unity even without uniformity—then this goal looks not just possible, but more promising for Catholicism and the nation. As Steven Krueger observes, "I think that there's something bigger going on and there is an opportunity for Catholics to take a step back and for the church to take a step back and to ask, 'What's happening to our society and what's happening to our democracy, upon which the democracies of the rest of the world depend?' And what I see is this black hole without truth, and the banality of evil playing itself out every day. The church could put itself in a position to make a mighty contribution toward healing our dystopian tribalism." Our current reality of polarization and everyday evil is not where most people want to be. And it is not where we have to be. Interviewees think that, with courage and intentionality, the church could play an important role in our nation's healing and eventual flourishing. The next chapter explores, in greater depth, two of the constellation of issues touched on here: Catholics' understanding of sex and family, especially as these touch Catholics' lived experiences and ministerial approaches.

5

Love

Many Catholics have had experiences in their lives that illustrate how Catholic families and their needs have changed faster than some of their church ministers recognize, fully appreciate, or want to acknowledge. For one of the authors, one such experience happened a few decades ago, in 1990, when he traveled to a Midwestern city to attend the first holy communion ceremony of his oldest niece, Kate. Because he arrived in town early, he decided to accompany Kate to the practice session held in the parish church for all the children who would be receiving holy communion for the first time (i.e., the "first communicants") at the Sunday Mass the following day. Most of the children were accompanied by a parent or another member of the family. The purpose of the practice session was to give families an opportunity to listen and observe as the director of religious education described the planned seating arrangement, and to show the children how to process down the aisle and toward the sanctuary to receive communion from the priest. Soon after everyone was settled in the pews for the practice session, the director began by describing that, in the reserved seating area, there would be three seats reserved for each family—one seat for the first communicant and two seats for the parents. Upon hearing this, Kate began to look perplexed and disappointed. As the child of divorced parents who had each remarried, she was counting on both her biological parents *and* their new spouses to attend her first holy communion ceremony. Without missing a beat, Kate raised her hand and asked the director: "Excuse me, but with only two seats available for the parents, which set of parents should I invite—my mother and her husband, or my father and his wife? I was hoping to invite all four." The director of religious education was quick to acknowledge the shortsightedness of reserving only two seats for parents, and told Kate that she should, in fact, feel free to invite both "sets of parents," and that the ushers would make sure there was ample seating for everyone.

Jump ahead three decades, and we can observe similar tensions between Catholic family ideals and Catholic family realities. A few years ago, an urban parish hosted its annual parish-wide gala celebration, in which all parishioners were invited to a dinner reception and dance on a weekend night in the spring. A few of the gay couples who are very active in the parish attended the event, and as usual, they were warmly welcomed by fellow parishioners they had gotten to know personally over the years. These couples felt very positive about their experiences that evening and appreciated being treated just like any of the other couples and families in attendance. Shortly after the event, however, when the parish posted photos of the gala in its online photo gallery, none of the photos featured them standing or sitting next to their partners, as many of the photos of the straight couples did. And there were certainly no photos of them dancing together. One of the gay couples raised this concern with a member of the parish staff, who explained the rationale behind the omission of certain photos. The message was clear: you are welcome here, but we cannot be too public or else we may cause scandal or receive a reprimand from the bishop.

These stories, although transpiring more than three decades apart, illustrate some of the challenges and dilemmas faced by the church and its ministers over the timeline of our surveys as they adapt to new family forms. On the one hand, church ministers want to be sensitive to the diversity of families so they can respond in ways that are welcoming, inviting, and inclusive. This is especially true of lay and ordained church ministers who, in recent years, have been responding affirmatively to Pope Francis's call for pastoral leaders to practice "accompaniment"—a practice designed to "meet people where they are" in life so they can feel welcomed and integrated into the life of the church even when their family situation is defined in official church teaching as "irregular," such as when they are either civilly married, living together, or divorced and remarried.[1] On the other hand, some ministers in the church, particularly those who are skeptical of the pope's emphasis on the practice of accompaniment, fear that publicly acknowledging these "irregular" situations gives legitimacy to the secularization of the family. Such ministers may think that the practice of accompaniment or other displays of welcoming and integrating Catholics in these "irregular" situations into the life of the church could create what church officials consider to be public scandal, especially if Catholics in nuclear families observe the active participation and reception of Catholics in "irregular" situations. The concern of bishops and church officials is that the public display of "irregular" family forms may "stoke misunderstanding of the church's teaching on marriage" or "stoke the perception of a double standard in the Church."[2]

Because these two approaches to responding to Catholics in "irregular" situations are often in tension with one another, when church ministers attempt to practice them in unison, they can leave some Catholics feeling only partly welcomed by the church. The message that these Catholics receive can be likened to a Catholic form of "don't ask, don't tell," or "you are welcome here, but just don't be too visible." These kinds of experiences can leave some Catholics feeling like their identities are being split or bifurcated, with a part of their self being stigmatized or cut off.

Since the first survey in this series in 1987, the characteristics of American families in general, and of American Catholic families in particular, have changed in a variety of ways. As the Pew Research Center reports and U.S. Census data confirm, compared to previous years, more adult Americans are delaying or forgoing marriage, more couples are choosing to cohabit rather than marry, an increasing share of children are living with an unmarried parent or with same-sex parents, and same-sex marriage, which is now legal across the United States, is becoming more common.[3] The 2020 U.S. Census reveals that 28 percent of all households are one-person households, which is more than double the percentage in 1960. Further, the numbers of single parents (divorced, widowed, and never married), blended families, multigenerational families, and interracial and same-sex marriages have all increased. Added to these changes is the fact that increasing percentages of the American population are postponing parenthood and having fewer children, while the percentage of gays and lesbians choosing to marry civilly and raise children is increasing. Based on the Current Population Survey, the U.S. Census Bureau reports that 15 percent of the 1.1 million same-sex couples in the United States in 2019 had at least one child under 18 in their household, compared with 38 percent of opposite-sex couples.[4] Among nuclear families, moreover, gender roles have shifted away from a breadwinner-homemaker model to a dual-earner couple who share more of the responsibilities of raising a family.

American Catholic families have been changing lockstep with the general population. The Pew Research Center reports that between 2007, when it conducted its first Religious Landscape survey, and 2014, when it conducted its second, the percentage of married Catholics declined from 58 percent to 52 percent while the percentage of never married Catholics increased from 17 percent to 21 percent, and the percentage of divorced or separated Catholics increased slightly from 10 to 12 percent.[5] Young Catholics today are also more likely than preceding generations to identify as lesbian, gay, bisexual, transgender, queer, or some identity other than straight (hereafter LGBTQ+).[6] Clearly, the same trends that characterize the American population—namely, declining rates of marriage, increasing rates of never marrying, and increasing percentages identifying as LGBTQ+—also characterize the American Catholic population.

These changes in the characteristics of American families correlate with changes in attitudes regarding family life. While some describe these changes as representing the decline of the family, increasing portions of Americans in general, and of American Catholics in particular, are accepting of these changes, with some even regarding them as "a good thing."[7] Sociologist Bella DePaulo, for instance, in studying singles in the United States, highlights some of the sociological benefits of having more singles in the population. Single people, DePaulo finds, are more likely than married people to encourage, help, and socialize with their friends and neighbors; visit, support, advise, and stay in touch with their parents and siblings; participate in civic groups; and volunteer for social service organizations, hospitals, and various educational and art organizations.[8] She uses these findings to suggest that not all changes in marriage and family patterns have negative outcomes; the increasing share of singles can actually be a "good thing" along some dimensions of societal well-being. Pew also reports that in 2022 a large majority of American adults (61%) believed that "same-sex marriage now being legal in the U.S. is a good thing for our society."[9]

In this chapter, we examine American Catholics' attitudes about a variety of issues related to marriage and sexuality, their levels of agreement with official church teachings in these areas, and how those beliefs have changed over time. We also examine the extent to which everyday Catholics, in their own moral decision-making about these issues, prefer to follow church leaders' publicly stated teachings, their individual consciences, or a combination of both. Additionally, we incorporate our interviewees' perspectives about how the church might respond to the new realities and unique challenges of America's diverse families.

The Church's Renewed Emphasis on Accompaniment

Just as the structure of American families has been in flux over the past several decades, so too has the Catholic Church's approach to—if not its formal doctrines about—issues of marriage, divorce, and sexuality.[10] Over the last decade in particular, Pope Francis, as noted above, has called on members of the church to "encounter" and has significantly elevated the importance of God's presence in the secular world by adopting a renewed posture of accompaniment toward those whose family lives do not resemble the church's ideals. As part of this approach, Pope Francis announced in 2013 that there would be a Synod on the Family. The purpose of the synod, as he outlined, was to listen to the experiences of the faithful with respect to issues of marriage, family, and sexuality, and to consider how the church might better respond to the realities facing contemporary families.[11]

As Michele Dillon has written elsewhere, the Synod on the Family and Pope Francis's response in his 2016 apostolic exhortation *Amoris Laetitia* ("*The Joy of Love*") illustrate a "postsecular sensibility."[12] By this she means that Pope Francis's emphasis on synodality, dialogue, and accompaniment represent a renewed pastoral approach that entails "meeting Catholics where they are." For Dillon, Francis's "postsecular sensibility" is evident in his desire to bring Catholic ideals, secular realities, and the social sciences into conversation with each other; his attempt to present church teachings in ways that are more accessible and relevant to the lives of everyday Catholics and the general public; and his insistence that the church respect the individual's lived experience, personal conscience, and prayerful discernment of God's will in their lives. In *Amoris Laetitia*, for instance, Pope Francis speaks directly to church leaders about the importance of inviting the faithful to consider and appreciate the church's teachings in light of their lived realities, rather than simply trying "to impose rules by sheer authority," which he believes is ultimately counterproductive.[13] He states:

> At times we have also proposed a far too abstract and almost artificial theological ideal of marriage, far removed from the concrete situations and practical possibilities of real families. This excessive idealization, especially when we have failed to inspire trust in God's grace, has not helped to make marriage more desirable and attractive, but quite the opposite. . . . We also find it hard to make room for the consciences of the faithful, who very often respond as best they can to the Gospel amid their limitations, and are capable of carrying out their own discernment in complex situations. We have been called to form consciences, not to replace them.[14]

Amoris Laetitia conveys Pope Francis's desire for the church to be more open to, and less threatened by, the lived realities of everyday Catholics and their families. He states that church leaders should do more to affirm the diversity and positive qualities of contemporary families, rather than "simply decrying present-day evils, as if this could change things."[15] This is evident in a variety of statements throughout the document. First, although he states that "the exclusive and indissoluble union between a man and a woman has a plenary role to play in society as a stable commitment that bears fruit in new life," he explicitly acknowledges and affirms a "great variety of family situations that can offer a certain stability," including the support that same-sex partners can provide to one another, even though such unions "may not simply be equated with marriage."[16] Second, with respect to Catholics who are divorced and remarried, he reiterates the conclusions of the Synod on the Family by calling the church to acknowledge the grace of God at work in their lives and inviting them, despite their "irregular" situation, to participate fully in the life of the Christian community. He states that divorced and remarried or cohabiting couples "are not excommunicated" from the church, but "should be made to feel part of the Church."[17] Although he does not explicitly state that the divorced and remarried should receive the Eucharist while attending Mass, he does state that church leaders should respond to Catholic couples in these "irregular" situations with "careful discernment and respectful accompaniment."[18] In short, Pope

Francis believes that Catholics in "irregular" family forms should be more fully integrated into the sacramental and community life of the church, and that even if Catholic couples are in situations that might be regarded as objectively sinful, the extent to which they are subjectively morally culpable depends on the particular circumstances and the particular individual's discernment and obedience to conscience. Such persons, the pope maintains, can still benefit from inclusion in the life of the church and "the help of the sacraments."[19]

Although *Amoris Laetitia* can be seen as presenting a hopeful message to Catholics in "irregular" situations, Dillon points out that the document "allows the accommodation of both doctrinal truths and changing realities."[20] In writing the document, the pope hoped to chart a middle path that would satisfy both progressive and conservative bishops. On the one hand, it extends an invitation to Catholics in "irregular" family forms to enjoy full integration into the church. On the other hand, by emphasizing the role of individualized pastoral discernment through what is referred to as the "internal forum," it stops short of granting public legitimacy to these "irregular family forms." Thus, Catholics who are civilly married, cohabiting, or divorced and remarried may, in conscience, participate in the life of the church, but only to the extent that, in church officials' terminology, they do not cause public scandal.

What is clear is that Pope Francis has attempted to build a more inclusive Catholicism that will engage the contemporary world by demonstrating an openness to dialogue and learning from the social sciences and the lived experiences of everyday Catholics. Both the report on the Synod on the Family and Pope Francis's apostolic exhortation *Amoris Laetitia* were published soon before our 2017 national survey of American Catholics. We turn now to our analyses of the survey. We examine the structure and form of Catholic families today, and their beliefs and attitudes about issues related to marriage and sexuality.

Family Arrangements among American Catholics

The 2017 survey from which we draw our data reveals that U.S. Catholics live in all types of family arrangements.[21] Over half of adult Catholics (56%) report being married, approximately one in five (23%) has never been married, one in ten (11%) is divorced or separated, approximately one in twenty (5%) is living with a partner, and another one in twenty (5%) is widowed. Moreover, 74 percent of the married Catholics in our survey are married to a Catholic spouse.

Pew's 2014 U.S. Religious Landscape Study (RLS) provides some additional data about U.S. Catholic couples that were not available in our own survey. Although our survey, like RLS, finds that approximately three quarters of married Catholics are partnered with a spouse who is also Catholic, RLS finds that of the 25 percent who are partnered with a non-Catholic spouse, 8 percent are partnered with someone from a mainline Protestant tradition, 5 percent are partnered with someone from an evangelical Protestant tradition, 3 percent are partnered with someone from another faith tradition besides these, and 9 percent are partnered with someone who is religiously unaffiliated.[22] These rates of religious intermarriage, as we will see, have consequences in terms of both the couple's ability to affirm their faith with one another and to socialize their children in the faith.

The RLS also reports that, at some point in their lives, one in four Catholics has gone through a divorce, one in ten has divorced and remarried, and close to half (44%) have cohabited with a romantic partner. Moreover, although approximately 90 percent of Catholics report being straight or heterosexual, nearly half (47%) of U.S. Catholics say they have a close friend or family member who is gay or lesbian, about 4 percent report being LGBTQ+ themselves, and another 2 percent say they "don't know" when asked about their sexual orientation.[23]

Today's Challenges for Socializing Children in Catholic Faith and Values

Alongside changes in American Catholic families have been shifts in the various pathways and opportunities available for the socialization, education, and formation of children in Catholic faith and values. Some of these shifts are caused by changes in the structure of the family itself and whether, in a two-parent household, both parents are Catholic. As Pew reports, based on its 2014 RLS, among those raised in a household in which Catholicism was the only religion of the parent(s), 62 percent remain Catholic as adults, whereas among those raised in a two-parent household in which only one of the parents was Catholic, only approximately 30 percent continue to identify as Catholic into adult-hood.[24] The same report reveals that those who were raised in religiously mixed households are less likely to say that religion was a significant feature in their lives when they were growing up. Further, according to Pew, when couples are in a religiously matched marriage (i.e., where they are of the same religion), they are more religiously observant, and if they are parents, they are more likely to practice their religion with their children, including attending religious services, praying, and reading scripture with their children, than are parents in a religiously mixed marriage.

Another traditional pathway for the socialization of children that has declined over the years is the geographic proximity of the extended family. Although there has been an increase in intergenerational house-holds, extended families are more geographically dispersed than they once were. One of the church leaders we interviewed, Monsignor Bill Young, who has spent his lifetime in pastoral ministry and currently serves as pastor at St. Vincent de Paul Catholic Church in Houston, Texas, has observed this trend over the years. "A lot of us grew up with extended families around us, grandparents, aunts, uncles, cousins, et cetera. Now everybody's all over, all over the country, and it takes a lot of time and expense to get with your family." Without the presence of this network of extended family members in the same location, parents may lack the support system they need to effectively share and model their faith to their children.

Another change that affects the intergenerational transmission of the faith is the diminishing access of Catholics to the Catholic educational system, as was noted earlier.[25] Between 1985 and 2022, the total number of Catholic elementary schools and elementary school enrollments in the United States declined by nearly 40 percent. In this same time period, the total number of Catholic secondary schools and secondary school enrollments declined by approximately 20 and 30 percent, re-spectively.[26] These declines have been attributed to geographic shifts in the Catholic population, parish closings, and rising tuition costs.[27]

Several interviewees express concern about what these trends mean for the transmission of the faith to the next generation. Helen Alvaré, a family law professor at George Mason University and member of the Holy See's Dicastery for Laity, Family and Life, states, "Catholic families are in a rocky transition between a time when parents could pass on their faith by ordinary Catholic practices—almost through osmosis—to a time when parents have to be intensely intentional, communicative, and dialogic with their children. You cannot count on the institutional church or on the larger world around you to assist your transmission of faith. . . . It used to be the case that you could count on Catholic schools or the church in general to perform those roles in faith formation, but not so much anymore." The point is that the decline in Catholic schools means that an important avenue for the formation of children in Catholic faith and culture is no longer as viable as it once was. Further, because enrollments in parish-based religious education and faith formation programs have decreased by an even larger percent over the same time period, faith formation today is almost entirely dependent on parents and families.[28]

Dr. Andrew Lichtenwalner, director of the Office of Formation and Discipleship in the Archdiocese of Atlanta and former director of the Secretariat of Laity, Marriage, Family Life and Youth at the USCCB, recognizes this and is leading a pilot program in his archdiocese designed to equip parents with tools needed to renew the Catholic culture of the home. He states:

> I love Catholic schools. I'm a product of them—or better, a beneficiary. In a Catholic school, you have an opportunity for a culture. A school has the time, the leadership, and the space to develop a culture with the students. However, for a parish faith formation program, where you might have one hour a week at most, you don't have the time to build and foster a culture there. The most important culture when it comes to lifelong discipleship, the most important one that needs to be renewed, is the culture of the home. If nothing is tapping into that, if the overall parish culture is not supporting healthy and holy homes and domestic churches, anything we do at faith formation, anything we do in youth ministry, frankly, is not going to have a full impact.

To renew the culture of the home, Lichtenwalner's pilot program is designed to accompany parents on the path of faith formation. Instead of simply handing a textbook to parents and suggesting that they read it with their children, parish catechists meet with parents where they are and equip them with tools and models for praying with their children and offering a personal witness of faith. John Prust, director of Family Life and Spirituality for the Diocese of San Diego, similarly recognizes this need to renew the faith culture of the home and uses the concept of the domestic church and the resources of organizations like the Peyton Institute for Domestic Church Life to do so.

American Catholic Attitudes about Marriage and Sexuality

Faith formation is not the only issue that arises when considering America's changing family forms. Catholics' understanding of their faith and what it teaches about marriage and sexuality also evolves and develops in tandem with changing sociohistorical circumstances. In this section, we examine what Catholics believe about who should be the locus of moral authority on five issues of marriage and sexuality. In cases where Catholics in different types of family arrangements exhibit distinct sets of beliefs, we highlight those differences by comparing responses across three primary subgroups—married Catholics ($n = 849$), never married Catholics ($n = 342$), and divorced and separated Catholics ($n = 158$). Respondents who identify themselves as "married" include married Catholics who may have had previous marriages that ended in divorce, annulment, or the death of their former spouse.

Our respondents were asked who should be the locus of moral authority—church leaders, individuals, or both individuals and leaders working together—on five issues of marriage and sexuality. Because four of these five survey questions were asked consistently between 1987, when the first survey in our series was conducted, and 2017, when the most recent survey was conducted, we can observe changes over time. As table 5.1 reports, between 1987 and 2017, everyday Catholics' locus of moral authority has shifted away from church leaders and increasingly toward the individual. This is true for all four measures, but the size of the shift toward the individual being the locus of authority is particularly large with respect to decisions about engaging in same-sex relations and sexual relations outside of marriage, which saw a 15 percentage point increase among those who believe that the individual alone should be the one to make these decisions; and re-marrying after a divorce without getting an annulment, which increased by 14 percentage points over this

TABLE 5.1: Catholics' Views on Who Should Have Final Say on Sexual Morality, 1987 and 2017.

		1987	2017	Change
A divorced Catholic re-marrying without getting an annulment	Church leaders	23%	17%	−6
	Individuals	32	46	+14
	Both	45	37	−8
A Catholic using artificial birth control	Church leaders	13	9	−4
	Individuals	64	68	+4
	Both	23	23	0
A Catholic who engages in same-sex relations	Church leaders	36	13	−23
	Individuals	43	58	+15
	Both	21	29	+8
A Catholic who engages in sexual relations outside of marriage	Church leaders	35	13	−22
	Individuals	44	59	+15
	Both	21	28	+7

Sources: 1987 and 2017 ACLS.

thirty-year time span. The decision to use artificial birth control shows the least increase in individual moral locus of authority—rising by 4 percentage points—but that is simply because American Catholics have long thought that this particular issue, more than all of the others, is one whose morality should be determined almost solely by the individuals involved. In fact, in 2017 only 9 percent of American Catholics believe that decisions about the morality of using artificial birth control rests with church leaders alone.

Some other features of this table are worth pointing out. While all four issues saw increases in the percentage of Catholics who believe that moral authority rests with the individual, two of the four also saw increases in the percentage of Catholics who believe that moral authority rests with both church leaders and individuals. For these two issues, the increases in shared moral authority are attributable to declines in the percentage of Catholics who believe that church leaders alone have the authority to judge these actions.

In order to examine how one's marital status correlates with one's locus of moral authority on these issues of marriage and sexuality in our 2017 survey, we compared Catholics of three different statuses—married, never married, and divorced and separated. Table 5.2 reports the results.

TABLE 5.2: Catholics' Views on Who Should Have Final Say on Sexual Morality, by Marital Status.

		Married	Never Married	Divorced/ Separated
A divorced Catholic re-marrying without getting an annulment	Church leaders	16%	20%	18%
	Individuals	43	48	53
	Both	41	32	29
A Catholic using artificial birth control	Church leaders	10	8	9
	Individuals	65	70	74
	Both	25	23	17
A Catholic who is considering having an abortion	Church leaders	15	12	9
	Individuals	51	60	63
	Both	34	28	28
A Catholic who engages in same-sex relations	Church leaders	15	11	10
	Individuals	56	63	63
	Both	30	26	27
A Catholic who engages in sexual relations outside of marriage	Church leaders	15	13	14
	Individuals	57	59	70
	Both	29	28	16

Source: 2017 ACLS.

Perhaps not surprisingly given their lived experience, divorced and separated Catholics are substantially more likely than married Catholics to believe that individuals alone should determine the morality of re-marrying after a divorce (53% to 43%, respectively) and the morality of using artificial birth control (74% to 65%, respectively). Compared to their married counterparts (51%), both the never married (60%) and the divorced and separated (63%) are substantially more likely to believe that individuals alone should determine the morality of an abortion. Never married (63%) and divorced and separated (63%) Catholics are also somewhat more likely than their married counterparts (56%) to believe that individuals alone should determine the morality of engaging in same-sex relations. Finally, with respect to the issue of having sex outside of marriage, a large majority of divorced and remarried Catholics (70%) believe that individuals alone should decide the morality of this action, compared to 57 percent of married, and 59 percent of never married, Catholics.

Overall, these patterns in the data are understandable. For instance, married Catholics, to the extent that they remain faithful to their partners, are arguably less likely to personally face having to decide the morality of engaging in same-sex relations or sexual relations outside of marriage. Divorced, separated, and never married Catholics, on the other hand, are perhaps more likely to experience situations in which they are actively discerning or deciding about such things as remarrying or having non-marital sex. When someone has life experiences that increase their (or their close friends') exposure to these realities, they perhaps have a greater proclivity to regard themselves as the final arbiter in judging their morality.

Another way we can examine Catholics' attitudes about issues of marriage and sexuality is through their responses to a series of questions in our survey about what is entailed in being a "good Catholic." Respondents were asked if they think a person can be a good Catholic without obeying the church hierarchy in its opposition to birth control and same-sex relationships, or without their marriage being approved by the Catholic Church. This latter question takes on additional meaning in this most recent wave of the survey because in 2015 the U.S. Supreme Court ruled in *Obergefell v. Hodges* that same-sex couples have a right to marry. As a result, when Catholics today think about the various types of marriages that are not approved by the Catholic Church, they are not just thinking about the civil marriages of divorced Catholics who did not have their previous marriages annulled; they are also thinking about the civil marriages of Catholics who have either decided not to have a sacramental marriage, or as is the case with gay and lesbian Catholics, are prevented from having a sacramental marriage.

Catholics' responses to these questions, like their responses in previous waves of our survey, indicate that the vast majority of Catholics "articulate a view of what it means to be a good Catholic that is largely independent of the church hierarchy's teachings."[29] Figure 5.1, which compares our survey results to those of other surveys, shows that Catholics' views on these issues are increasingly independent of church teachings, with increasing majorities saying that a person can be a good Catholic without obeying the Church hierarchy's opposition to birth control (70% in 1987 and 81% in 2017) or same-sex relationships (55%

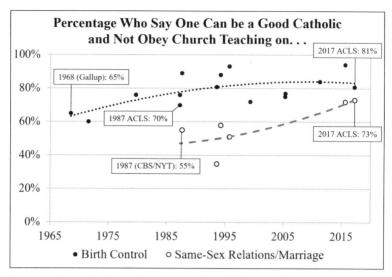

Figure 5.1: Attitudes Toward Being a Good Catholic Regarding Birth Control and Same-Sex Relations/Marriage.
Sources: Published results from various polls and the authors' analysis of data sets.

in 1987 and 73% in 2017). The upward trend line is particularly dramatic with respect to the issue of same-sex relationships, which shows a nearly 20-percentage-point increase since 1987.

Although not reported in this figure, a large majority (77%) of respondents to our 2017 survey also stated that a person can be a good Catholic without their marriage being approved by the Catholic Church, up from 61 percent in 1993. These responses—beliefs about birth control, same-sex relationships, and the need for a Catholic sacramental marriage—all indicate that Catholics are increasingly likely to say that a person can still be a good Catholic without adhering to the Church's official teachings regarding these issues.[30]

The data presented in table 5.1 and figure 5.1 present clear evidence of Catholics' increasing reliance on their own lived experiences and individual, informed consciences in making decisions about different issues related to marriage and sexuality. This parallels what Dillon describes as an increasing "postsecular sensibility" among everyday Catholics in the United States. Unlike members of some Protestant evangelical churches who might commit themselves to literalist interpretations of scripture or certain "fundamental moral truths," everyday Catholics believe that, especially regarding issues of marriage and sexuality, they do not need to adhere to all the ideals presented in official Catholic Church teachings in order to regard themselves as "good Catholics." They may be guided in their thinking by what the church teaches, but they are also guided by their own lived experiences, by modern understandings of marriage and sexuality derived from the behavioral and social sciences, and by their own consciences.

While some might regard this as a type of "cafeteria Catholicism" in which individuals "pick and choose" what beliefs they want to adhere to, this would, we think, be a mischaracterization when applied to every Catholic who disagrees with a teaching. For some Catholics, especially those most engaged with their faith, moral decision-making is not simply a matter of holding onto preferred teachings and disregarding the rest; rather, it is recognizing that there are multiple considerations to balance, and an individual's personal circumstances and everyday life experiences can also be a source for understanding God's will in one's life. Knowing how deeply a particular Catholic engages the resources of her tradition may be a better measure of her commitment to Catholicism than whether she happens to agree or disagree with a church teaching.

Now that we have examined what everyday Catholics think about the morality of these issues of marriage and sexuality, we turn our attention to specific issues that appear to be of concern to both the everyday Catholics in our survey and the interviewees. These issues relate to the challenges faced by divorced Catholics and their children, the church's response to the increasing number of single Catholics (including those choosing to cohabit with a partner rather than marry), and the increasing number of Catholics identifying as LGBTQ+, getting civilly married, and raising children. Analyzing these data reveals the issues that concern both everyday Catholics and our interviewees. As we will see, many ordained and lay church leaders desire to respond to concerns among the laity in ways that strike a balance between the pastoral practice of accompaniment on the one hand and, on the other, the need to proclaim the church's teachings clearly and accurately, notwithstanding ambiguities in the discernment and application of church teaching.

Divorced and Separated Catholics and Their Children

The Catholic Church teaches that "the purpose of the sacraments is to sanctify men, to build up the Body of Christ and, finally, to give worship to God."[31] In these ways, the sacraments strengthen one's faith through the reception of God's grace and express one's faith in the act of worship. Thus, the sacraments "express and develop the communion of faith in the Church."[32] The church further teaches that participation in the sacraments and the reception of the Eucharist during Mass is important for the spiritual well-being of the faithful.[33] By receiving communion, Catholics are, in accord with Catholic theology, receiving the body and blood of Christ. Given the deep-seated significance of the Eucharist and the Mass in the socialization and lived experiences of everyday Catholics, it is understandable that the vast majority of Catholics in our survey (76%), regardless of their marital status, agree that the sacraments of the church are essential to their relationship with God.

Recognizing both the importance that the church assigns to reception of the Eucharist, and Catholics' desire to participate fully in the sacraments, including reception of communion, the church's recent Synod on the Family opened dialogue among the bishops about the possibility of allowing divorced and remarried Catholics to receive communion. While the Synod on the Family and Pope Francis's response in *Amoris Laetitia* stopped short of opening this door completely, Pope Francis did explicitly state that "divorced people who have not remarried . . . ought to be encouraged to find in the Eucharist the nourishment they need," and he called on pastoral ministers to respond to those who are divorced and remarried with "careful discernment and respectful accompaniment."[34] By calling on church ministers to assist the divorced and remarried in this way, the pope is alluding to the "internal forum" whereby individual Catholics, in consultation with their pastor, may discern a path that is most in line with their well-formed conscience.[35]

Our 2017 survey explicitly asked Catholic respondents their opinion about this key issue discussed during the 2014–15 Synod on the Family—i.e., whether Catholics who have divorced and remarried should be able to receive holy communion. Over three-quarters (78%) of Catholics reported that they either strongly agreed (44%) or somewhat agreed (39%) that divorced Catholics who remarry without an annulment should, in consultation with a priest, be able to receive the Eucharist. Only 22 percent reported that they somewhat disagreed (13%) or strongly disagreed (9%). Clearly, the overwhelming majority of Catholic respondents believe that divorced and remarried Catholics should be allowed to receive communion. This view is also consistent with findings from the 2017 and prior laity surveys indicating that approximately two-thirds of respondents believe that one can be a good Catholic while not adhering to church teaching on marriage and divorce.[36]

Our survey did not include direct measures of whether Catholics who are divorced or separated feel excluded or stigmatized in the church, but their responses to pertinent survey questions, the reports of some of our interviewees, and prior literature on divorced Catholics suggest that these feelings are common. One of the clearest indicators in our survey data that divorced and separated Catholics may not feel as at home in the church is seen in their response to the question "How important is the Catholic Church to you personally?" As table 5.3 shows, divorced and separated Catholics (25%) are somewhat less likely than never married Catholics (31%) and substantially less likely than married Catholics (38%) to claim that the church is among the most important, if not the most important, parts of their lives. Moreover, those who are divorced and separated (36%) are also somewhat more likely than never married Catholics (31%) and substantially more likely than married Catholics (24%) to say that the church is either not terribly important, or not important at all, to them personally.[37]

The data from our survey also reveal that divorced and separated Catholics are substantially less likely than married Catholics to be registered as a member of a parish, to give financially to their parish or to other Catholic organizations or causes, to attend Mass regularly, and to be involved in their parish beyond attending Mass. Certainly, part of the reason for divorced and separated Catholics' lower levels of support and involvement in the church is the absence of a spouse who can encourage and support these practices. For instance, married Catholics are more likely than divorced and separated Catholics to say that pleasing or satisfying someone close to them, like a spouse or parent, is an important reason for their Mass attendance. And part of the reason may be that divorced and separated Catholics do not derive as much enjoyment from participating when they do it alone. But it is also likely the

TABLE 5.3: Catholics' Views about the Importance of the Church to Them Personally, by Marital Status.

The Catholic Church is . . .	Married	Never Married	Divorced/ Separated
Among the most important, if not the most important, parts of my life	38%	31%	25%
Quite Important to me, but so are many other areas of my life	37	39	39
Not terribly important to me, or not very important at all	24	31	36

Source: 2017 ACLS.

case that these lower levels of commitment and engagement in parish life among the divorced and separated is due to their feeling excluded or even stigmatized because of their "failed marriage." Our data sources support this as a plausible explanation.

Interviewees speak about the feelings of alienation, exclusion, and stigma among some, though certainly not all, divorced and separated Catholics, and suggest that ministers sympathetically accompany them on their journey. Deacon Ray Dever, for instance, notes that he sees "divorced individuals who have widely different reactions to their situation and to their relationship with the church. . . . Some feel totally stigmatized and outside of the church, even though they may have done nothing wrong in accordance with the church teachings. Then, on the other extreme, there are many people who are not in conformance—someone who is divorced and remarried without an annulment—who are just saying 'I'm still participating. I know I'm supposed to get an annulment, but I don't care. I'm going to receive communion.'" Deacon Dever believes that the most pastoral approach to these various situations is for ministers to be sympathetic. "Divorce is probably the most traumatic experience that many people experience in their lives honestly, and so it really cries out for accompaniment, of just walking with them and not hitting them over the head with the rules." Helen Alvaré concurs, saying that "Divorce is like going through a death" because "at some point you've gone from having a great love to none." The first thing the church should do when someone experiences a divorce, Alvaré states, "is to be there for them, to make them understand that they are still beloved . . . to sit with them the same way that we sit with widows. . . . And I mean the debate about communion is like eight steps down the path." While Alvaré, like Dever,

believes that the most important role of the church is to accompany divorced Catholics by sitting with and listening to them, she does not think
that relaxing the rules restricting access to communion by divorcees who
have remarried without an annulment should be as high a priority.

However, for Frank DeBernardo, director of New Ways Ministry, the
issue of access to communion is more critical to the church's ministry of
accompaniment: "Divorced Catholics experience an uncertainty about
how welcome they are because there are so many conflicting messages,
and the biggest conflicting message is, 'You can come to church but you
can't receive communion.'" DeBernardo acknowledges that the church's
restrictions on receiving communion apply only to Catholics who have
divorced and remarried without an annulment, but he suggests that
not all Catholics are aware of this distinction, "A lot of people feel that
the church's teaching about divorced and remarried people applies to
all divorced people," which can cause the divorced to think they might
"find a much better welcome at other Christian churches." Clearly, these
church figures believe priority should be given to the ministry of accompaniment—of simply being present with Catholics during their naviga-
tion of divorce. At the same time, some church leaders believe that the
church should either present its teachings more clearly in order to avoid
confusion, or relax its restrictions on reception of communion, so all
divorced Catholics—including those who are remarried with or without
an annulment—know that they are welcome in the church.

Relatedly, another area of confusion and sometimes disappointment
among divorced Catholics is the church's teachings and practices regarding annulments. Research shows that the vast majority of divorced Catholics choose not to seek an annulment and, if they decide to remarry,
to do so outside of the church.[38] Sociologists attribute this low interest among divorced Catholics in seeking an annulment to two factors.[39]
First, some Catholics regard the practice of annulments as dishonest,
especially if they believe their marriage was a valid bond that simply
broke down over time. To receive an annulment in an ecclesial court requires establishing the grounds for the nonexistence of a valid marriage
from the outset, which many divorced Catholics and non-Catholics are
unwilling to do.[40] Secondly, many divorced Catholics who have gone
through the annulment process report that the process itself fails to de-
liver on the kind of healing and renewal that they were seeking in the

process.[41] These experiences are confirmed by some of our interviewees. Katie Gleason, coordinator of campus ministry for the Diocese of Lansing and a member of her diocese's synod task force, describes the input her diocese received from divorced Catholics:

> We had a really high response rate from divorced Catholics who felt that they were no longer welcome, felt judged, or like they couldn't show their face after the divorce. Socially, the divorce had messed up their relationships. Along those lines, annulments were an area of a lot of confusion and a lot of hurt. Even though we as church bill it as an opportunity to heal, unfortunately people experience it as just a lot of legal paperwork. Then, they get a letter in the mail that says, "Congratulations." But now what? I just dug into my life and into my pain, I got ahold of my ex from how many years ago, but now what? There isn't great communication, and you kind of hope that maybe the pastor is doing that, but people feel let down. The reality is it seems very legalistic. So, one thing the church could do to show its support for those who are divorced or whose marriages have been annulled is to add an element to the annulment process that reaches out to the person and provides some follow up. Like, here's some divorce and remarriage groups, or here's a healing retreat, or something. But unfortunately, we stop at the point of processing the paperwork and we don't do that next step. It could be as easy as . . . having that in the annulment paperwork, so when they open the letter saying "you got your declaration of nullity" there's also a list of recommended books or counselors, and an invitation for Catholics to consider seeking therapy or counseling for whatever issues emerged in the process, such as substance abuse or whatever it happens to be. There could be a low contact way of offering someone a bridge where obviously there's brokenness.

Based on responses like this from our interviewees, as well as testimonies presented in other sociological research on the topic,[42] it is clear that the church's current teaching and practice of annulments may, in some instances, inflict additional emotional trauma rather than help heal the wounds of a painful separation.

Interviewees, while acknowledging these concerns among divorced Catholics themselves, also express a need for the church to be attentive to the negative experiences of children. Andrew Lichtenwalner, for instance, states that families that "don't have a mom and dad together have a lot more needs, and you have to offer more specific accompaniment." Based on his work with an organization that serves the needs of adult children of divorce, he claims that it is a "myth that children are resilient following a divorce," and describes how the church, by better assisting parents during and after a divorce, can help prevent long-term negative effects of divorce on children.

Single Catholics and Cohabiting Catholics

Single and cohabiting Catholics, like divorced Catholics, may not always feel at home in their parishes simply by virtue of church messages and symbols that prioritize marriage and the nuclear family. Our 2017 survey did not have a sufficient number of respondents who reported living with a romantic partner ($n = 78$) for us to conduct meaningful statistical analyses. We are, however, able to compare the levels of parish involvement among Catholics who are married, never married (single), and divorced and separated to see if distinct patterns emerge among the never married. As we saw in table 5.3, never married Catholics are somewhat less likely than married Catholics to state that the church is among the most important, if not the most important, part of their lives. And like divorced and separated Catholics, never married Catholics are substantially less likely than those who are married to give financially to their parish and other Catholic organizations, and to attend Mass regularly. Interestingly, however, never married Catholics are substantially more likely than those who are married, divorced, or separated to do volunteer work with the poor or other vulnerable groups in society, a finding that supports the results of DePaulo's research reported earlier.[43]

A few interviewees describe ways the church could more effectively affirm its single members. One way, according to Dr. Andrew Lichtenwalner, is for the parishioners to reach out intentionally to include people in diverse states of life in their social interactions within the parish. He reflects on how he and his wife do this at their parish: "For instance, we have young kids. It's natural for us to gravitate towards other families with younger kids in order to connect similar experiences. But it's also important to connect with those people around us that aren't there with a family and to get to know them, spend some time with them, talk with them, invite them over." By sharing this example, he is suggesting it as one way that parish communities can be more inclusive of people who are single. Frank DeBernardo discusses how ministers can showcase in their teachings and homilies some of the prominent single people in the Bible, including Mary Magdalene and Martha of Bethany. The point these leaders are making is that there are ways for the church to affirm the lives and contributions of single people, and by doing so, make them feel more a part of the parish community.

In terms of addressing the issue of cohabitation, some interviewees describe how the church and its ministers can do a better job of inviting cohabiting couples and couples who are civilly but not sacramentally married to consider taking the steps toward sacramental marriage, which, in cases where two baptized Christians have already been civilly married, means having their marriages "convalidated." Part of the welcoming posture of the church in these cases, according to Lichtenwalner, is for ministers to be proactive and say to parishioners who are in civil marriages "If you happen to be in this situation, we'd love to have you come to a session just to learn more about how your marriage might be recognized in the church." According to Lichtenwalner, even among those who are showing up on Sundays, there are a good number of people who could benefit from that type of proactive pastoral response. Simply by inviting people to these types of information sessions shows that the parish is thinking about them.

When speaking about the issue of cohabitation, Helen Alvaré focuses on the church's teachings with respect to sexuality: "Much of what the church teaches about sexuality is rarely well thought out and articulated by church ministers," and as a result, "people don't really have an understanding of where our teachings come from." For Alvaré, the heart of Catholic teaching on marriage is having a couple remain committed to one another in order to take care of each other and their children in a stable relationship. In other words, it is mission focused. For her, many people who have not taken the time to learn the origins of the church's teachings about marriage and family have a misperception that the church's teachings are some kind of purity code and that Catholics "hate sex" when it is not in the form of marriage. This, she believes, overlooks the church's fullest teachings about marriage and family, which would hold up the marriage commitment as the "most loving arrangement for romantic partners and for their children" because it offers them the "stable relationship needed to flourish."

This parallels what interviewee Dr. Julie Rubio, professor of Christian ethics at the Jesuit School of Theology at Santa Clara University, elaborates. According to Rubio, many people in the church focus too much on "what families are rather than what families do." She says that if you look closely at what the church teaches about sex, love, and families, "the church spends quite a bit of time focusing on what the mission of the family is supposed to be in terms of prayer, service, engagement, and sex. But these teachings do not often get emphasized at the parish and diocesan levels, and as a result people lose sight of what the primary mission of the family is, and instead get caught up in what families are." In expressing these concerns, both Alvaré and Rubio are suggesting that if church ministers focus more on what families are called to do—i.e., the mission of families—then that moves the focus away from which family structures are ideal.[44] All Catholic families are called to pursue the most loving and stable environments for romantic partners and their children.

LGBTQ+ Catholics and Those Choosing to Marry Civilly and Raise Children

Some interviewees also talk about the dilemmas facing the church with respect to inclusion of LGBTQ+ Catholics and their families. They talk about the absence of visible role models of people who have successfully integrated their Catholic and LGBTQ+ identities, and the tensions between recognizing the social benefits of civil same-sex marriage and upholding the church's teaching that sacramental marriage is reserved for a union between one man and one woman. For instance, Katie Gleason states that she believes that the church has done a poor job with respect to how it approaches LGBTQ+ Catholics in two ways. First, "We've sort of pretended that homosexuality doesn't exist within our ranks," as is evident, she claims, in the number of priests who identify as gay but who are prohibited from talking openly about it. According to Gleason, when we fail to be open about this reality, "we don't have access to celibate examples of lived homosexuality." As a result, without providing public examples, "all we're doing is telling people intellectually you should choose celibacy, but we're not going to show you any successful celibates in this area because we're going to pretend they don't exist." Secondly, she says it is a good thing that LGBTQ+ people in our society are living with more freedom, less shame, and greater access to benefits. "It's good that people don't have a risk of their job, or their health, or being attacked or something along those lines. It's good that we've had a movement that better protects LGBT people and potentially their mental health. But we as church don't believe in same-sex marriage because we don't believe that it qualifies for the grounds of a sacramental marriage. But we also haven't come up with a good way to articulate that, and to articulate the empathy that we have for people who are not able to live within the bounds of our sacramental expectations." This, she believes, puts pastoral ministers in somewhat of a bind. Church leaders need "to develop that language that is not yet out there for people in ministry to use." Simply put, Gleason does not believe the church has "a pastoral language or a pastoral program to meet the needs of the world we're in right now." She, like other interviewees, believes that the church needs to develop better ways of addressing these issues that prioritize the pastoral practice of accompaniment.

Like Gleason, John Prust believes "it would be wonderful" if more gay priests came out and publicly acknowledged their sexuality. "I think people would appreciate that. If some of our priests would just come out, people would see that some of our really holy priests—priests that people look up to—are also gay [and celibate]. And then you're providing a good model, and it would also bash the narrative that there's a connection between homosexuality and the sex abuse crisis."

Developing a pastoral language that simultaneously seeks to be welcoming to LGBTQ+ Catholics and their families while upholding the church's teachings on sexuality and sacramental marriage is a challenging task. Perhaps nowhere is this more evident than with respect to the issue of the legalization of same-sex marriage. Using data from other surveys, figure 5.2 shows the increase in support among American

Catholics for legal same-sex marriage over the last thirty years. In 1992, approximately 31 percent of American Catholics supported the right of same-sex couples to legally marry.[45] By 2023, this number had risen to 65 percent of American Catholics.[46] And as figure 5.3 shows, the increase is true for every generation, while also fueled by deaths among more traditional pre-Vatican II Catholics and simultaneous growth among relatively liberal Millennial and iGen young adults. The fact that so many American Catholics support this right while the Vatican continues to stand against it presents a dilemma for the church. On the one hand, church ministers are being asked to adopt the pastoral practice of accompaniment, but on the other hand, church doctrine makes it hard to implement this commitment.

In addition to the perceived inconsistencies in the church hierarchy's approach to legal same-sex marriage is the wide variation in how individual American bishops respond to members of the LGBTQ+ community. In some dioceses, LGBTQ+ lay ministers or church employees who are open about their sexual orientation or gender identity, or who are discovered to have entered into civil same-sex marriages, might be asked to resign or be fired, while in other dioceses similar ministers and employees are retained or perhaps even held up as role models. Father James Martin, editor-at-large of the Jesuit magazine *America*, speaks about this and other inconsistencies in how the church approaches LGBTQ+ issues:

> A lot of pastors are not interested in really listening to LGBTQ people or considering their situations. Primarily it's because they don't know them that well. I often use the example of married couples using birth control. Pastors generally know them and the complexity of their lives. So, they do not thunder from the pulpit against birth control, nor do they condemn people and say they can't come to communion. Why? Well, because they recognize that good Christian couples in their consciences have made decisions to use birth control. They know them, they trust them, and they respect their consciences. They also know that 80 percent of Catholics feel that it's not a moral problem. In the case of the LGBTQ person, they don't know them, they don't know their consciences, they certainly don't respect their consciences.

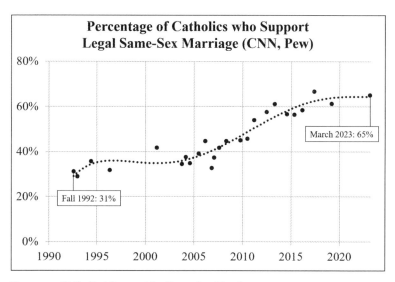

Figure 5.2: Catholics' Support for Same-Sex Marriage, 1992–2023.
Sources: 1992–1994: CNN/*Time* Magazine. 1996–2003: Pew Research Center.

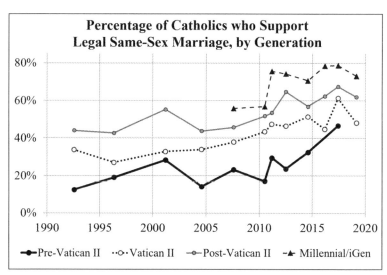

Figure 5.3: Catholics' Support for Same-Sex Marriage by Generation, 1992–2019.
Sources: 1992: CNN/*Time* Magazine. 1996–2019: Pew Research Center.

Dr. Julie Rubio similarly recognizes that this lack of consistency in how the church approaches these issues can be problematic. "If a bishop or other church leader is going to deny employment to a Catholic who is in a same-sex relationship, that bishop or church leader should also deny employment to a Catholic who is using artificial contraception or who is divorced and remarried." Similar to previous leaders who wanted the withholding of communion from politicians to be consistently applied (and not only to the abortion issue), interviewees argue that if bishops or priests are going to withhold sacraments or deny employment for violating sexual teachings of the church, this practice should be applied consistently, not simply where it is convenient or popular.

Another inconsistency mentioned by church leaders is pastors' varying approaches to same-sex couples with children. Even though the USCCB stated clearly in its 2006 document *Ministry to Persons with a Homosexual Inclination* that "the church does not refuse the sacrament of baptism to these children," Father Martin mentions that he receives "emails all the time from people saying the pastor wouldn't baptize my kid because we're a same-sex couple."[47] Santa Fe Archbishop John Wester has seen this issue arise in his diocese and describes how he needed to sensitize some of the clergy to be more receptive of same-sex couples. According to Wester, some clergy had expressed hesitancy in baptizing the children of same-sex couples, fearing that they could not be good models for their children in their faith formation. In Wester's perspective, church ministers should be happy that same-sex couples, some of whom have probably had negative experiences in the church, would even consider presenting their children for baptism. He advised these clergy to not turn these same-sex couples away, but to welcome them and assist them in forming their children in the Catholic faith.

Another issue facing some contemporary Catholic families is how to respond when a family member, such as teenager or adult child, expresses a different gender identity. One interviewee, Deacon Ray Dever, faced this situation himself when one of his own children, who was raised Catholic, attended Catholic schools, and even served as an altar server, revealed her transgender identity while she was away at college.

Dever recently asked his daughter why she no longer practices Catholicism, and she responded by showing him a popular meme that basically conveyed the message, as Dever describes it, "if this isn't good for you, why are you staying?" Dever suggests that this is the perspective of many young people today. Unless they feel like the church is somehow affirming who they are, they are not staying. Parents and grandparents who grew up during a time when Mass attendance was seen as an obligation may not understand this perspective, according to Dever. "Younger generations need to see why they should be there," and for this, Dever states that "there needs to be more emphasis on just living the good news, on being a community—a joyful, inclusive, loving community—that people want to be a part of. Telling them 'you've been baptized Catholic and you have an obligation to be here' just doesn't fly anymore." Sociologist Dean Hoge and colleagues found that this was true of young adult Catholics twenty years ago.[48] Young adult Catholics are not as skilled as previous generations in discerning what is core to the faith and worth staying for from what is unimportant or even peripheral, as well as discerning something they can dissent from while maintaining their Catholic identity.

When asked his perspective on where the church is at in its understanding of the experiences of the transgender community, Deacon Dever states that the "church is in its infancy with understanding this issue," but that he's optimistic because "there's more recognition within the church that they have a lot to learn." According to Dever, because "gender dysphoria is not something that is readily understandable by most people who are totally comfortable with their gender," and because science is uncovering new understandings of this reality, it is especially important for lay and ordained church ministers to educate themselves about it, to learn what the social and behavioral sciences reveal, and to practice accompaniment, "A tremendous amount of research is being done on the whole issue of gender identity right now, and there are respected researchers and medical professionals who should be a part of the church's discussion about this because they really understand the issues much better, and those people have really not been consulted at all, they're not even part of the conversation." In making this statement, Dever is exhibiting the pastoral, collaborative sensibility that has characterized Francis's papacy.

Implications

This chapter has shown that American Catholics continue to rely on their own lived experiences and individual, informed consciences in making decisions about issues related to marriage and sexuality. Today, large numbers of everyday Catholics do not feel they need to adhere to all the ideals presented in official Catholic Church teachings in order to regard themselves as "good Catholics." They may be guided in their thinking by what the church teaches, but they are also guided by their own lived experiences, by modern understandings of marriage and sexuality derived from the behavioral and social sciences, and by their own consciences.

One area in which this is especially clear is with respect to Catholics' attitudes showing overwhelming support for legal, same-sex marriage. Most Catholic laity have long abandoned the notions that family life should resemble the nuclear family ideal and that sexual expression should be reserved solely for a man and woman who are united in sacramental marriage and open to the creation of new life. They believe that modern families, in all their diversity, are equally called to foster loving, stable environments wherein romantic partners and their children can flourish, and many invite the church and its members to assist them in pursuit of that mission.

While some may interpret these trends as reason for despair, others interpret them as signs of hope. Either way, interviewees suggest that accompaniment and encounter require ministers who are willing to really get to know the members of their communities by listening attentively to their concerns and experiences. It also requires them to be courageous. Dr. Andrew Lichtenwalner makes this clear, stating:

> The church today needs to be courageous. There's nothing to fear in encountering people, and we know not everybody embraces the fullness of what the church teaches. We know that there are Catholics also who struggle with the church's teaching in visible ways. We're all sinners, that's a basic fact. Some Catholics struggle more with certain aspects of the teaching. The key is that we all are called to grow. Rather than approaching difficult situations and scenarios in fear, the church (we ourselves) should approach them with confidence. If we are motivated by the love

of God, if we are motivated by the love of Jesus Christ, by the gospel, there's nothing to fear, even when circumstances are difficult. . . . Coming from that perspective of faith, people of faith shouldn't be afraid to deal with difficult questions and scenarios. That has certainly been the approach of Pope Francis, an approach which I think so many people really appreciate—the fact that he zeroes in on the heart of the gospel message. The importance of welcoming, and accompanying, and loving in the truth. Respecting the dignity of the individual, and having that as the core—meeting the person first—which gives proper context to what should follow.

One of the most recurring themes that emerged during our interviews was the difficulty church ministers face in trying to strike a balance between the pastoral practice of accompaniment and all that it entails—a welcoming demeanor toward all people, an openness to the diversity of family forms and relationships, and pastoral sensitivity—and upholding and proclaiming the church's teachings clearly and accurately. Some leaders speak about their desire to receive, in Gleason's words, a new "pastoral language . . . to meet the needs of the world we're in right now." They believe this new pastoral language should offer models for parishes and their ministers who seek to overcome the tension they feel, and the church-perceived "public scandal" they wish to avoid, when publicly welcoming individuals and communities whose consciences are at odds with some of the church's teachings and ideals. There seem to be ways for the church to chart a path forward that is consistent with church teachings, respectful of today's diverse family forms, and responsive to the evolving *sensus fidelium* (or sense of the faithful) regarding issues of marriage, family, and sexuality. Successful efforts will require engaging the church's teachings more fully on the primacy of the individual's informed conscience and relating those teachings directly to the lived experiences and distinct circumstances of today's Catholics.

6

Trends

Several young adult Catholics, well-dressed and professional in appearance, are taking turns speaking in front of a camera. With the help of a professional videographer, they are making a high-quality promotional video featuring testimonies of their experiences in a program called Fellowship of Catholic University Students (or FOCUS). All of them are recent college graduates and their role in the program is as "missionaries," a title given to all program participants engaged in the work of evangelizing on college campuses. One of the men sits in front of the camera and states: "I've appreciated having a flexible schedule so I can fully participate in the sacraments and holy hours and pour myself into evangelizing others. It's an experience I will carry on for the rest of my life." Another young man sits in front of the camera and describes how, after joining the program, he wondered what people would think about him when they see or hear the title "missionary" attached to his name, especially since as a Harvard graduate, he could be working in a lucrative profession. He states: "The other job opportunities I had were great and very well paying, but they really just paled in comparison to the joy and satisfaction I've experienced as a missionary." A woman who was a scholarship athlete in college relates, "I had financial job offers on the table, the prospect of law school. I could have even gone and played soccer internationally. . . . But now I'm working in and around one of the biggest and one of the most successful athletic departments in the country. I'm working with student athletes who, despite their accolades and their successes, are starving for Christ, and I'm there to serve them. . . . I want to help them to realize that their identity is not in their sport but rather in the fact that God created them."

These young men and women, called FOCUS "missionaries," are assigned in teams to a college or university where they lead the campus FOCUS chapter and live together in community on or near the campus. They share the responsibility of raising donations to cover their own living expenses and rent. The missionaries' primary responsibility is evangelization, and they do this by reaching out to students on the campus and inviting them to Bible studies, prayer groups, or various social activities typical of any college club. Missionaries also teach students themselves how to recruit peer-to-peer, although they seldom, if ever, use the word "recruiting" to describe their activities. Instead, they might say, "spreading the gospel" or "evangelizing." FOCUS is modeled to some extent after Campus Crusade for Christ, the nondenominational evangelical Protestant organization whose approach to evangelization is to spread the faith student-to-student.

Observing this FOCUS community and others like it at work on college campuses, and listening to the testimonials of their missionaries, raises a number of questions: How vibrant are the faith lives of young Catholics today? Are the commitment and passion seen in FOCUS missionaries typical of younger generations of Catholics? What are the prospects for college students or other young adult Catholics retaining their faith into adulthood and through the life course? These questions animate this chapter. As we will see, the young missionaries in this vignette are atypical among everyday young Catholics in their levels of commitment to the faith. However, their efforts to spread that faith illustrate a theme that will arise later: the significance of social networks in sustaining religious commitment. This chapter examines several long-term trends and generational changes among everyday Catholics, trends that may provide insight into the direction Catholicism is heading in the near future. The first section of the chapter focuses on trends in religious commitment, especially Mass attendance. The second examines the effects of Catholic education on later religiosity in adulthood. And the third compares men and women on their religious attitudes and practices, with special attention given to whether Catholic women have become, over time, more alienated from the church and more skeptical of its leaders and teachings.

Religious Commitment over Time

Perhaps the most frequent question we receive as sociologists of religion is: Why are fewer Catholics, especially young people, practicing their faith? And why are more of them leaving the church altogether—that is, no longer even calling themselves "Catholic?" We do not have a simple explanation, but we can describe what is happening in sociological terms and place it in the context of larger trends in religion.

Mass Attendance

A starting point is to ask when Mass attendance began to decline. Available data suggest that attendance began to decline in the late 1950s or early 1960s. It is difficult to know this for sure, however, because survey questions about church attendance were rare before the 1950s; the decline could have preceded the 1950s. Figure 6.1 shows Gallup data on the percentage of Catholics and Protestants saying that they had attended church in the previous seven days. Starting in 1955 and continuing until 2004, Gallup asked about church attendance multiple times each year (usually at least four times) and published a yearly average. In 1955, 74 percent of Catholics reported that they had attended in the previous week.[1] As figure 6.1. shows, the steepest drop took place roughly from the mid-1960s to the early 1970s, when attendance fell from 71 percent in 1964 to 55 percent in 1973. For a time, it appeared that the decline may have ended.[2] But now looking back over a longer period of time, we can see that it did continue to slip—just much more gradually. Although Gallup has asked about church attendance infrequently since 2004, surveys such as the GSS confirm that there was a slow, nearly linear decline in Catholic attendance until very recently. The recent downturn in attendance is due primarily to COVID-19; as the figure shows, it occurred among Protestants as well as Catholics. The newest data (as of mid-2023) suggest there has been only a slight increase in attendance since the end of the pandemic among each of these two groups. Jeffrey Jones of Gallup writes: "At this point, it does not appear that church attendance will revert to pre-pandemic levels."[3]

The year 2002, when the sex abuse scandal became public, also saw a drop in Mass attendance, but only temporarily. This effect is somewhat difficult to see in figure 6.1 because it was spread out over late 2002 and early 2003. It is more apparent in individual surveys from that time period.[4] In March 2002, 47 percent of Catholics told Gallup they had attended church in the past week. By December 2002, the percentage fell to 41 percent, and by February 2003 to 35 percent. But in November, it rebounded to

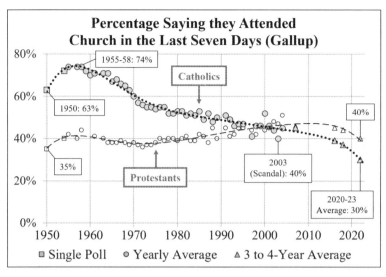

Figure 6.1: Church Attendance During the Prior Week, 1950–2017.
Sources: Various Gallup publications.
Note: From 1955 to 2004, Gallup asked about church attendance multiple times each year and published an average for the year.

45 percent. During this period there was very little change in Protestant attendance. It is surprising how short-lived this effect was, given the magnitude of the scandal and Catholics' anger over it. But some attitudes of Catholics at the time show a parallel decline and rebound. For example, CARA surveys found that Catholics' satisfaction with the "leadership of the U.S. bishops" fell sharply during Spring 2002, bottomed-out in January 2003, but then returned close to original levels by Spring 2003.[5] Our own analysis of GSS data finds that the proportion of Catholics expressing "a great deal" of confidence in "organized religion" was 32 percent in 2000. It fell abruptly to 19 percent in 2002, but then rebounded to 28 percent in 2004. Comparing the temporary effect of the sexual abuse scandal on Catholics' Mass attendance to the longer-lasting effect of COVID-19 resonates with other findings in this book: sometimes the factors that most influence Catholics are external rather than internal to the church.

Setting aside the recent impact of COVID-19, observing generational categories helps to illuminate the long term-decline in Mass attendance since the early 1960s. Using data from the General Social Survey, figure 6.2 shows the percentage of Catholics who, across time, say they attend church at least weekly—for each of the generational categories in our analyses. The steep decline in attendance that started in the mid-1960s took place among almost all the generations.[6] In other words, older and younger Catholics alike reported attending less frequently than they had in the past. However, the more gradual decline that has continued since the early 1970s has occurred primarily because of a generational replacement. For most years between 1972 and the late 1990s, the majority of older pre-Vatican II Catholics (those born before 1928) reported attending weekly or more. Despite year-to-year, random ebbs in the data, the percentage of this cohort attending weekly fluctuated only slightly over the course of about a quarter century. In comparison, about 40–50 percent of the younger pre-Vatican II Catholics reported attending weekly. Again, the trendline for this generation, like that of the older pre-Vatican II Catholics is fairly flat, meaning that this generation's level of attendance changed little after 1972.

This same pattern continues for the three successor generations, with each attending at a lower rate than the preceding generation. (It is still too early to draw strong conclusions about iGen, but in 2021 their

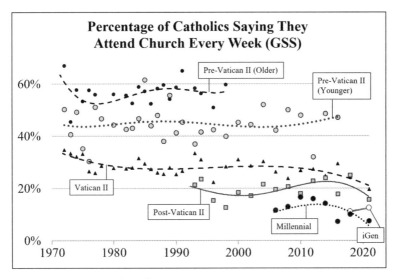

Figure 6.2: Mass Attendance by Generation, 1972–2001.
Source: Authors' analysis of GSS data.

attendance sat between that of Millennials and post-Vatican II Catholics.) The Vatican II generation is the only generation that exhibits a notable drop in attendance over time. But the change is still rather modest—from 35 percent in 1972 to 24 percent in 2018 and then to 20 percent in 2021.[7] Given these patterns, it is clear that the pattern of gradual decline is a result of the older generations being replaced by younger generations, each of which has a lower Mass attendance rate. In other words, the younger generations have always been less religiously active and they will likely continue to be.

It is noteworthy that a similar cross-generational decline in religious participation is evident in most Western European countries among both Protestants and Catholics. Rarely do people who are very devout suddenly lose their religion and become atheists. Rather, parents fail to pass on quite their same level of religiosity to their children, and thus the next generation is, on average, a little less religiously-committed. From modern survey data, we know that religious decline has been advancing in most of Western Europe since at least the 1960s.[8] But indirect evidence suggests that in many countries it goes back much further. For example, in predominantly-Catholic France, a very gradual decline in church attendance appears to have begun by the 1930s or 1940s, a decline which then accelerated in the 1960s and 1970s.[9] In mostly-Protestant Great Britain, church membership and church attendance probably started declining by at least the 1930s.[10] And in Protestant areas of Prussia, it probably started falling in the late 1800s.[11] The point is that what we observe in U.S. Catholicism is not unique. And in the past century, there are few, if any, examples of Catholic (or Protestant) religious leaders in any Western country reversing religious decline once it gained momentum.

Generation and Reported Reasons for Infrequent Mass Attendance

In chapter 1, we reviewed reasons that infrequently-attending Catholics cite for not attending Mass more often. Table 6.1 breaks down these responses by generation. Several cross-generational differences make intuitive sense. The older Catholics are, the more likely that they say health problems prevent them from attending. Older people are also *less*

TABLE 6.1: Reasons for Not Going to Mass More Often, by Generation.

	Pre-Vatican II	Vatican II	Post-Vatican II	Millennial	iGen
Work/family responsibilities	15%	31%	48%	60%	46%
Just not a religious person	29	40	35	44	50
Not a mortal sin to miss Mass	15	30	27	29	43
I'm too busy	3	15	28	44	39
Health reasons	42	32	24	20	13
Inconvenient Mass schedule	9	18	20	26	47
Sermons are poor	3	24	20	19	15
It's boring	6	18	17	24	15

Source: 2017 ACLS.

likely to describe themselves as too busy, especially those who are at or near retirement age. Post-Vatican II and Millennial Catholics—those currently in the prime years of career and parenting—are unsurprisingly most likely to cite work or family responsibilities. There are a few other notable cross-generational differences. Members of the emerging iGen generation are most likely to say that an inconvenient Mass schedule keeps them from attending more often (though we caution that there are relatively few iGen members in the sample). Few pre-Vatican II Catholics cite negative aspects of the Mass itself (i.e., sermons being poor or the Mass being boring).

Is there evidence of an increase in irreligious attitudes regarding Mass attendance? Overall, the differences among the middle three generations (Vatican II, post-Vatican II, and Millennial) are not large, and so we would not describe any emergent trend as being "systematic" or "consistent" from one generation to the next. That said, it is notable that, when asked their reasons for not attending Mass more frequently, pre-Vatican II Catholics are *least* likely to cite the belief that missing Mass is not a mortal sin, and iGen Catholics are most likely to do so. Similarly, pre-Vatican II Catholics are least likely to say they are "just not a religion person," and iGen Catholics are most likely to do so. More than any other response, this item may reflect a loss in faith. Indeed, the majority of Catholics who cite this as a reason for not attending Mass more frequently also say the Catholic Church is "not terribly" or "not at all" important to them.

Importance of the Church in Catholics' Lives

Another central aspect of religious commitment is the subjective attachment Catholics feel to the church and the sense of significance it plays in their lives. The American Catholic Laity Surveys allow us to examine whether this feeling has also declined over time. Table 6.2 shows the importance that Catholics place on the church in their lives, in 1987 and 2017. The results show a decline, but not a particularly severe one. In 1987, 49 percent of Catholics said the church is either the "most important" or "among the most important" parts of their life (this percentage combines the first two rows of the table). By 2017 it had fallen to 37 percent.

Not surprisingly, the subjective importance of Catholicism is highly correlated with Mass attendance. But the correlation is by no means perfect. Who are the people who say the Catholic Church is relatively important to them but do not attend Mass regularly? One way to answer this question is through the reasons that infrequent church-goers give for not attending Mass more frequently. This group of Catholics tends to point to health problems or to family or work responsibilities as reasons they do not attend more often. They are not especially likely to offer "negative" reasons, such as Mass being boring or sermons being poor.

This question reveals generational differences, although these are not as large as in the case of Mass attendance (see table 6.3). In 1987, pre-Vatican II Catholics placed considerably more importance on the church than did either Vatican II or post-Vatican II Catholics. This was especially the case for older members of the pre-Vatican II generation: 70 percent said the church was either the "most important" or "among the most important" parts of their life. In the 2017 data, iGen stands apart from all older Catholics; just 26 percent say the church is either the "most important" or "among the most important" parts of their life. Again, we should be cautious when analyzing these data because relatively few members of this generation have entered adulthood, and none were older than about 23 when surveyed. Among the three generations represented in both the 1987 and 2017 surveys, only younger members of the pre-Vatican generation exhibit a notable change across time, falling from 53 to 41 percent.

TABLE 6.2: "How Important is the Catholic Church to You Personally?"

	1987	1993	2005	2011	2017
The most important part of my life	13%	11%	11%	11%	10%
Among the most important parts of my life	36	33	33	28	27
Quite important to me, but so are many other parts of my life	38	40	37	41	38
Not terribly important to me	9	10	13	17	19
Not very important to me at all	3	6	5	4	6

Source: 1987 to 2017 ACLS.
1999 is excluded from the table because response categories for this question differed that year.

TABLE 6.3: Importance of the Catholic Church, by Generation.

Percentage Saying the "Most Important" or "Among the Most Important" Parts of their Life

	1987	1993	2005	2011	2017
All Catholics	49%	43%	44%	38%	37%
Pre-Vatican II, Older	70	69			
Pre-Vatican II, Younger	53	53	58	49	41
Vatican II	41	44	36	39	37
Post-Vatican II	37	30	46	38	36
Millennial			35	35	37
iGen					26

Sources: 1987 to 2017 ACLS.

Leaving the Catholic Church

Figure 6.3 uses GSS data to show trends in disaffiliation from Catholicism from 1973 to 2018.[12] For each year, it shows the percentage of adults who were Catholic when they were teens but who have since left the church—either because they converted to a different religion or because they now have no religion. Again, there is a considerable amount of year-to-year fluctuation in the data, due partly to sample sizes. But the trend lines show a clear rise in both types of disaffiliation, trends which in turn are understandable in light of the continuing steady increase in religious disaffiliation in the U.S. since the late 1990s.[13]

In 1973, 10 percent of those raised Catholic had since joined another religion. This proportion was gradually rising by the 1990s. It was 13 percent in 1991, and 15 percent in 1996. With the data available, it is difficult to be certain why this increase was happening, but we can identify a few factors that likely contributed. Many conversions occur due to marriage; when a couple with differing religions marry, one of them sometimes switches to the religion of the other.[14] At this time, the proportion of young Catholics marrying non-Catholics was increasing, albeit very gradually. Another probable factor is growth in the Hispanic population; Hispanic Catholics are generally more likely than whites to convert to other religions. Some sociologists have also pointed to the increase in the divorce rate during the 1970s, arguing that the church's prohibition on divorce and remarriage (without annulment) alienated some divorced Catholics.[15] Whatever the case, the rate of out-conversion appears to have leveled off, starting around 2008. Since then, it has remained at about 16 to 18 percent, though that is still considerably higher than in the 1970s. These losses have not been offset by people converting into Catholicism. In recent decades, the proportion of Catholics who report having been raised in a different religion (or none at all) has been holding steady at about 7 to 8 percent. According to the church's official records, adult baptisms and reception of adults into full communion actually peaked in 2000 and have since been declining.[16] Sociologist Ryan Burge estimates that by 2032, U.S. Catholicism will likely have more members over the age of 60 than members between 18 and 45. This is a point at which the absolute number of Catholics is likely to start falling, absent a substantial increase in Catholic immigrants.[17]

The proportion of Catholics *leaving religion completely* and becoming "Nones" began to rise slightly later. This can be seen by comparing the two trendlines in figure 6.3. During the 1970s and 1980s, the proportion of Nones hovered between 4 and 9 percent. An evident upswing began during the 1990s. By 2010 it had risen to 12 percent, and by 2018 to 18 percent. Clearly, Catholics are part of a larger trend in the American public. The proportion of the U.S. population identifying with no religion began to rise rather suddenly during the early 1990s and has steadily continued to the present day.[18] In 1991, eight percent of Americans reported no religion; by 2023, this figure was 33 percent.

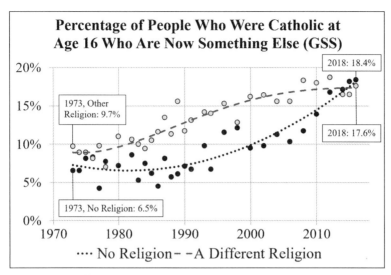

Percentage of People Who Were Catholic at Age 16 Who Are Now Something Else (GSS)

1973, Other Religion: 9.7%

2018: 18.4%

2018: 17.6%

1973, No Religion: 6.5%

···· No Religion – – A Different Religion

Figure 6.3: Disaffiliation from Catholicism, 1973–2018.
Source: Authors' analysis of GSS data.

No obvious precipitating "event" occurred in the early 1990s, but sociologists are in general agreement that the increase is partly political in nature.[19] Besides having had a weak attachment to religion in the first place, those who report no religious affiliation are disproportionately political moderates and liberals. Sociologists have documented that this increasing rejection of religion was, at least initially, a negative reaction to the religious right and its rise to prominence in the 1980s. In other words, weakly-religious Americans chose to stop identifying themselves as Christian due to Christianity's increasing association in the public eye with cultural conservatism.[20] Those raised Catholic, too, are much more likely to become Nones if they are politically liberal— but for Catholics this actually goes back well before the 1990s. For the combined GSS years of 1973–1979, 18 percent of cradle Catholics who described their political views as "liberal" or "extremely liberal" had left Catholicism and become Nones. This compares to just 4 percent of those who described their views as "conservative" or "extremely conservative." For the combined years of 2008–2018, the corresponding percentages are 34 percent of liberal cradle Catholics and 9 percent of conservatives (in other words, each proportion has roughly doubled from the 1970s).

Sociologists Carol Ann MacGregor and Ashlyn Haycook compared political attitudes among former Catholics who have left the church, lapsed Catholics (those who are relatively inactive but nevertheless continue to identify as Catholic), and practicing Catholics.[21] Their analysis offers suggestions regarding the specific aspects of political liberalism that may result in people feeling distant or alienated from the church. Compared to practicing Catholics, they found that lapsed and former Catholics are more likely to believe that churches are too involved in politics and too focused on rules and judgment. Lapsed and former Catholics are also much more likely to hold a pro-choice position on abortion as well as to support same-sex marriage.

A final noteworthy point in figure 6.3 is the apparent absence of an effect from the sexual abuse scandal of 2002. If the scandal had caused a non-trivial number of Catholics to leave the church, one would expect to see a rather sudden acceleration of the upward trends in disaffiliation, starting in 2002 or shortly after. But no such acceleration appears in the data. Between 2002 and 2008, the proportion of former-Catholic Nones increased from 10 to 12 percent. A bigger increase actually occurred between 2008 and 2012, from 12 to 17 percent. A large 2012 survey, conducted by the Public Religion Research Institute, asked former Catholics why, in their own words, they had left the church. Just 4 percent mentioned clergy sexual abuse.[22]

Using the General Social Survey, table 6.4 explores the characteristics of people who have left Catholicism in recent years. It combines data from the years 2008 to 2018 in order to attain adequate numbers of individuals in each subgroup. Men are a little more likely than women to have become Nones (20 percent and 13 percent, respectively). This is consistent with trends among the general public and reflects the fact that women, on average, are more religiously-committed than men.[23] Among racial and ethnic groups, Asians and Pacific Islanders are most likely to have remained Catholic (72 percent). Black respondents are most likely to have left the church; just 55 percent remain Catholic. However, subdividing Hispanics by country of birth reveals that those born in the United States are about as likely as Blacks to remain Catholic (56 percent remaining). Hispanics born in the United States are among the most likely to have converted to another faith (28 percent).

TABLE 6.4: Disaffiliation from Catholicism by Selected Characteristics (Among Those Who Were Catholic at Age 16).

	Still Catholic	A Different Religion	No Religion "Nones"
All who were Catholic at age 16	66%	17%	16%
Race and Ethnicity			
White (not Hispanic)	64	17	18
All Hispanics	63	24	13
Born Outside the United States	69	21	11
Born in the United States	56	28	16
Mexican Ancestry	75	14	12
Puerto Rican Ancestry	54	31	15
Central American Ancestry	66	21	13
Black	55	23	23
Asian or Pacific Islander	72	20	9
Gender			
Male	64	16	20
Female	68	19	13
Generation			
Pre-Vatican II	81	12	7
Vatican II	65	22	13
Post-Vatican II	66	18	16
Millennial	64	15	22
iGen	68	7	24
Political Party			
Democratic[a]	66	14	20
Independent	64	17	18
Republican[a]	70	21	9

Source: Authors' analysis of the combined 2008–2018 GSS.
[a] Including Independents who call themselves "close to" the party.

Historically, Catholics who converted to other religions usually became mainline Protestants. Several reasons explain this. One is broad structural similarities between Catholicism and some mainline churches such as Episcopalian and Lutheran denominations (e.g., having holy communion and calling their clergy "priests").[24] Another was the allure of upward social mobility at a time when mainline membership was a marker of high social status.[25] By contrast, Hispanics who leave Catholicism today disproportionately join evangelical Protestant churches.[26] Contextually, this is understandable given that evangelicalism is vigorous in many Latin American countries, worship in some evangelical traditions such as Pentecostalism favors an expressiveness valued by Hispanics, and evangelical churches are noted too for the strong community support they provide their members.[27]

Comparing results by generation shows a pattern that parallels what we saw earlier for church attendance. Each successively younger cohort has a greater outflow to the None category than the one preceding it. Ten percent of Vatican II cradle Catholics are now Nones. Twenty-two percent of Millennials are Nones. And already, so are 24 percent of iGen. Granted, some members of iGen may eventually return to the church as they move beyond college age and perhaps marry. But we hypothesize that returners will be a minority. As discussed above with the case of Mass attendance, this pattern of gradual, cross-generational decline is how "secularization" of society has proceeded in Western European nations such as Great Britain,[28] where about half the population now has no religious affiliation.[29]

Effects of Catholic Education

Previous books in this series discussed Catholic education in depth, and some of the material we present here is a review of what is already known. But we also draw attention to a new question: whether the impact of Catholic education has changed across generations. Adult Catholics who attended Catholic school are, on average, a little more religiously committed than others. For example, they are more likely to be weekly Mass attenders. But for obvious reasons, it is not easy to infer a causal relationship. Highly religious parents are more likely than less religious ones to send their children to Catholic school. Other aspects of growing up in a more religious family might result in greater adult commitment. For example, one study found that if Catholics' parents frequently spoke with them about religion when they were children, they were more likely to be religiously active as adults.[30] Academic-quality studies on Catholic schooling—the ones that give researchers the most confidence—include information about the religiosity of one's parents and upbringing.

One finding from these studies is that adolescence seems to be more important than childhood.[31] Attending Catholic grade school *by itself*— that is, with no further Catholic schooling above the elementary level—is not correlated with greater religiosity, such as Mass attendance, in adulthood. But attending Catholic high school *is*, even after controlling for family religiousness. This is especially the case for those who spent at least three years at a Catholic high school; there is less of a correlation for those who attended for a year or two before switching to a public or other non-Catholic school. Similarly, attending a parish youth group during one's adolescence is also correlated with adult religiosity. Why do adolescent experiences matter and not those of earlier childhood? A likely answer is that the teen years are the time that young people first start thinking maturely about religion and deciding for themselves whether to accept or reject it.[32] It is also a time when peer influence starts to become important for young people's values and behavior, a topic we return to later.

Research findings on effects of attending Catholic college are somewhat mixed. It is a challenging topic to study, because young people who choose a Catholic college may already be more religiously committed than others. On the whole, however, the evidence points to such colleges producing a positive effect on Catholics' religious commitment later in adulthood.[33]

Catholic High School and Current Mass Attendance

Data from the American Catholic Laity Surveys can illustrate the correlations between adult religious commitment and attendance at Catholic high school and Catholic college. Drawing on the 2017 survey, table 6.5 shows the relationship between Catholic high school and Mass attendance by generation. Analysis is limited to those who were Catholic as children.[34] Among everyone, 54 percent of those who attended a Catholic high school now go to Mass at least once a month (see the first line of figures in the table). This contrasts with 43 percent of those who did not attend Catholic high school, a difference of 11 percentage points. For the pre-Vatican II generation, a relatively large effect is apparent. Eighty-four percent of pre-Vatican II Catholics who attended Catholic high school go to Mass at least monthly, a difference of 22 percentage

TABLE 6.5: Catholic High School and Current Mass Attendance, by Generation.

Percentage who Report Attending Mass at Least Once a Month

	Attended a Catholic High School	Did Not Attend	Difference
All those raised Catholic	54%	43%	+11
Pre-Vatican II	84	62	+22
Vatican II	52	46	+6
Post-Vatican II	54	45	+9
Millennial	49	38	+11

Source: 2017 ACLS, supplemented by data on pre-Vatican II Catholics from the 2011 ACLS.
Only respondents who were Catholic as children.

points from those who did not.[35] For the other generations, the effect is comparatively modest: a difference of 6 percentage points for Vatican II, 9 for post-Vatican II, and 11 for Millennial. In other words, Catholic high school seems to have had a bigger impact on pre-Vatican II Catholics than on all those who came after.

It is worth pausing to ask why those who attended Catholic high school tend to be more religiously committed than others—even after accounting for the religiosity of their parents. In our experience, many people assume it is because Catholic schools successfully teach young people about the faith. It is probably true that graduates of Catholic high schools know more about church teaching than others. For example, they are more likely to know what the church teaches about the real presence of Christ in the Eucharist (and to believe it).[36] But the educational component of Catholic high school is not necessarily what leads their graduates to be more religiously active as adults. We mentioned earlier that participation in a parish youth group is positively correlated with adult religiosity. Similar findings are evident for Protestant teens who participate in church youth groups.[37] Yet most research suggests that Catholics who participate in parish religious *education* classes during their teen years are neither more nor less religiously active than others as adults.[38]

An under-appreciated aspect of Catholic high schools and Catholic youth groups is that they bring religious young people together. When friendships form, teens can reinforce one another's faith. We suspect, but cannot be certain, that this is more important than the content of religious education in Catholic high schools. There is something of a parallel in social science findings on political changes that some young adults exhibit during college—most often, but not always, adopting more liberal attitudes. People often assume that such changes result primarily from the content of a college curriculum (or more specifically, from exposure to the ideas of liberal professors in the classroom). But much research suggests that it is not the only factor. Probably at least as important are peer effects that occur organically as college students interact with one another socially.[39]

Catholic College and Current Mass Attendance

Table 6.6 shows the relationship between Mass attendance and having attended a Catholic college or university. To achieve an adequate sample size, this analysis combines the 2005, 2011, and 2017 American Catholic Laity Surveys. It is limited to respondents with at least some college education. Among these individuals, going to a Catholic college shows a stronger overall correlation with monthly Mass attendance than we saw above for high school. Sixty-nine percent of those who ever attended a Catholic college (including for graduate or professional degrees) now go to Mass at least once a month. This compares to 51 percent who never attended a Catholic college—a difference of 18 percentage points. The most notable result in the table is that this difference remains relatively large among the younger two generations:

TABLE 6.6: Catholic College and Current Mass Attendance, by Generation.

Percentage who Report Attending Mass at Least Once a Month

	Attended a Catholic College	Did Not Attend	Difference
All those raised Catholic	69%	51%	+18
Pre-Vatican II	84	62	+22
Vatican II	60	46	+7
Post-Vatican II	71	45	+19
Millennial	65	42	+25

Source: Combined 2005, 2011, and 2017 ACLS.
Only respondents with at least some college education.

19 percentage points for post-Vatican II and 25 percentage points for Millennial. We must exercise caution in comparing tables 6.5 and 6.6, because they are based on different subsamples; the former is limited to those who were raised Catholic and the latter to those who attended college. But, it appears that for the younger two generations, attending a Catholic college may have a bigger impact on religiosity than attending a Catholic high school.

The apparent positive effects of attending Catholic college are no doubt encouraging for Catholic leaders, but it is important to keep in mind that relatively few Catholics today attend Catholic institutions. In our survey, only 8 percent of all respondents under the age of 30 have attended a Catholic college. When further limiting the sample to those under 30 with at least some college education, the percentage rises only to 20 percent.[40] And among this group, White Catholics are twice as likely as Hispanic Catholics to have attended a Catholic college (24% compared to 12%). There are probably a number of reasons that Hispanic students are less likely to enroll in Catholic colleges. Almost certainly, having lower average incomes and the consequent challenge of affording tuition is an important factor. Another is that much of the growth in the Hispanic population has occurred in southern states that have fewer Catholic colleges and universities than the Northeast or Midwest.

Catholic Women and Attitudes about Equality

The 1970s saw the rise of Catholic activists who spoke out in favor of greater involvement of women in the leadership of the church. Most contentious, perhaps, were calls for the church to ordain women as priests and deacons. For example, the Women's Ordination Conference, founded in 1975, first received significant mention in the news when it held a vigil during Pope John Paul's II 1979 visit to the United States. Such developments led to concerns that women's dissatisfaction with their position in the church might grow to such a point that they would leave Catholicism in large numbers. Such an exodus never occurred. As we saw earlier in this chapter, men are still slightly more likely to leave the church than women. Writing in the 1980s, Andrew Greeley offered a more nuanced appraisal of the situation. He argued that Catholic women were in the rather conflicted situation of being, on average,

TABLE 6.7: Differences Between Catholic Men and Women on Selected Religious Practices and Attitudes.

	Women	Men	Difference
2017 American Catholic Laity Survey			
Attends Mass at least once a month[a]	51%	44%	+7
Prays every day	59	42	+17
Goes to reconciliation (confession) at least yearly[a]	29	30	−1
Is "very" satisfied with the leadership of . . .			
Your parish priest	40	32	+8
Your local bishop	31	24	+7
The bishops of the United States	21	15	+6
Pope Francis	64	51	+13
Views the following as "essential" to being Catholic:			
Devotion to "Mary, the mother of God"	66	53	+13
The obligation to attend Mass once a week	44	35	+9
Engaging in daily prayer	57	42	+15
Participating in devotions such as Eucharistic adoration or praying the rosary	47	36	+11
The necessity of having a pope	61	51	+10
A celibate male priesthood	28	23	+5
Favors ordination of women as priests	67	70	−3
2015 Pew Survey of Catholics and Family Life			
When praying, mainly says memorized prayers[a]	17%	27%	−10
Thinks Pope Francis is "too liberal"	15	24	−9
Rates Pope Francis as "good" or "excellent" in addressing the needs and concerns of women	68	62	+6
Thinks the church will "probably" or "definitely" ordain women by the year 2050	37	46	−9

[a] Percentages are limited to those under the age of 75 because of a skewed gender ratio among seniors.

more active and committed in their faith while simultaneously being more angry with the institutional church and its leaders.[41]

Table 6.7 examines how well this description of Catholic women holds up today. It compares women and men on several factors that are relevant to this question. Most of the comparisons are drawn from our 2017 survey of Catholics. We supplement it with a few questions from a 2015 Pew survey of Catholics.[42] First, there are indications that women remain somewhat more religiously-committed than men. They still attend Mass slightly more frequently than men, something that has been the case as long as surveys have asked about the topic. As the first line of the table shows, 51 percent of women report attending at least once a month, compared to 44 percent of men, a modest difference of 7 percentage points.[43] Our 2017 survey shows no gender difference for participating in the sacrament of reconciliation, although some other surveys find that women go to confession a little more frequently than men. Perhaps the single largest difference between Catholic women and men is the frequency of personal prayer. Fifty-nine percent of women report praying every day, compared to 42 percent of men. And as shown in the second half of the table, Pew finds a difference in *how* women and men pray. Men are a little more likely to say that they mainly recite memorized prayers, as opposed to having a personal conversation with God (or engaging in both these forms of prayer).

Finally, we see little evidence in table 6.7 that women are uniquely unhappy with the institutional church or with their exclusion from the priesthood. They are more likely to describe themselves as "very" satisfied with the leadership of their pastor, their bishop, and the U.S. bishops as a whole—and even more so with the leadership of Pope Francis. Although in the case of Francis, this could be interpreted as approval of his seeming openness to (modest) change in the church. As the second half of the table shows, men are a little more likely than women to view Francis as "too liberal." The difference between the sexes on ordination of women is small, just 3 percentage points. In fact, going back to the 1970s, polls have failed to find a gender difference on this issue in either direction. While this result may seem surprising, women are generally a bit more likely than men to support traditional Catholic teachings. So, if there is any underlying tendency for women to express greater support for women's ordination, it might be offset by a greater theological "conservatism." On the other hand, the Pew survey finds that women are slightly more pessimistic about ordination of women actually happening in the future. Forty-six percent of men think women's ordination will be approved by the church by the year 2050. Just 37 percent of women think so.[44] This could reflect skepticism about the openness of the institutional church to women's concerns and reforms.

Looking back across time reveals that Catholic support for women's ordination grew very quickly from low levels during the 1970s and 1980s. Figure 6.4 illustrates this, using results from many different national surveys taken over the years.[45] The first time Catholics were asked about women's ordination was in a 1971 Gallup survey of Catholics sponsored by *Newsweek* magazine. At that time, just 22 percent of Catholics supported women in the priesthood. But the proportion increased dramatically during the next two decades before leveling off in the early to mid-1990s. Since then, even as younger Catholics have slowly been replacing older ones, it is noteworthy there has been little change, either across time or generations. Average support for women's ordination has consistently hovered in the low 60s.

Comparing these results with support for a married priesthood shows that favorability toward women's ordination started out much lower but then grew more quickly. The first survey to ask about allowing priests to marry was another *Newsweek*-sponsored poll conducted in 1967. Already nearly half of Catholics (48 percent) were in favor. In the aftermath of Vatican II, with so many other changes underway, the topic was being openly debated in Catholic circles as a realistic possibility. As figure 6.5 shows, support for married priests rose slowly during the 1970s and 1980s. One way of looking at the results is that these two decades were a period in which Catholics' attitudes about women priests were "catching up" to their already more liberal stance on a married priesthood. However, the latter leveled off in the 1990s at a few percentage points higher (close to 70 percent) than that for women's ordination.

A number of reasons help illuminate the sudden burst of support for women's ordination in the early 1970s and its rapid growth to the 1990s. It could have been part of the larger liberalizing shift in attitudes occurring around the same time, such as those regarding premarital sex discussed earlier. Another, probable explanation is that attitudes on this particular topic were uniquely influenced by the women's rights movement and the public activism of that decade, as well as by the ratification of the Equal Rights Amendment by the House of Representatives in 1971 and the Senate in 1972. Interfacing with women's political activism in the 1970s, Vatican II's emphasis on the importance of lay participation in the church, and the laity's obligation to engage on issues that concern the good of the church "according to the needs of the times," may have

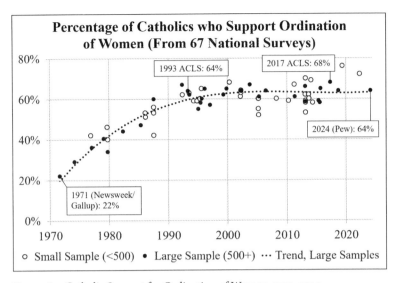

Figure 6.4: Catholic Support for Ordination of Women, 1971–2024.
Sources: Various polls, both published results and authors' analyses of data sets.

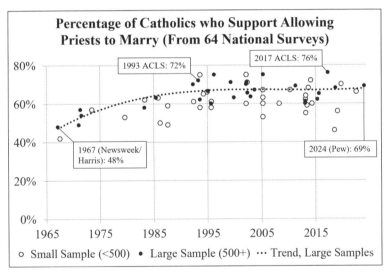

Figure 6.5: Catholic Support for a Married Priesthood, 1967–2024.
Sources: Various polls, both published results and authors' analyses of data sets.

further motivated the surge in Catholic women's advocacy in the 1970s for women's ordination.[46] Some survey data from the 1980s appears consistent with the notion that concerns about women's equality in the church were one factor in growing support for this movement. A 1987 ABC News poll asked Catholic women: "As a woman, do you feel you are being denied your full role in the Roman Catholic Church because the church forbids the ordination of women as priests?" Forty-five percent of those who favored ordination of women said yes to this question. (Not surprisingly, very few of those who favored an all-male priesthood said yes—just 3 percent.)

Though men and women today differ little on women's ordination, there is a subset of both genders who appear frustrated and disappointed (if not exactly angry) over the issue. In the 2022 survey by the Associated Press and NORC,[47] 34 percent of Catholics who support women's ordination say they disapprove of "the way Pope Francis is handling church doctrine on women in the priesthood." This is despite the fact that only 17 percent of these Catholics hold an unfavorable opinion of the pope.

Kate McElwee is executive director of the Women's Ordination Conference. She reflects on Francis's leadership and a gesture of inclusion made by the Vatican as part of the Synod process:

> In 2015, Pope Francis said that he would not appoint a woman as head of a dicastery [i.e., a Vatican department]. But more recently he's said that any lay faithful could lead a dicastery. So that little evolution is very encouraging to me. Pope Francis, we know, is a man who has changed his mind. I'm not sure if we will see women's ordination under his papacy, but he seems to be opening the conversation in more generous and courageous ways than we've seen in many years. The Vatican synod website put the Women's Ordination Conference campaign on there among institutional resources. That was completely shocking to me. It sends a message that this is part of the conversation that the church needs to be having, that this is part of the communal discernment. I find little pieces of hope like that to be very sustaining.

McElwee adds that, for some of her organization's members, those sorts of gestures are not enough: "I've found that the Women's Ordination Conference is often the last stop for women, before they leave the institution of Catholicism completely." Religious activists such as the young women who join WOC are outliers in that they are among the most ideologically discontented with the church and most committed to reform. But they also tend to exemplify the growing trend of young liberals leaving Catholicism for broadly "political" reasons.

A few months after these remarks, Pope Francis did, in fact, appoint three women to the Dicastery for Bishops, a body that advises him on which priests to elevate to the role of bishop. Asked if she wished to comment on this development, McElwee's praise was muted: "This is an important step in removing all barriers to women's full participation in the life of the church. This encouraging shift creates greater opportunities for co-responsibility and collaboration between men and women. However, without gender parity within the Vatican's dicasteries, women will continue to confront a culture of clericalism and sexism that has long thrived within those walls. I must also point out the irony that women may now aid in selecting bishops, a role that they themselves are prohibited from holding on account of their gender." McElwee's feelings are ultimately mixed. She is appreciative of the tone Francis takes on women's issues and of the Vatican's recognition of the Women's Ordination Conference in the Synod process. But she is conscious that the changes he has instituted are small and, at best, incremental. She adds that to sustain hope, it is necessary to take a long view when it comes to change within the Catholic Church: "It's a long-haul movement, and this will take time."

Implications

This first section of this chapter reviewed generational trends in Catholic religious commitment. Mass attendance has been in decline for many decades, and since the 1980s this decline has occurred primarily through gradual cohort replacement. The rate at which cradle Catholics leave the church has increased since the 1970s. Today, Hispanics born in the United States are among those most likely to convert to another religion, often evangelical Protestantism. Since the early 1990s, there has been a particularly steep increase in Catholics choosing to identify with no religion at all, which is most common among young people and men. There is also a political element to the rise of the Nones. They are disproportionately Democrats and tend to reject traditional Catholic teachings on topics such as abortion and same-sex marriage.

What, if anything, can be done to improve the odds that younger generations of Catholics engage more fully with and stay active in the church as adults? It may be an obvious point, but the habits inculcated by one's parents are among the most important factors: when parents make religion an integral part of family life, take their children to Mass, involve them in religious activities, and generally set a good example by practicing the faith themselves, those habits may endure over the life course. Simply put, having religious parents increases the likelihood that, as an adult, a person will hold onto their faith and be religiously active.[48] Odds of success seem to increase for people who grow up in a two-parent household in which both parents, not just one, are religious.[49] But given both the increase in single-parent families and in the numbers of those not affiliated with any religion, having two religiously practicing parents is an increasingly unlikely scenario. Thus, perhaps, a more synodal as well as a revived Eucharistic-centered church—as envisioned by the USCCB 2024 Eucharistic Congress—might help revive families' and children's religious formation.

Nothing is guaranteed, of course. Bishop Larry Kulick of Greensburg references this fact in the course of discussing synodal listening sessions taking place in his diocese:

> We break into small groups, and I'll take time and go around to each group. So many people, a lot of whom are older, say to me, "Bishop, I did everything I was supposed to do as a parent. I sent my child to Catholic school. I sent them to religious education. We went to Mass every weekend. My children are not connected to the church." And a lot of them are saying that it's not that their children are running to the megachurches or other places. They are, as we hear in the statistics all the time, "Nones." They're just not engaged. These parents are feeling great remorse about that. They kept saying, "How do we get younger people re-engaged? How do we get them back in the pews?"

Bishop Kulick continues, relating that many such parents experience guilt, a sense that they have failed not only their children but also the church itself for not successfully passing down the faith. As should be obvious from the data, such self-recrimination is unwarranted; declining religiosity has taken on an inter-generational momentum of its own.

We are often asked if "fallen away" Catholics would return to the church or to regular Mass attendance if Catholicism moderated on some of its more divisive stances. If traditional, orthodox teachings are a source of alienation for some individuals who have left the church, would they return if the hierarchy relaxed some of its strictures? MacGregor and Haycook suggest this might be the case: "If the church were to become more progressive on social issues such as same-sex marriage, some Catholics with lingering affiliations may well find themselves more at home in the pews."[50] On the other hand, this might be a difficult needle to thread. It would risk disaffection of conservative Catholics, who are currently overrepresented among the most active and committed members of the church. Moreover, the experience of mainline Protestant denominations in the U.S. provides a cautionary tale. Total mainline membership began falling in the mid-1970s and has continued to do so despite these denominations adopting a number of liberal positions. For instance, the Episcopal Church took a stand in favor of abortion rights in 1967, began ordaining women in 1977, and allowed its priests to bless same-sex relationships in 2012. But its membership trajectory, which had started to drop in the 1960s, never reversed course. Today, remaining Episcopalians are mostly elderly, and sociologist Ryan Burge predicts the denomination "will very likely be on life support" by 2040.[51]

A competing argument is that Catholicism should move in the opposite direction and model itself on the religious counter-culturalism of evangelical Protestantism. For many decades, while mainline denominations bled members and fewer and fewer Catholics attended Mass weekly, conservative Protestant denominations experienced growth in membership and had congregations brimming with highly-involved members. Frequency of church attendance among evangelicals gradually increased from the 1980s through the first decade of the new century (the increased Protestant attendance evident in figure 6.1 is due entirely to evangelicals). Sociologist Christian Smith argued that evangelicalism's strength arose partly because it consciously placed itself in opposition to secular liberalism.[52] Viewing itself as "embattled" against a dominant, fallen American culture allowed the movement to thrive. In comparison to mainliners and Catholics, evangelical members remained relatively conservative on many matters of sexual morality; moreover, this conservatism was central to its vitality. However, evangelicalism's ability to maintain traditional beliefs was due in large part to its insularity, especially among regular church-attendees. The most committed evangelicals interacted primarily with each other, and their congregational leaders fiercely discouraged individualism and autonomy on topics of sexual morality.[53] We are skeptical that this model can realistically be duplicated in Catholicism. Today's Catholics are well-integrated into secular culture and (at least among whites) are more highly educated than evangelical Protestants. Additionally, Catholicism does not share the strict biblical literalism integral to an evangelical worldview.

If anything, trends in the last two decades should provoke more doubt about the possible success of Catholicism in attempting to follow this path. While the overall proportion of the population that self-identifies as evangelical has remained constant, fewer of those who embrace this label are regular church attendees than twelve to fifteen years ago.[54] This is partly because the label has taken on a purely political connotation, drawing in some political conservatives who are not particularly religious.[55] It also remains unclear to what extent evangelicalism will continue to hold the line on moral conservatism. Acceptance of same-sex marriage has increased sharply among evangelicals since 2004, approaching two-thirds of those aged 18 to 35.[56] There has also been a small but measurable drop in evangelical support for a total abortion ban since the Supreme Court ruling in *Dobbs*.[57]

Although many of the overall trends in U.S. religion are quite sobering, Catholicism has its own distinctive institutional and theological resources that might help it forge a more vitalized future; we have already noted the opportunities provided by a theology of encounter, the Eucharist, and synodality. Additionally, there are tentatively encouraging findings from our analyses. For today's younger generations, attending Catholic college may have a stronger positive effect on future Mass attendance than attending Catholic high school. That was not necessarily the case for older generations. Similarly, the fervor of American youth participation in the Catholic Church's World Youth Day (held most recently in Lisbon in 2023) is encouraging. These socialization channels, though weaker perhaps than family religious formation, might help mitigate the impact of the current changes in marriage and family life; as

Pew documents, the under-40 never married population (at 25 percent in 2021, compared to 20 percent in 2010 and 6 percent in 1980) is the highest it has ever been in American history.[58] Clearly, young people are starting "adult" activities a little later in life—for example, living independently from their parents, marrying (if at all), and having children (if any).[59] An obvious implication is that college is a time to reach young adult Catholics. Father Dennis H. Holtschneider is a Vincentian priest and president of the Association of Catholic Colleges and Universities. He echoes our findings on the positive effects of Catholic colleges, and reflects on ways they may be able to do better:

> In the U.S., about 10 percent of college-age Catholics attend a Catholic university. If they do so, past studies have shown that they are more likely to attend Mass as adults, more likely to have their children baptized, and more likely to pursue ordination or religious life. That said, there is room for these institutions to redouble their efforts to introduce students to church life while they are enrolled. Catholic campus ministry programs are terrific in serving student populations that come to Mass, or show up at the campus ministry offices or the tables at "student organization days." They certainly "advertise" their programs in all the usual places. Unlike their more evangelical equivalents, however, they do not as often "cold call" on students in the dorms, stop by tables in the cafeteria, or attend large student gatherings to meet students and invite them to Mass. There is room for our universities to step up the invitational nature of our evangelism.

Holtschneider also notes that some Catholic colleges have replaced requisite coursework in Catholic theology with more general religious studies requirements. Though perhaps done with the admirable intentions of accommodating non-Catholic students, there may be trade-offs. Priest and sociologist Paul Sullins finds that students tend to be more religiously-committed at Catholic colleges that require more Catholic coursework.[60] Of course, it is also critical for the church to develop Newman Centers and a visible presence at public and non-Catholic private colleges and universities, so that a broad array of students have the opportunity to explore or continue their engagement with Catholicism.

Research supports the inference that peer networks are important for the religiosity of adolescents. And we suspect this is likely true for young adults, too. An implication is that outreach to younger generations of Catholics does not necessarily need to be focused on catechesis or religious education. Tracey Lamont is director of the Loyola Institute for Ministry at Loyola University, New Orleans, and is a professor of Religion and Young Adult Ministry. Previously, Lamont spent several years as a parish young adult minister. She argues that an important step is simply bringing young adults together:

> People doing ministry with young people, sadly, want a textbook and an outlined curriculum made for them, and they don't want anything other than that. I get it; it's a hard ministry. But if we don't start rethinking and reimagining what we're doing with young people, nothing's going to change. It's only going to get worse. . . . COVID in many ways democratized faith for young adults because they took to Facebook groups, to Facebook Live or to Zoom. They were forming their own ministry [to each other], apart from any church or diocese, because they wanted connection. There was one group called something like The Catholic Couch Community. They had around 200 young people from around the country logging on to join them. They just wanted to pray with other people every night of the week. They were not necessarily attached to any formal religious organization. I feel that there are many lost opportunities to find all these young adults who care deeply about their faith and who are also struggling, maybe because all their friends have left the church. What can we [older Catholics] do? Just listen. Invite young people to share openly. Promise them it won't be weaponized against them, and just take to heart what you hear.

Lamont also relates that, in her ministry experience with listening sessions, young people can sometimes benefit from hearing older Catholics share their own faith struggles. For example, a generational divide may be bridged by hearing members of the pre-Vatican II generation share their own difficulty in coming to terms with the church's position on birth control many decades ago. Young people can see in this a reflection of their own concerns with church teaching. This approach presents a contrast to a catechetical model of simply instructing young people about the church's position on an issue like contraception, or perhaps a more contemporary issue such as same-sex relationships. Lamont adds: "It is phenomenal to hear from people who are 80 years old something so similar to what 27-year-olds [themselves] are saying. There's such a ripe opportunity for intergenerational ministry here." This somewhat counterintuitive approach suggests that reaching out to young adults does not always have to involve ministry with them as a group set apart from the rest of the community.

Finally, evidence on disaffiliation from Catholicism offers some implications for ministry with Hispanics. Hosffman Ospino is a professor in the School of Theology and Ministry at Boston College. He has also conducted social research on young Hispanics. He argues that attempts to staunch the outflow of Hispanic Catholics from the church have often focused on the wrong individuals. As our analyses show, it is members of the second (and later) generations who are most likely to leave. But Ospino notes that ministerial efforts have often targeted first-generation immigrants and immigrant-majority parishes. Second-generation Hispanics are more likely to be in more racially diverse parishes. Ospino also emphasizes that, while many Hispanics who leave Catholicism become Nones, even more are drawn to small evangelical Protestant congregations. He describes some of the reasons for this:

> Why do they join those communities? There are many reasons. The churches are smaller. In a big Catholic church with thousands of people coming to Mass, you're just one more number. But in a church with 40, 50, or 60 people, you are *someone*, and they pay attention to you. One of the most basic needs a person has is to be recognized. Another reason is a level of autonomy in reading and interpreting the scriptures. The Catholic Church is a fascinating tradition, but it's very restrictive when it comes to dogma, our understanding of Jesus, and interpretation of the scriptures. And in those [other] churches the pathway to leadership is faster and easier. You see a lot of young, [former] Catholics who were pastoral leaders in their parish communities who have become evangelical pastors because they wanted to go to the next level of leadership. You don't even have to wait to become a priest to start one of those churches. And if you're a woman, ordination is a no-no in the Catholic Church, at least for now. Only two blocks away from the Catholic parish where I worship,

there is a small evangelical church that has three women as co-pastors. And boy, that church rocks! It's unbelievable. People in my Catholic parish community see that and ask: "Why can we not serve in that capacity in the Catholic Church?"

An obvious implication is that, if the reasons Hispanics leave Catholicism tend to differ from those of young white liberals, different approaches may be required in reaching out to them. Ospino's observations about the draw of leadership opportunities in evangelical churches, especially for women, also ties back with another theme of this chapter: women's attitudes about their collective position in the Catholic Church. Whatever the theological and sociological merits of greater leadership roles for women in Catholicism, it seems clear that local and national churches need to be proactively responsive to the changing context, composition, and everyday circumstances of Catholics if the church is to be reinvigorated.

Many church leaders do make a concerted effort to reach out to Hispanics and women, to meet them as equals, and to recognize the talents they offer to the church. David Bonnar, bishop of Youngstown, gives examples from his own ministry:

> The role of women in the church is so important. Women can see things that we don't often see as men, and they can bring out the best in us. I was blessed to work at Saint Bernard's [one of my assignments before becoming a bishop] with a large lay staff, most of whom were women. It was one of the highlights of my priesthood. I was at a school board meeting this past week. I walked in and it was all men except for one woman. And at the end when I had to give my remarks, I said, "If I didn't know any better, I would think that this is an all boys' school. I think that we need to balance this out." . . . When I came to Youngstown, I discovered that there is a large, growing Hispanic community, here. So I've been studying Spanish for the past year with a private tutor because I want to be able to speak their language.

Despite the sometimes discouraging longitudinal trends documented in this chapter, examples like these give us hope about the future.

Conclusion

With data that reach across thirty years and analyzed through the six themes of church, authority, race, citizenship, love, and trends, much has been discussed in the preceding pages. Although we discovered general patterns, these were often qualified with the nuances, ambiguities, and complexities that perpetually mark human and social life. We wanted to convey both the larger trends and the smaller, telling exceptions in this story. Keeping in mind both our scholarly and practitioner readers, each chapter concluded by providing both theoretical and pastoral implications. These implications should by no means be considered an exhaustive list of the relevance of the findings, but they offer a starting point for considering the significance of the data.

This conclusion follows suit. Rather than offering a summary that concisely restates what has come before, we have distilled three catalysts. These are areas that we believe the data indicate that, if discussed in-depth, offer fertile ground to re-imagine Catholicism's role and significance in the lives of Catholics and in the American landscape. These catalysts have very practical ramifications for Catholic leaders and provide intellectual insights for scholars. We begin our analysis at the level of the parish, focusing on major ideas that are relevant for this manifestation of Catholicism. Our second catalyst examines Catholicism at a more national level, raising questions that connect to the Catholic Church as it is perceived as an institution. Expanding further, our third catalyst takes a closer look at polarization, considering what a way forward might look like not only for Catholics, but also for the nation as a whole.

Our concluding analysis is grounded in the philosophical, sociological, and theological tradition of personalism. Personalism takes many diverse forms, but these each share a person-centered lens of analysis. Foundational to personalism is that each person—who is an ontological reality—has intrinsic value and inviolable dignity, is fundamentally unique and irreplicable, and is inherently relational and social. This theoretical system insists that any analysis must start with—and be grounded in throughout—an accurate notion of the human person. Personalism offers not just sociological insights but also has much congruence with Catholic theology, and so has the ability to speak to both scholarly and everyday Catholic readers. It can be used to analyze persons, groups, and institutions. The theory has roots in Aristotle and St. Thomas Aquinas and their virtue-based approach to understanding flourishing in human life; not surprisingly, flourishing and growth are central concepts in the psychology of adult development. We now turn to the first of our three catalysts, the parish.

Parish

The importance of the parish cannot be overstated. The parish is the nexus between the institution of Catholicism and everyday believers. When the parish experience is vibrant, the individual and collective experience of Catholicism is vibrant; when it is weak, adherents may not have as deep or as meaningful of a connection to their faith. In short, the parish experience can make or break Catholics' relationship to their faith, to religion, and to God. Granted, just over half of American Catholics attend Mass a few times per year or less frequently—signaling that they have little parish contact—but a large minority have at least monthly contact with their parish. This is the locus for institutional Catholicism to impact Catholics and civic life, as well as to learn the concerns of the faithful. To overlook or neglect the parish is to miss the most relevant institution for the most active Catholics.

Turning to the slight majority who identify as Catholic but infrequently attend Mass, this reveals empirically what many already know intuitively: many are leaving Catholicism. Pew Research Center found that for every adult who converts to Catholicism, 6.5 Catholics leave; this is far more than any other denomination studied.[1] Although our survey respondents who identify as Catholic but do not attend Mass regularly are different in important ways from those who no longer identify as Catholic, both phenomena are considered a loss to building and sustaining Catholic community. We also reported that the various channels of loss are many: cross-generational loss in the transmission of the faith, disagreeing with a teaching, drifting, and more. There is no single or easy solution. A multi-pronged approach is necessary for Catholic leaders—locally, nationally, and globally—to mitigate the tremendous loss the church continues to experience.

One insight that emerges in the context both of vibrant parishes and mitigating attrition is the importance of Catholic relationships and networks in predicting and maintaining religiosity. From attending a Catholic university to being involved in a youth group (as distinct from religious catechesis that takes a more educative tone) to having two religiously-involved parents, the more explicitly and deeply Catholic a person's social networks are, the more likely they are to remain Catholic as they age. This is corroborated elsewhere. For instance, Stephen Bullivant demonstrates that the gradual diffusing of once densely Catholic social networks—a fact of modernization and globalization—preceded major Catholic disaffiliation in Britain and the United States.[2] Bernard Lee found that most Catholics name the explicit purpose of the group as the reason why they initially join a small group (e.g., joining a Bible study group to learn more about scripture), but they name the relationships and community as their most compelling reason for staying.[3] Relationships make that shared world more important, and when relationships are lacking, the salience of the world withers.[4]

How might the fundamental importance of relationships in Catholics' faith journeys shape parish approaches? This has some overlap with the belonging, believing, behaving model of ministry discussed in chapter 1. Clearly, relationships, acceptance, support, and emotional closeness need to be central in parish life. Of course, not everyone will know each other, but there should be a sense of affective closeness that fosters familiarity among parishioners.

None of this means that the "traditional parish" as a place of spiritual formation is thrown to the wayside. Instead, it involves a rethinking of the ways these theological beliefs are likewise relevant for our lived, relational reality. It means that on feast days—like the Immaculate Conception, Divine Mercy, the Holy Family, the Transfiguration, and the Holy Trinity—not simply reminding everyday Catholics of the abstract theological principles involved, but also what these mean for their lives and the world they share. For instance, for the feast of Corpus Christi each year, it means reminding the faithful that the Eucharist not only binds them to Christ, but also unites them into one "Mystical Body" and "commits [them] to the poor."[5] Thinking about the three-year Eucharistic Revival that the USCCB launched in 2022, it would be a missed opportunity if this effort is confined only to teachings on transubstantiation and does not include a theology of communion that connects the Eucharist to an inclusive and diverse body of believers as well as to an ethics for everyday life.

Turning to personalism more explicitly, parishes might find that they offer more significant ministries and experiences for their parishioners if they start every effort by asking a fundamental question: What does a more human-centered experience of church look like? This does not mean taking worshippers' focus away from divine matters and becoming narcissistic. It simply means taking personhood seriously. Dr. Timothy O'Malley, Academic Director at the Notre Dame Center for Liturgy, offers some things to think through in the context of liturgy: "It's this communion that's received and then this gathering, with all of its concrete materiality: infants and young people and screaming children and putting up with one another. And bodies. Bodies that breathe and sometimes smell and other things. All the materiality of the human condition, of course, the materiality of the church. This all makes it meaningful. It's in this space—not in some sort of abstract, self-constructed space—that divine love becomes present and dwells among us." To make parishioners aware of the significance of gathering means to make liturgy not simply spiritually significant, but also humanly significant, raising their awareness of God's grace present in the gathered community.

The idea that the human person is inherently spiritual is an anthropology present in both Catholic teaching and among the interviewees, with retired journalist and author Paul Wilkes retorting to survey respondents who said they are not religious, "Not a religious person? Of course they're a religious person. You [parishes] just haven't hit the spot yet." To be sure, there are substantial numbers of Americans—23 percent—who are averse to organized religion,[6] and 18 percent who have unfavorable views of Catholics.[7] Wilkes, Catholic anthropology, and personalism are not naive to this fact. However, these interviewees (and we as authors) maintain that there is a fundamentally spiritual dimension to being human. Questions about morality, meaning, purpose, and other existential yearnings are universal human concerns.[8] Understandably, however, there is no universal way to meet these fundamentally human longings. And the narrower and more prescriptive any religion is with its practices, the more it misses connecting with and accompanying substantial numbers of people whose particularities warrant different spiritual practices.

This raises questions: Do Catholics—as individuals or as an institution—see these needs? And if, as personalism argues, human action is motivated by the pursuit of *perceived* goods, are there additional needs that Catholicism sees that people are missing because of misidentification? And what might be Catholicism's blind spots? An important dimension to answering these questions is the qualification of "perceived needs." A person may benefit greatly from a feeling of belonging and having a better understanding of how the Eucharist connects to her life, but if she feels like she is drowning in student debt, Catholicism is simply a distraction. If parishes consider how they might be more expansive and innovative in thinking through how they might meet the identified and legitimate needs of those who show up at the parish doors, they could have much to offer. Jesus models a ministry that allows people to name their own needs, even when these are more "human" than "spiritual."[9] Given the deep history of Catholic aid to those in need—both domestically and internationally—there is ample reason to view financial, educative, health, or other types of assistance as integral to the scope of Catholic ministry. Also, even as disaffiliation is rising, other forms of spirituality are likewise rising. Except for the years impacted by COVID-19, the number of Americans earning their pilgrim's stamp on the Camino de Santiago, a popular pilgrimage route in Spain, has been steadily increasing, from 810 in 2007 to 7,382 in 2019.[10] The Catholic Church would be wise to take note of this and see how it might help people fulfill the spiritual needs that pilgrims and others are looking to meet.

Institution

Our second catalyst is the Catholic Church as a larger—global, but especially national—institution. Interviewees voiced concerns about statements made by individual bishops or the tenor of discussions at national meetings of the body of bishops. Interviewees referenced major official statements as well as quotes from individual bishops in both secular and Catholic media. Our interviewees examine these well-publicized accounts through a variety of lenses, particularly through relevance, optics, hypocrisy, and evangelization. Regarding relevance, many observe that the priorities of the bishops do not align with everyday Catholics' concerns; they wonder whether bishops have a proper pulse on the lives of Catholics. Regarding optics, they refer to strong statements or actions—typically made by individual bishops—that some argue show little to no pastoral sensitivity, which repels many away from Catholicism. Hypocrisy is most vehemently discussed in the context of child sexual abuse—its perpetration and systematic cover-up—but also emerged regarding neglect of other pressing issues, like not adequately addressing systemic racism. Each of these makes the Catholic Church less attractive and stunts the capacity of Catholics to evangelize. These mistakes or oversights of relevance, optics, and hypocrisy not only challenge the faith of highly-committed Catholics; they also pave an exit path for many Catholics as well as make Catholicism less attractive to non-Catholics who otherwise, perhaps, might more willingly engage as citizens with the church's large body of social justice teaching.

To elaborate this focus on relevance, optics, hypocrisy, and evangelization, the previous chapters raised a variety of related concerns. Interviewees are concerned that there is substantial dissonance between the priorities of bishops and church officials and the lives of the everyday faithful. The sex abuse scandal is an extreme but illustrative example of this. Not only were priests, who were purportedly committed to sacrifice and care for others, exploitative of their ministerial trust; but also the bishops, who were aware of this and quietly moved the perpetrators from parish to parish, abused their power, and enabled further victimization. The sexual abuse crisis is huge because of the damage caused to the victims and their families as well as to the moral credibility of the church as a whole; many Catholics reason that if bishops cannot get something this morally obvious correct, what right do they have to weigh in on anything? Silence on the virulent and even deadly racism in the country is another example of dissonance that has deeply wounded Catholics for centuries and is just beginning to be discussed in earnest.

Sexual teachings or poor preaching are less extreme and visceral but still important examples of dissonance; priests and other leaders are seen as out of touch with lay Catholics' lived experiences. Catholics' attitudes on artificial contraception, divorce, and abortion in certain cases were distinctive until about the 1960s, when Catholic attitudes came to look more like those of Americans generally. To continue to talk about contraception in the categories and terms that most have heard (e.g., natural law or obedience to authority) strikes many as out of touch. Contraception became an individual conscience issue for pre-Vatican II Catholics; for many, it simply distanced them from the church hierarchy by reminding them where they part ways. Similarly, Catholic teaching on same-sex relationships is also understood as an issue of individual conscience among all but the oldest generation of Catholics. Vatican II and post-Vatican II Catholics have supported same-sex marriage for some years, and young Catholics are entering adulthood already very much in favor of it. None of this is to say that church teaching on these issues should change. We simply note that church teachings on these matters lack cultural and psycho-emotional resonance with the experiences of American Catholics.

Another concern is that the bishops do not speak in a unified voice when helping Catholics discern how to bring their faith into public life; some say that abortion is the preeminent issue and must take first priority, whereas others claim that this is one among many important life issues and emphasize inter-issue connections. Interviewees wonder how Catholics or the general public will know the breadth of Catholic teaching on the common good when only a handful of issues get media play.

Interviewees also express concern about whether Catholics and the general public perceive the Catholic Church as welcoming or condemning. They wonder how conditional the welcome is in some parishes or how judgment, or a fear of judgment, affects people's willingness to engage Catholicism. Connected to this was whether Catholics themselves are excited or feel good about Catholicism. While this might seem rather trivial, consider what happens when people have a great dining, movie-going, or volunteer experience. They go again and again, they tell their friends about it, they carve out time and money to make sure it does not end up on the back burner. And for an outstanding parish, they would additionally get more involved and want their life and beliefs to align with the mission and vision of that house of worship. But rare is the Catholic who has this much enthusiasm for their parish or Catholicism as a whole. What might Catholicism as an institution consider in light of all this?

In the 2021–2024 synod, Pope Francis named the risks—formalism, intellectualism, and complacency—and opportunities—in becoming a synodal church, a listening church, and an affectively close church. These prompt important considerations. Namely, there is a relationship between risk and opportunity. When at a critical moment of decision—we use the term "crossroads"—if people move thoughtfully, intentionally, and creatively, they are more likely to manifest the potential opportunity. If they are haphazard, thoughtless, or distracted at the crossroads, they are more likely to actualize the risk.

Although people often flag the word "crisis" as alarmist language, political philosopher Hannah Arendt uses this word in a different way, "A crisis forces us back to the questions themselves and requires from us either new or old answers, but in any case, direct judgments. A crisis becomes a disaster only when we respond to it with preformed judgments, that is, with prejudices. Such an attitude not only sharpens the crisis but makes us forfeit the experience of reality and the opportunity for reflection it provides."[11] She distinguishes between a crisis and a disaster. Both begin as a crisis, that is, an event that begs for reflection on fundamental questions. A crisis becomes a disaster when people attempt to forgo thoughtful dialogue, research, and consideration in their response and instead react with prefabricated answers. This is a serious moment in the American Catholic Church and, for those who care, it warrants serious discernment.

This connects to personalism. Often what is objectively deleterious for people still has elements or approximations of the good; these positive elements are what attract people to things that may be ultimately destructive for them.[12] For example, a college student might have a one-night stand with a total stranger out of a desire for intimacy. Intimacy is good for persons, but this fleeting encounter is unlikely to meet that need. Additionally, this anemic approximation of intimacy further postpones flourishing as well as confuses or disheartens one or both persons.[13] We can be misguided as we pursue imagined goods, sometimes horribly so. Sociologist Christian Smith touches on one particular human experience that can cloud people's notion of the good: vulnerability.[14] Every human person, at every moment, is vulnerable. There are three common responses to this vulnerability: fear, denial, and trust.

Although Catholicism is an institution, not a human person, personalism can be applied to institutions and larger social constructs and communities. And these personalist insights apply here. Every organization, every community of persons, is vulnerable. Decisions must be made, often without complete information, that may lead to the thriving or diminishment of the organization, as well as that of the people or communities the organization touches. If fear or denial undergirds the choice, this decision may be based on a misunderstanding about how to pursue what is good. But if trust leads the decision, that which leads to flourishing is clarified.

Let us examine fear, denial, and trust in turn.

A response rooted in fear would be reactionary. Threats and enemies would be identified and attacked or strictly avoided. These threats may be internal to Catholicism (e.g., a dangerous theology that is seeping into parishes) or they may be external (e.g., the secular press). An American Catholicism that is combative or sectarian makes no sense given the institution-building, collaboration, and transformative spirit it has shown in the last century. Pope Francis's theology of encounter and his ecclesiology of the church as a field hospital, consistent with Catholicism's long tradition as a publicly engaged church, render isolationist efforts contrary to a theologically Catholic engagement with the world. Given the many pressing human-societal challenges (e.g., the devaluation of human life, climate change, poverty), their effective amelioration will require an approach grounded in trust.

Denial might look very similar to fear, but it would have a lighter emotional intensity than a purely fear-informed response would. Denial allows the actor to forgo either accountability or internal suffering that would be required in accepting reality for what it is. Denial is antithetical to human flourishing because human flourishing is deeply grounded in reality. Denial is manifest when Catholic officials are only able to identify threats that are external to Catholicism (e.g., hostility or indifference toward religion), with little that leaders can do about them. Denial might also be a diminishment of these findings or a denial of the severity or implications for the future (e.g., "It's not that bad, it's really always been like this."). It is true that the American church has always faced challenges.[15] But our and others' survey data show real shifts over time in important measures of religiosity as well as Catholic attrition. To respond lukewarmly and without innovation is precisely what Arendt cautions against.

A wholly different response is one rooted in trust. Trust places the relevant aspects of reality in their proper perspective and lends the actor confidence that all will be well, even if the desired outcome does not materialize. It grounds the actor or the institution in the faith that they will do their part and they can depend on others to do theirs; even when a person's piece is complete, they believe this effort is part of a larger project that will be continually built upon. Trust allows the actor to fully see what is at stake, what the challenges are, and what more is required, without feeling overwhelmed by how daunting and difficult the road ahead will be. To live a life in trust is to employ other virtues as well, such as hope, generosity, gratitude, courage, prudence, humility, and most of all, love. Knowing that one is loved makes trust possible, even given the real hardships and obstacles of life.

What could an institutional response of trust look like for Catholicism in the United States? First of all, it would require an "eyes wide open" approach to reality, and this might begin with accountability. Sometimes an organization may wish to remain silent on past errors. This might be motivated by embarrassment, guilt, or a desire to keep focused on the future with a commitment to do better. Recalling data from the chapter on authority, Catholics who believe that most church leaders are enforcing the new child protective policies are less likely to say the sex abuse scandal damaged their perceived moral authority of the leaders. Catholics, therefore, are more trusting of Catholic leaders the better informed they are of the policies. We could imagine how this would likewise apply to racism. Transparency—being open and honest about the ways the Catholic Church in the United States has excluded or directly harmed various racial and ethnic groups—would be an honorable first step away from denial and toward accountability. Widely discussing parish, diocesan, and national reconciliation efforts (especially at parish levels) would bring hope and healing to many. While these sorts of efforts are happening, helping more people to become aware of them, as well as how they have shaped policies (e.g., perhaps a diocese increased the required number of intercultural courses taken in seminary), are key to ensuring that a broader array of Catholics understand the progress being made.

An institutional response of trust also entails healing intergroup relationships. Just as interpersonal relationships are key to growing and developing parish life, intergroup relationships are important for the wholeness of the church as an institution as well as its relationship to other social actors. Relationships are healed through apology and reconciliation. Apologies include words spoken that admit the wrongdoing and express contrition; to demonstrate sincerity, these are followed by real actions and reparations. Reconciliation involves those who were wronged acknowledging the apology, and, if they choose, opting to be involved in the reparations process. Efforts are underway with sex abuse survivors and Catholic communities of color, with a long road to healing expected. Discussions and actions aimed at being more inclusive of women at all levels of the church are likewise shaping the ways Catholicism is moving forward. For example, previous synods have allowed only men to vote—be they bishops, priests, or brothers; women could only participate as auditors.[16] With the 2021–2024 Synod on Synodality, 70 voters were non-bishops, with half of these women.[17] To the disappointment of many Catholics sympathetic to the LGBTQ+ community, reconciliation efforts here have been minimal. Although the Catholic Church teaches that society may not discriminate against people due to their sexual orientation,[18] many felt the need for more engagement after the church's relative silence following the 2016 Pulse massacre, which killed 49 and wounded 53 patrons in a gay nightclub. Only twelve bishops issued statements.[19]

Beyond more formal efforts of apology and reconciliation are other practices of restoration the Catholic Church could pursue. Some of these are at the policy level. Priestly formation requirements as well as ongoing professional development could include intercultural courses that spend more time examining racial injustice and assuring intercultural competence. Parishes, dioceses, and national bodies could be more aware of the various populations they serve—according to race, gender, age, and other characteristics—and work to ensure that their leadership reflects the composition of these communities.

Restorative efforts could also take shape in a more programmatic way. This could take the form of penitential pilgrimages, in which participants visit various places in their diocese that were significant places of exclusion or sanctuaries of inclusion, and learn about the harms that have been caused in the past as well as ongoing reparations. Parishes or dioceses could create landmarks of apology—such as statues or other art—to mark the sins of their past as a reminder of what can happen as well as who they would rather be. Further, if "church" is the whole community of believers, then members share in both the victimhood and the infliction of past harms. Catholics should grieve alongside victims of sexual abuse, racial injustice, hate crimes, and more, as well as openly apologize to individuals or groups when Catholic policies or actions taken by leaders contributed to such injuries and injustices. Restorative practices can also be incorporated within the liturgy. Just as the water sprinkling rite of the Easter season reminds Catholics of Christ's resurrection, their own baptism, and new life, there may be ways to bring historical memory and reconciliation into devotional practices or the liturgy itself. One such effort is the USCCB's recent creation of a stations of the cross—a devotional practice remembering the events before, during, and after Jesus's crucifixion—that helps Catholics connect these fourteen stations to contemporary racism.[20] These sorts of efforts not only help Catholics connect their faith to the specific issue, but form Catholics to better connect their faith to everyday life more generally.

Restorative projects must include opportunities for friendship. Recalling earlier chapters, interviewees continually amplify the power of friendship in personal and collective faith journeys. One of our interviewees, Dr. Ansel Augustine, director of the Office of Black Catholic Ministries of the Archdiocese of New Orleans, explicitly affirms that Catholics of different racial and ethnic backgrounds need to be in each other's spaces. This means not just inviting Catholics of color into White Catholics' spaces but having all the church readily integrating into one another's spaces. Imagine parishes hosting encountering events. For instance, perhaps for the month of November—Black Catholic History Month—a parish serving Black Catholics would invite Catholics from across the diocese to special events during and after their 10:00 Mass. Liturgy and preaching would showcase the parish's understanding of what it can mean to be both Black and Catholic.[21] Following the Mass, there could be a speaker who talks about a specific aspect of Black Catholicism. There would be time for discussion, in which attendees could process what they had heard and learn more about the liturgy and the topic. The morning could culminate in a potluck social, where people from across the diocese mingle with the host parishioners. At these events, the next hosted event could also be announced. Similar events could be held to celebrate the Feast of the Vietnamese Martyrs, Oktoberfest, Lunar New Year, Las Posadas, San Lorenzo Ruiz, the Feast of St. Kateri Tekakwitha, and more. The important thing is that this learning and formation is reciprocal and happens alongside friendship-building. This technique does not need to be limited to issues of race and ethnicity, but could also include bridge-building across ability, generation, economic class, immigration status, and more. Returning to personalism, rarely will any of these encounters be smooth or easy, but transformative experiences can happen when participation is mutually rooted in trust. Other virtues to draw upon for these restorative occasions—at the level of policy, program, or friendship—are courage, humility, self-awareness, compassion, patience, honesty, hope, and love.

Similar efforts of listening and attentiveness to needs beyond the church are likewise an important step in trust. Immersion experiences or less formal but intentional encounters can spark a concern in people about an issue that previously escaped their awareness. This engagement can get Catholics more involved in the *ad extra* dimension of church life—living the church's mission in the world. They can come to care and learn more about the human persons affected by local, regional, and national problems. These efforts can also bring a church community closer together. For example, we have heard of a Catholic program that pairs host families with a family trying to climb out of poverty; this "just out of poverty" phase is an especially critical time, as one unfortunate event could mean slipping back into poverty. The host family is an important support in this time. They are expected to help as they are reasonably able, perhaps picking up the kids from school when the family car breaks down or watching the baby while a parent is at a job interview. Importantly, they have the family over for a meal once each month, just to enjoy each other's company. This creates a real friendship between the families, and the unequal power between benefactor and beneficiary gradually fades as each family comes to celebrate and support one another in the ups and downs of daily living. Further, we have also learned of a faith-sharing group that collectively elected to host a family. This endeavor not only connected the family in need with more people, but it brought the faith-sharing group closer together in this shared effort; the *ad intra* and *ad extra* dimensions of being church can overlap. These examples demonstrate that a church that listens well to its members and the world in which it is embedded is a vibrant, relevant, and attractive church.

Polarized or Contested?

Personalism also illuminates a way to get past political differences. Although political differences among Americans are very real, as are the differences in political priorities and theological emphases among American Catholics and their leaders, they point to underlying goods. By considering their shared goods and concerns, Catholics and other Americans can become more aware of what connects them, even amid real differences. And, from a personalist perspective, the binding quality of these core concerns is far more powerful than the divisive quality of the areas of disagreement.

The 2021–2024 Synod on Synodality sparked frank and open discussions among Catholics of all persuasions. These discussions caused Catholics to pause and look at both forgotten and taken-for-granted aspects of their faith with new and intentional eyes. Dr. Timothy O'Malley asks rhetorically, "What does it mean to recover a tradition?" While he asks this in light of liturgical discussions, it bears on Pope Francis's intention that from the synod should emerge not another church, but a different church.

One theme that is at least implied in several chapters is that being Catholic entails an embracing of both unity and diversity. Catholics definitely exhibit differences of opinion. Some of these are theological, based on different Christologies, eschatologies, ecclesiologies, and more. Some differences are rooted in culture, be these generational, regional, or racial/ethnic. Some are political, and can manifest as opposition or, more mildly, as different priorities. Some differences relate to ideas about what constitutes a legitimate family, even if not a sacramental marriage.[22] Catholics can and have used distinctions of these kinds to highlight or foster division. Matthew Kelly, founder of Dynamic Catholic, observes that this division is readily apparent: "The bishops can't agree on anything. The priests can't agree on anything. A parish can't agree on anything. We can't agree on anything." Even with elements of the faith that are rarely contested (e.g., human persons as *imago dei*), it is easy to only identify and experience the contested areas. Further, unity is not the same as uniformity. Unity and diversity can co-exist, and this mutualism actually increases the depth and the breadth of Catholicism, as it would for any organization that can hold these tensions. Catholics here and in other, previously-cited studies find the sacraments and Jesus to be particularly unifying elements of their faith. Kelly continues, pointing out that division has frustrated the mission of the church, "Until we can agree that something is more important than disagreeing on everything, unfortunately, I think we are stuck. And I think that's the bigger question, how do we get unstuck?" With the formal completion of the 2021–2024 Synod on Synodality, dioceses, parishes, and persons now need to decide how to implement these ideas. In their discernment, Catholics would do well to continually return to beliefs they share in common as they also come to understand, appreciate, and cultivate solidarity across differences and consider what their common beliefs all mean for Catholicism in the present era.

John Carr, founder of Georgetown University's Initiative on Catholic Social Thought and Public Life, shares these thoughts on church leadership: "There's two kinds of leadership. One is if you think we've lost, if you think the culture has completely overwhelmed us—on life, on religion, on morality—then the temptation is to hunker down to try and preserve and protect, but also to judge and condemn." Going back to personalism, this first model is similar to an imagination in which moral choices are clouded by fear. He continues, "The other way of leading is if you're convinced Catholicism has what the world or the nation needs—on human life and dignity, in terms of justice, peace, solidarity—then engage and persuade. And you listen and you learn. And Pope Francis is an 'engage and persuade, listen and learn' kind of leader." This second model reflects a personalist ethic rooted in trust.

An important implication here is that sometimes these two fundamental orientations can themselves be a source of contention. Those animated by fear may believe that those animated by trust do not see the challenges as a threat. They might even believe that those who trust *embrace* the threats, seeing them as a social positive. This difference in orientation can create an overwhelming lacuna between these leadership models and foster hostility and aggression between leaders. It is possible that some leaders dismiss the challenges as less significant than they really are (but this would then slip into an orientation of denial, not the trust that Carr describes). More likely, those animated by trust see the challenges, threats, and real dangers as they are. However, they have tremendous faith in redemption and the transformative power of evangelization and encounter. This faith pushes Pope Francis and leaders like him into spaces and conversations that alarm some people, including fellow bishops.

It is no secret that there is division within the episcopate and their acceptance of Francis's way of leading the Catholic Church. Although all the popes since Paul VI or their Vatican offices (dicasteries) have received dubia, the dubia connected to the Synod on Synodality and the Synod on the Family received much attention and appeared to push back on some of Francis's initiatives in a public way rather than simply request clarification. On American soil, a disapproval of Pope Francis's direction may manifest as simply a lukewarm reception of his pronouncements or non-participation in the 2021–2024 synod. More unequivocally, a small but vocal portion of the laity openly reject him, manifest in "not my pope" T-shirts and hashtags; a handful of bishops and priests have likewise voiced strong opposition. However, despite the media attention on the few who are taking the strongest stance against him, as our data show, the vast majority approve of his leadership. More mildly, there are some Catholic leaders who are concerned with Pope Francis's methods or policies and may desire more dialogue, different techniques, or greater clarity, but in a way that does not signal disunity with the pope; this approach of "unity while disagreeing" was apparent when the bishops of Africa and Madagascar stated that they would not, as a conference, bless same-sex couples.[23] This signals that disagreement with a choice or statement of Pope Francis does not necessarily mean that there is disunity or doubt in his authority. The diversity in this paragraph illustrates both the spectrum of enthusiasm for the pope's policies and direction as well as the range of responses and their implications for unity.

Any of the leaders in the Catholic Church, regardless of their alignment with Pope Francis on a particular issue, may fall into the fear or trust models that John Carr described. And yet they are all called to work together. How might these differences in a fear or trust orientation be navigated? One approach that may reduce the friction between these two types of leaders is to have conversations that name the challenges at hand. Stark differences in priority and pastoral approach will continue to exist if apprehensions and risks seem to be unrecognized by Pope Francis and the leaders promoting his ideas. But there is the possibility that the apprehensions of those who most disagree with the pope would be quelled, at least in part, if other leaders named and acknowledged those same concerns, which could lead to greater collegiality and less suspicion than is currently experienced.

Another challenge, however, is that Catholics, in many ways, are becoming indistinguishable from mainline Protestants; given this situation, how can Catholicism offer anything uniquely Catholic to American life? High commitment Catholics may hold the clue to what this contribution might look like. Denying that there are serious challenges faced by Catholicism as well as that the stakes are tremendously high undermines the efforts currently being made, and is a dangerous basis for future choices.

Turning to the polarization in the wider society, some interviewees mentioned that because Catholic teachings do not neatly align with either political party, Catholicism has the potential to serve as a neutral space for dialogue and the healing of polarization in contemporary times. Remembering that high-commitment Catholics are more likely than other Catholics to part ways with their party and align themselves with Catholic teaching further amplifies this possibility. High-commitment Catholics are already navigating their faith and their politics in nuanced ways that prioritize their commitment to their faith. At the same time, they still identify with their party, which indicates an ability to empathize with people who think differently from themselves on some issues. Another finding worth touching on here is that, as with Americans generally, political differences among Catholics follow lines of race.[24] Because of this, certain experiences (e.g., being a victim of anti-Blackness) may not be on the cognitive radar for some at the start of a conversation. Catholics need to consider what needs to be illuminated for productive conversations to happen when their political differences follow racial lines. This is obviously relevant for conversations concerning racial justice, but it would also affect conversations and imagined ways forward on issues that affect racial and ethnic communities to different degrees, like migration, criminal justice, health care, housing, labor, access to public services, and more.

Steven Krueger, president of Catholic Democrats, continues this "neutral space" line of thinking with hope, "Something we can all be striving for to help guide our civic actions is to imagine that we are all part of co-authoring a book today, that is written with a futuristic retrospective twenty-five to fifty years from now, that would be entitled *How the U.S. Catholic Church Healed Division within Itself, and Helped Save the Country and Democracy in the Process without Losing Its Soul.*" Krueger begins by inviting everyone to think as though their fate is shared in a grand project. He envisions the Catholic Church, even amid its own problems, still ushering in healing for the nation. He continues, claiming that this endeavor will take imagination, collaboration, and hope. He closes his thought with a reflection: "We need to continue to be a church of hope. We need to remind ourselves in this process that we are an Easter people." He highlights the possible role American Catholicism might take in healing itself and the democracy in which it is embedded. Catholics, because of their political breadth, may be uniquely situated to show others what it means to bring faith to politics beyond sound bites, and beyond ways that consistently align with one party or another.

Catholicism—and religion broadly—should not absent itself from political conversations. As Michele Dillon writes elsewhere, we are now living as a global community with more complex problems. The problems we face are no longer the domain of one field of experts. Solutions rely upon the analyses of a number of experts and, once coupled with the ethics and principles that Catholicism offers the public at large, can help remedy societal ills while also revitalizing the church's relevance.[25] This frame has been applied to the climate change issue, showing that solutions are enhanced when they come from a collaboration of scientists, economists, sociologists, policy makers, theologians, and other experts.[26] The Catholic Church best serves the common good when it speaks as one expert among many, combining its expertise with that of others. This approach should not be limited to climate change or other environmental issues, but could be applied to a number of social concerns including racial justice, supporting families and neighborhoods, governmental budgets, physical and mental health, immigration, and more. The Catholic Church at various levels—parish, diocese, and national church—might consider how it has done well in staking a claim in these conversations, where it has failed to do this well, and how any failings might be improved. Additionally, in light of polarization, great care should be taken to ensure that these conversations do not exacerbate an already hostile climate; Catholic leaders and Catholics themselves should be cognizant of the difference between being political and being partisan if they aim to heal polarization.

Religion can provide resources for countering the polarizing impulses of our social and political climate. These resources can be in the form of fundamental religious beliefs (e.g., the dignity of the human person, shared by nearly all world religions), but also in the form of the unifying and depolarizing characteristics of many of the social interactions that take place inside of religious congregations.[27] This can provide a model for American society more broadly. As a step toward healing polarization, Americans might search for what basic, shared, binding elements would unite them. Like Jesus and the sacraments for Catholics, often what is held most deeply in common is not what is most often discussed; that which is taken for granted is often not top of mind.[28] We have common experiences that transcend partisan commitments: hobbies, struggles with physical and mental health, treasured friendships, uncertainties about the future, a sense that we try to do the right thing, ups and downs of child-rearing, positive childhood memories, aging, favorite TV shows, feeling that money and time are in short supply, funny stories from bad jobs, desire for meaningful employment, high school, infertility and miscarriage, acts of kindness, relocating to places without extended family, family recipes, fresh starts. There are many elements of our lives, both ordinary and significant, that are shared with countless others. Our successes and our struggles are remarkably similar. Americans want similar things: loving families, safe neighborhoods, good education and opportunities for our children, and to believe and think what we want. Rather than having conservatives hurl insults like "snowflake" and "libtard," and liberals dismissing conservatives as hateful and ignorant, some deeper conversations that start with shared aspects of our humanity can begin the first steps in lessening polarization.

Catholics, especially high-commitment Catholics, because they navigate a faith of tension and paradox may in fact have the opportunity to pave the way toward not just political healing, but also a more flourishing society. What would a political community founded on solidarity, the common good, encounter, and—for Catholics—a Catholic interpretive lens look like? How would a less stark polarization look different from where we currently are? What happens if we could disagree with people, but still have an affinity for them, and maybe even love them? Can we as a country move from where we are now to where Veronica and David, the pair who opened this book, are: meeting for lunch, disagreeing, sharing in celebrations, and mourning with one another?

Rather than providing this book with an ending, we have opted to frame this conclusion as a beginning. The future of Catholicism can be allowed to unfold following trend lines, as if fate has already written its destiny. Or it can be written by the protagonists who know Catholicism best, from everyday Catholics to prominent leaders to those in between, like Veronica and David. In considering the findings presented here, we believe that Catholicism is at a crossroads and that its future is without certainty, promises vagaries, and is rich with both frightening and amazing possibilities. It is open. This seemingly boundless openness is, no doubt, both exciting and terrifying. And if flourishing is the aim, efforts must be guided by trust and love. For a religion that believes that God's very essence is love, and that the Holy Spirit moves in creative, generative ways, this aim should easily elicit assent and perhaps offer a guiding star far beyond the closing of the synod in 2024. Does U.S. Catholicism have the leadership, the focus, the tenacity, the cohesion, and the trust to discern what manifesting this love and flourishing among its 73 million believers might look like? This is Catholicism's crossroads.

ACKNOWLEDGMENTS

Many people and organizations deserve our gratitude for such a tremendous project. Beginning with the funders, we thank the Louisville Institute, The Anderson Foundation, The National Catholic Reporter Publishing Co., Alfred & Kathleen M. Rotandaro, Kevin J. Healy, and the Kathleen Blank Reither Trust for their generous gifts supporting the administration of the 2017 survey. Thank you so much for recognizing the importance of this research; we hope that you believe the findings are well worth your investment.

Major thanks go out to New York University Press's Senior Editor Jennifer Hammer and the responsive team at NYU Press. Thank you for your interest early on in the project; nothing is more motivating for diving into a large project than knowing that a publishing company believes in your work and wants to help disseminate your findings. From overseeing the project to choosing an appealing cover to attentive copyediting, your fine work has helped ensure that this book is as polished as it is. We also appreciate the feedback of the anonymous reviewers who saw things we did not and helped us think through the analyses at levels both large and small.

We want to thank our institutions and colleagues. First, we thank our various academic homes: the Center for Religion and Civic Culture and the Institute for Advanced Catholic Studies at the University of Southern California (Maureen Day), the University of South Florida (James Cavendish), the Center for Applied Research in the Apostolate at Georgetown University (Paul Perl and Mary Gautier), the University of New Hampshire (Michele Dillon), and The Catholic University of America (William D'Antonio). We appreciate the collegiality, conversations about the data and findings, and the many ways our institutions directly and indirectly supported this project in all its phases. Second, our thanks go out to our colleagues beyond our institutions that encouraged us in scholarly and relational ways, especially those whose research informed this work. But we also cannot overstate the importance of colleagues who acted as sounding boards, whether for analytical perspective or to help us solve (or at least laugh at) the latest setback in this whole process. Thanks to colleagues absolutely includes the co-authors; we share in our appreciation of one another and of the various roles each of us played in the research and writing process. The cooperation and good company we shared has resulted in a book that is better than anything any of us would have written in isolation.

Our heartfelt thanks go out to the over 1,500 Catholics who agreed to take part in the national survey and share their responses on a variety of beliefs and practices related to Catholicism. In wave after wave, your experiences as "everyday Catholics" are incredibly informative to a wide audience. And for the first time, we get to thank the interviewees—many of whom were familiar with the previous books—who said they looked forward to the ways these interviews might enhance our analysis. We hope you find that they, in fact, did; we certainly think so! Thank you so much for being extremely generous with your time, insights, and pointing us to additional resources, even amid your busy schedules. Some met with us outside of their working hours, others simply "squeezed us in," some even took a moment out of their family vacation; however you managed to work us into your busy lives, we are thankful.

The authors each want to thank those who were important during the research and writing process. I, Maureen, want to start by acknowledging the faith that Mary and Michele had in inviting me (even as a relatively early career scholar) to lead the writing phase of the project. I remember reading, as an MA student in 2003, the third of the American Catholic Laity books, and wistfully thinking that one day—many decades from now—I might find my name on one of these books. Your vote of confidence assured me that I would help carry on this amazing legacy in the way that it deserved. To all my co-authors: You. Rock. Really, what would this have been without our frantic group texts as we approached our various deadlines? Thanks also to friend-colleagues beyond my co-authors—Jerome Baggett, Tricia Bruce, Jeff Burns, Kate DeConinck, Thu Do, Stephen Fichter, Richard Flory, Tom Gaunt, Paddy Gilger, Brett Hoover, Matt Manion, Tia Pratt, Susan Reynolds, Lucas Sharma, Scott Thumma, Porsia Tunzi, Jonathon Wiggins, and Richard Wood; all of you help me keep my academic life deeply human (and without the human foundation, the academic piece is anemic). Lastly, thanks to my family. First, to my departed father—who offered me my first glimpse into everyday Catholic life and helped me view society from "the big picture"—and my mom—whose superlative goodness and generosity continue to point me to the "little things" that make life beautifully tender and human. My sister, my niece, and my cousin's "Fuller family" keep the joy coming and my spiritual wheels turning. My godfather and his wife in Singapore, from whose house I wrote portions of this book, and their amazing extended family is a gift that words cannot capture! My adult child, Veronica, for eighteen years has made our home into a place of fun and hospitality, despite our crazy schedules and occasional piles of foster dog poop! My teen, David, has a devoted, caring, and gentle spirit and inspires deep affection in those closest to him (me included!). My husband, Joseph, is quick to hug and is my steadfast partner in anything fun (even if his definition is less inclusive than mine, ha!). You are all three so amazing, and my life—scholarship included—is so much richer because of the love you bring. Big, fat heaps of gratitude to you . . . and even more love!

I, James, would like to thank the co-authors of this book for their trust in inviting me to be a part of this project and their steady support throughout its production. With so many distinguished scholars among the current and previous authors in the book series, it is truly an honor for me to join them, and I hope I have made them proud. I also express my appreciation to my mentors and friend-colleagues in the sociological enterprise, most especially Mark Chaves, Kevin Christiano, Michael Welch, David Leege (now deceased), Donileen Loseke, Thomas Gaunt, Fred Kniss, Christopher Ellison, Melissa Wilde, Michael Emerson, Paula Nesbitt, James Spickard, Gerardo Marti, Rachel Kraus, and Tia Noelle Pratt. I am also indebted to the members of Sacred Heart Parish's Racial Justice Committee and Open Doors Ministry and to numerous friends and spiritual companions—Jeremy King, Brian Lemoi, Maureen Connors, Robert Schneider, Sabrina Burton, Michael Cooper, Cathy Cahill, Antonio de Varona, Mark Morris, Michael Driscoll—whose curiosity and insights on Catholic life and faith helped inspire and guide me during my analyses and writing. And finally, to my family and loved ones who have been a constant source of support intellectually, emotionally, and spiritually, most especially: my mother, Joann, and my late father, John; my Godmother, Judy Moore, and my late Godfather, Thomas Miller; my brothers and sisters; and my soulmates Cagdas Agirdas, Kumar Jairamdas, and Carlos Valerio Gutierrez.

I, Paul, thank the Center for Applied Research in the Apostolate for institutional support. Many of the historical analyses and trend graphs in this book could not have been done without data sets having been made publicly available by many different polling organizations—and without archives hosting those data online. Among the most helpful for my work on this book are the Association of Religion Data Archives (ARDA) and the Inter-university Consortium for Political and Social Research (ICPSR) at the University of Michigan. I am particularly grateful for data made available by the Pew Research Center and for the archiving work of the Roper Center for Public Opinion Research at Cornell University.

I, Michele, am deeply grateful for the work of co-authors on prior American Catholic Laity Surveys; the energetic and generous leadership of Andrew Greeley in establishing the centrality of religion questions in the University of Chicago National Opinion Research Center's General Social Survey, and to him and Mike Hout for their impactful contributions to the sociology of religion and especially to deepening the understanding of American Catholicism; to Mary Gautier, a warm friend and colleague; to Maureen Day for her enthusiasm and also—along with Jim Cavendish and Paul Perl—for the many ways they exemplify cordiality and engaged scholarship. My family, as always, is foremost in enriching my daily life.

I, Mary, would like to thank the original authors of the American Catholic Laity series for having the faith to take a chance on me for the fourth book in the series. William D'Antonio, who led the project, from first book to sixth book. Dean Hoge, Ruth Wallace, and James Davidson have all passed on, but their spirit lives on in the data and in the question wording. Oh, how I loved the spirited debates over question wording! Though he did not take an active part in the writing of this sixth volume, Bill still played a vital role in raising funds for the project and shepherding us through the data collection and data analysis. Bill also wrote a piece from the data on the Catholic vote in the 2016 election, that was published in the National Catholic Reporter. I want to thank Michele Dillon for stepping up as a coauthor for the fifth book in the series and for seeing this sixth book through to fruition, even when the rest of us had run out of steam. Finally, major gratitude is due to Maureen Day, who innocently asked me, "So, how can I help with this sixth book on American Catholic Laity?" Little did she know what lay in store for her . . . I am so very proud of the work that you all have done to bring this to completion. Thank you all, Maureen, Michele, Paul, and Jim, for a job well done!

APPENDIX A

Survey Instrument and Basic Frequencies

Percentages may not total 100 due to rounding.

Q1. When did you become Catholic? As an . . .

- ∘ Infant (under age 1): 78
- ∘ Child (ages 1–12): 12
- ∘ Teenager (ages 13–17): 2
- ∘ Adult (ages 18 or older): 8

If Q1 = 4 (adult convert):

> Q1a   Did you go through the Rite of Christian Initiation of Adults (RCIA), the formal process that brings adult converts into the Catholic Church?

- ∘ Yes: 67
- ∘ No: 33

Q2. As a Catholic, how essential is each of these to your vision of what it means to be Catholic? Would you say the following is or are essential to the faith, somewhat essential, or not essential at all?

	Essential to the faith	Somewhat essential	Not essential at all
A. Devotion to Mary the mother of God	58	31	12
B. A celibate male clergy	24	28	48
C. The necessity of having a Pope	56	30	14
D. Engaging in daily prayer	48	35	17
E. Charitable efforts toward helping the poor	49	40	11
F. Belief in Jesus's resurrection from the dead	74	19	7
G. The obligation to attend Mass once a week	37	34	29
H. Private confession to a priest	32	34	34
I. Participating in devotions such as Eucharistic Adoration or praying the rosary	37	41	22

Q3. Please indicate whether you strongly agree, somewhat agree, somewhat disagree, or strongly disagree with each of the following statements.

	Strongly agree	Somewhat agree	Somewhat disagree	Strongly disagree
A. The sacraments of the Church are essential to my relationship with God	40	36	16	8
B. Catholics can disagree with aspects of Church teaching and still remain loyal to the Church	49	38	9	4
C. Divorced Catholics who remarry without an annulment should, in consultation with a priest about their situation, be able to receive Holy Communion	44	34	14	9
D. Individuals who are terminally ill and in great pain should have a legal right to doctor-assisted suicide	28	36	18	18
E. It is important to me that younger generations of my family grow up as Catholics	35	40	17	8

Q4. Next, we are interested in your opinion on several issues that involve the moral authority in the Catholic Church. In each case we would like to know who you think should have the final say about what is right or wrong. Is it Church leaders such as the pope and bishops, individuals taking Church teachings into account and deciding for themselves, or both individuals and leaders working together?

	Church leaders	Individuals	Both together
A. A divorced Catholic re-marrying without getting an annulment	17	46	37
B. A Catholic using contra-ceptive birth control	9	67	24
C. A Catholic who is consid-ering having an abortion	13	55	32
D. A Catholic who engages in gay or lesbian sexual relations	13	58	29
E. Sexual relations outside of marriage	14	58	29

Q5. Please indicate whether you strongly agree, somewhat agree, somewhat disagree, or strongly disagree with each of the following statements.

	Strongly agree	Somewhat agree	Somewhat disagree	Strongly disagree
A. Most pastors don't know how to reach out to laity to get them involved in parish life	9	44	38	9
B. Most Catholics don't want to take on leadership roles in their parish	13	54	28	5
C. Catholic parishes are too big and impersonal	9	35	41	16
D. Catholic Church leaders are out of touch with the laity	11	46	33	10
E. On the whole, parish priests do a good job	31	57	10	2

Q6. Please indicate your level of satisfaction with the leadership of each of these.

	Not at all satisfied	Only a little	Somewhat satisfied	Very satisfied
A. Pope Francis	5	10	28	57
B. The bishops of the United States	7	23	52	18
C. Your local bishop	6	19	48	28
D. Your parish priest	5	16	42	37
E. Lay leaders in your parish	5	21	53	22

Q7. Catholic bishops often speak out about politics and elections, as well as about policy issues like health care, immigration, and foreign affairs. Which of the following best describes how you typically respond to bishops' statements in these areas?
- ○ The bishops' views are irrelevant to my thinking about politics and public policy: 36
- ○ I consider what the bishops have to say about politics and public policy, but ultimately I make up my own mind: 55
- ○ I try to follow the bishops' guidance and instructions on political and public policy matters: 9

Q8. Please indicate whether you strongly agree, somewhat agree, somewhat disagree, or strongly disagree with the American bishops on each of the following issues.

	Strongly agree	Somewhat agree	Somewhat disagree	Strongly disagree
A. Support for expanding government-funded health insurance	38	33	16	13
B. Opposition to the death penalty	21	31	29	19
C. Support for making the immigration process easier for families	38	34	18	10

Q9. The following statements deal with what you think it takes to be a good Catholic. Please indicate if you think a person can be a good Catholic without performing these actions or affirming these beliefs. Can a person be a good Catholic:

	Yes, can be a good Catholic	No, cannot be good Catholic
A. Without going to Mass every Sunday	80	20
B. Without obeying the Church hierarchy's opposition to artificial contraception	83	17
C. Without obeying the Church hierarchy's opposition to abortion	64	36
D. Without obeying the Church hierarchy's opposition to gay/lesbian sexual relationships	74	26
E. Without believing that in the Mass, the bread and wine really become the body and blood of Jesus	45	55
F. Without their marriage being approved by the Catholic Church	77	23
G. Without donating time or money to help the poor	63	37
H. Without believing that Jesus physically rose from the dead	34	66

Q10. When you have an important moral decision to make, which, if any, of the following activities or sources do you usually look to for guidance:

	Always	Sometimes	Rarely	Never
A. I pray or meditate about it	40	36	14	10
B. I talk to a close family member	37	43	14	6
C. I talk to my local priest	6	19	32	43
D. I talk to trusted friends	28	48	15	8
E. I read the Catechism of the Catholic Church	6	20	28	46
F. I read papal statements or encyclicals	3	15	27	55
G. I visit the website of my diocese or of the U.S. Catholic bishops	3	10	23	64
H. I look at/read Catholic media	5	22	29	44

Q11. At the present time, do you think religion as a whole is increasing its influence on American life or losing its influence?
- Increasing its influence: 12
- About the same as always: 35
- Losing its influence: 53

If Q11 = 1, 2, or 3:

Q11a. All in all, do you think this [religion increasing influence, losing influence, or staying the same] is a good thing or a bad thing?
- A good thing: 42
- A bad thing: 59

Q12. At the present time, do you think Catholicism is increasing its influence on American life or losing its influence?
- Increasing its influence: 9
- About the same as always: 40
- Losing its influence: 51

If Q12 = 1, 2, or 3:

Q12a. All in all, do you think this [Catholicism increasing influence, losing influence, or staying the same] is a good thing or a bad thing?
- A good thing: 42
- A bad thing: 58

Q13. For each of the following areas of Church life, please indicate whether you think the Catholic laity should have the right to participate or should not have the right to participate.

	Should	Should not
A. Deciding how parish income should be spent	80	20
B. Deciding how diocesan income should be spent	73	27
C. Helping select priests for their parish	76	24
D. Helping select bishops for their diocese	68	32
E. Deciding about parish closings	75	25

Q14. How important is the Catholic Church to you personally?
- ○ The most important part of my life: 9
- ○ Among the most important parts of my life: 26
- ○ Quite important to me, but so are many other areas of my life: 38
- ○ Not terribly important to me: 21
- ○ Not very important to me at all: 6

Q15. In the past six months, how often have you engaged in the following activities?

	Not at all	Occasionally	Regularly
A. Giving financial contributions to my parish	41	31	28
B. Being involved in my parish beyond attending Mass	61	26	13
C. Volunteering in my community	52	35	13
D. Doing voluntary work with poor people or other vulnerable groups in society	64	29	7
E. Engaging in interfaith or ecumenical gatherings	69	26	6
F. Financial contributions to Catholic organizations or causes	46	35	19

Q16. How regularly do you pray, apart from Mass?
- ◦ More than once a day: 15
- ◦ Daily: 36
- ◦ Occasionally or sometimes: 35
- ◦ Seldom or never: 14

Q17. How often, if ever, do you participate in the Sacrament of Reconciliation (Confession)?
- ◦ Seldom or never: 56
- ◦ Less than once a year: 16
- ◦ Once a year: 12
- ◦ Several times a year: 12
- ◦ Once a month or more: 4

Q18. Are you currently registered as a member of a Catholic parish?
- ◦ Yes: 60
- ◦ No: 40

Q19. Aside from weddings and funerals, about how often do you attend Mass?
- ◦ At least once a week: 29
- ◦ Two or three times a month: 10
- ◦ About once a month: 9
- ◦ A few times a year: 22
- ◦ Seldom or never: 31

IF MASS ATTENDANCE IS AT LEAST ONCE PER MONTH:

Q20. People go to Mass for different reasons. Please indicate whether or not each of the following is an important reason you go to Mass.

	Yes, important reason	Not an important reason
A. The Church requires that I attend	41	59
B. Mainly, it's a habit	46	54
C. I want to please or satisfy someone close to me, like a spouse or parent	27	73
D. I enjoy being with other persons in our church	60	41
E. I enjoy taking part in the service itself and experiencing the liturgy	86	14
F. I feel a need to receive the sacrament of Holy Communion	82	18

IF MASS ATTENDANCE IS A FEW TIMES A YEAR OR
SELDOM OR NEVER:

Q21. Is there a particular reason why you don't go to Mass more often? Please indicate whether or not each of the following is an important reason you don't attend Mass more often.

	Yes, important reason	Not an important reason
A. It's boring	19	82
B. It's not a mortal sin to miss Mass	28	72
C. Sermons are poor	19	81
D. Work/family responsibilities	45	55
E. I'm too busy	29	71
F. Health reasons	25	75
G. Inconvenient Mass schedule	22	78
H. Just not a religious person	40	60

Q22. Now here are four statements about the priesthood. After each, please indicate whether you strongly agree, somewhat agree, somewhat disagree, or strongly disagree.

	Strongly agree	Somewhat agree	Somewhat disagree	Strongly disagree
A. It would be a good thing if priests who have married were allowed to return to active ministry	42	39	13	7
B. It would be a good thing if married men were allowed to be ordained as priests	42	35	14	9
C. It would be a good thing if women were allowed to be ordained as permanent deacons	39	40	13	9
D. It would be a good thing if women were allowed to be ordained as priests	35	34	16	14

Q23. On a scale from one to seven, with "1" being "I would never leave the Catholic Church," and "7" being "Yes, I might leave the Catholic Church," where would you place yourself on this scale?

1	2	3	4	5	6	7
I would never leave the Catholic Church						Yes, I might leave the Catholic Church
44	17	9	13	9	5	4

Q24. Which of the following most closely reflects your political position?
- I am very conservative in matters involving politics: 14
- I am moderately conservative: 26
- I am a moderate: 32
- I am moderately liberal: 19
- I am very liberal in matters involving politics: 10

Q25. With which political party do you generally identify?
- The Republican party: 29
- The Democratic party: 44
- The Green party: <1
- The Libertarian party: 3
- The Tea party: <1
- Other party: 1
- [Do not read]: Do not identify with a political party: 22

Q26. Do you approve or disapprove of the way Donald Trump is handling his job as President?
- Approve: 36
- Disapprove: 63
- [Do not read]: Don't know/neither approve nor disapprove: 2

Q27. Did you vote in the presidential election in November 2016?
- Yes: 76
- No: 24

If Yes to Q27:

    Q27a. For whom did you vote?
- Donald Trump: 43
- Hillary Clinton: 48
- Jill Stein: 1
- Gary Johnson: 4
- Another candidate: 4

If Yes to Q27:

> Q27b. What role did religion play in your decision to vote for the person you did?
>
> (Percent choosing each response)

- ° I voted for my candidate because of his/her religious beliefs: 4
- ° I voted for my candidate because of my religious beliefs: 10
- ° I voted for the candidate that my pastor/bishop recommended: <1
- ° Religious beliefs played no part in my decision: 86

Now a few questions for statistical purposes.

IF MARRIED:

Q28. Is your spouse Catholic?

- ° Yes: 74
- ° No: 27

Q29. Did you ever attend a Catholic school or college for any of your education?

	Yes	No	If yes, median number of years attended
A. Attended Catholic elementary, middle, or junior high school	39	61	8
B. Attended Catholic high school	19	81	4
C. Attended Catholic college or university	9	91	4

Commitment Index:

- ° High: 20
- ° Medium: 64
- ° Low: 16

DEMOGRAPHICS

Gender:

- ° Female: 52
- ° Male: 48

Race/Ethnicity:

- ° White, non-Hispanic: 56
- ° Black, non-Hispanic: 3
- ° Other, non-Hispanic: 5

- Hispanic: 35
- 2+ races, non-Hispanic: <1

Age:
- 18–24: 9
- 25–34: 18
- 35–44: 17
- 45–54: 18
- 55–64: 19
- 65–74: 11
- 75+: 9

Generation:
- Pre-Vatican II: 7
- Vatican II: 27
- Post-Vatican II: 33
- Millennial: 27
- iGen: 6

Education (Highest Degree Received):
- Less than high school: 16
- High school: 31
- Some college: 26
- Bachelor's degree or higher: 28

Current Employment Status:
- Working, paid employee: 57
- Working, self-employed: 7
- Not working, temporary layoff: <1
- Not working, looking for work: 27
- Not working, retired: 20
- Not working, disabled: 3
- Not working, other: 9

MSA Status:
- Metro: 91
- Non-Metro: 9

Region (Based on State of Residence):
- Northeast: 25
- Midwest: 21
- South: 29
- West: 25

APPENDIX B

List of Interviewees

Helen M. Alvaré   Professor of Family Law and Law and Religion at George Mason University

Dr. Ansel Augustine   Director of the Office of Black Catholic Ministries of the Archdiocese of New Orleans

Maka Black Elk   Executive Director for Truth and Healing at Red Cloud Indian School

Bishop David Bonnar   Bishop of the Diocese of Youngstown

Fr. Robert Boxie   Chaplain at Howard University

Fr. John Burger, S.S.C.   Former Director of the Missionary Society of St. Columban, U.S. Region

John Carr   Founder of the Initiative on Catholic Social Thought and Public Life at Georgetown University and former Director of the Department of Justice, Peace, and Human Development at the USCCB

Christopher Check   President of Catholic Answers

Sandra Coles-Bell   Executive Director of National Black Sisters' Conference

Cardinal Blase J. Cupich   Cardinal Archbishop of the Archdiocese of Chicago

Francis DeBernardo   Executive Director of New Ways Ministry

Dcn. Ray Dever   Permanent Deacon in the Diocese of St. Petersburg, Florida, and frequent speaker on issues of faith in the LGBTQ community

Fr. Frank S. Donio, S.A.C.   Founding Director, Catholic Apostolate Center; Executive Director of the Conference of Major Superiors of Men of the United States (CMSM)

Bishop Mario Dorsonville-Rodríguez   Bishop of the Diocese of Houma-Thibodaux, Chairman for the Committee on Migration

Dr. Michele Dunne   Executive Director of the Franciscan Action Network

Bishop Daniel E. Flores   Bishop of the Diocese of Brownsville, Chairman of the USCCB Committee on Doctrine

Yohan Garcia   Catholic Social Teaching Education Manager at the USCCB

Katie Diller Gleason   Coordinator of Campus Ministry for the Diocese of Lansing

Cassie Guardiola   Youth Outreach/Marketing Specialist at the JPII Life Center

Dr. Linh Hoang, O.F.M.   Professor of Religious Studies, Siena College

Fr. Dennis H. Holtschneider, C.M.   President of the Association of Catholic Colleges and Universities

Ken Johnson-Mondragón   Director of Pastoral Engagement at the California Catholic Conference

Matthew Kelly   Founder of the Dynamic Catholic Institute

Steven Krueger   President of Catholic Democrats

Bishop Larry Kulick   Bishop of the Diocese of Greensburg

Tracey LaMont   Director of the Loyola Institute for Ministry, Professor of Religious Education and Young Adult Ministry, Loyola University New Orleans

Dr. Andrew W. Lichtenwalner   Director of the Office of Formation and Discipleship, Archdiocese of Atlanta

Fr. James Martin, S.J.   Editor-at-Large, *America*

Dr. Bob McCarty   Adjunct Professor of Pastoral & Youth Ministry, University of Dallas, Former Chief Operating Officer of the Catholic Mobilizing Network

Michael McDonnell   Interim Executive Director and former Communications Manager, Survivors Network of those Abused by Priests (SNAP)

Cardinal Robert McElroy   Cardinal of the Diocese of San Diego

Kate McElwee   Executive Director of the Women's Ordination Conference

Dan Misleh   Founder of Catholic Climate Covenant

María del Mar Muñoz-Visoso   Executive Director, Secretariat of Cultural Diversity in the Church at the USCCB

Dr. Joan Neal   Deputy Executive Director, NETWORK: Advocates for Justice, Inspired by Catholic Sisters

Dr. Timothy O'Malley   Professor of the Practice, Theology, University of Notre Dame

Dr. Hosffman Ospino   Associate Professor of Hispanic Ministry and Religious Education, Boston College

Nicole Perone   National Coordinator of ESTEEM

Russ Petrus   Co-Director of FutureChurch

John Prust   Director, Office for Family Life and Spirituality, Diocese of San Diego

John Michael Reyes   Director of Adult Spirituality, St. Ignatius College Preparatory

Sr. Theresa Rickard, O.P.   President of RENEW International

Kerry Robinson   President and CEO of Catholic Charities USA

Deborah Rose-Milavec   Co-Director of FutureChurch

Joan Rosenhauer   Executive Director, Jesuit Refugee Services

Julie Hanlon Rubio   Professor of Christian Social Ethics, Jesuit School of Theology of Santa Clara University

Linda Ruf   CEO, JPII Life Center

Dr. Stephanie Russell   Vice President for Mission Integration at the Association of Jesuit Colleges and Universities

Dr. Stephen Schneck   Retired faculty member and former Director of the Institute for Policy Research & Catholic Studies at The Catholic University of America

Tara Segal   Associate Director of University Ministry, Dominican University

Jason Simon   President, The Evangelical Catholic

Bishop John Stowe, O.F.M. Conv.   Bishop of Lexington, KY

Susie Tierney   Executive Director of JustFaith Ministries

Archbishop John C. Wester   Archbishop of the Diocese of Sante Fe, New Mexico

Dr. C. Vanessa White   Associate Professor of Spirituality and Ministry at Catholic Theological Union

Paul Wilkes   Retired journalist, author of *Excellent Catholic Parishes*

Msgr. Bill Young   Pastor, St. Vincent de Paul Catholic Church, Houston, Texas

Johnny Zokovitch   Executive Director of Pax Christi, USA

NOTES

INTRODUCTION

1 Identifying details of this story have been changed, but they are based on a real friendship.

2 A legitimate concern was that these leaders might offer interviews that were more like a collection of sound-bites than thoughtful responses. However, the great majority did not feel rehearsed or contrived. The leaders spoke in a very spontaneous way: changing gears or backing up in the middle of their response, pausing mid-sentence and looking to the side to really consider what they wanted to say, laughing at their "lessons learned" over the years, and so forth.

3 Deborah Rose-Milavec and Russ Petrus, Co-Directors of FutureChurch, were interviewed simultaneously.

4 We include demographic disclosures—most often racial and ethnic identities within the chapter on race—but do not do this elsewhere if participants did not disclose their racial identity as well as connect this to their response. Catholics of color comprise 28 percent of our total sample.

5 "Frequently Requested Church Statistics," Center for Applied Research in the Apostolate (CARA), accessed June 12, 2023, https://cara.georgetown.edu.

6 Ibid.

7 "America's Changing Religious Landscape," Appendix C, Pew Research Center, May 12, 2015, www.pewresearch.org.

8 James L. Heft and Jan E. Stets, *Empty Churches: Non-Affiliation in America* (New York: Oxford University Press, 2021), 3.

9 "African Immigrants in U.S. More Religious than Other Black Americans, and More Likely to be Catholic," Pew Research Center, December 7, 2021, www .pewresearch.org.

10 Mark M. Gray, "Were U.S. Catholics Raptured Again?" *Nineteen Sixty-Four* (blog), Center for Applied Research in the Apostolate (CARA), October 31, 2012. http: //nineteensixty-four.blogspot.com.

11 Frank Hobbs and Nicole Stoops, *Demographic Trends in the 20th Century: Census 2000 Special Reports,* (Washington, DC: U.S. Government Printing Office, 2002), 49, www.census.gov.

12 James D. Davidson, Andrea S. Williams, Richard A. Lamana, Jan Stenftenagel, Kathleen Weigert, William Whalen, and Patricia Wittberg, *The Search for Common Ground: What Unites and Divides Catholic Americans* (Huntington, IN: Our Sunday Visitor Press, 1997); and William D'Antonio, James D. Davidson, Dean R.

Hoge, and Katherine Meyer, *American Catholics: Gender, Generation, and Commitment* (Walnut Creek, CA: Alta Mira Press, 2001).

13 "Frequently Requested Church Statistics," Center for Applied Research in the Apostolate (CARA), retrieved May 12, 2023, https://cara.georgetown.edu. The total number of Catholic elementary schools dropped by 2,950, from just over 7,700 schools in 1985 to approximately 4,750 in 2022. The total number of Catholic secondary schools has dropped by 250, from 1,425 in 1985 to 1,175 in 2022.

14 Charles E. Zech, Mary L. Gautier, Mark M. Gray, Jonathon L. Wiggins, and Thomas P. Gaunt, *Catholic Parishes of the 21st Century* (New York: Oxford University Press, 2017), 7-11. Migration from other countries is also very significant and will be discussed in chapter 3.

15 Andrew Greeley, William C. McCready, and Kathleen McCrout, *Catholic Schools in a Declining Church* (Kansas City, MO: Sheed and Ward, 1976), 60–65; Andrew Greeley, *Religious Change in America* (Cambridge, MA: Harvard University Press, 1989); and Charles Morris, *American Catholic* (New York: Times Books, 1997).

16 These percentages likely do not quite represent the true percentages in the overall Catholic population, as the 1987 survey was conducted only in English. By the time of the 2017 survey, respondents could select English or Spanish as their preferred language for the survey.

17 Because there are just a few iGen respondents in our 2017 survey, we rely on data from large surveys by the Pew Research Center for the racial and ethnic composition of iGen in this figure.

1. CHURCH

1 Because confidentiality was required of synod participants in the San Diego diocese, this composite vignette was created using diocesan materials that are available to the public, especially the final synod report. All parish names are fictitious. The other vignettes in this book are conventional sociological vignettes, using media or firsthand accounts.

2 Pope Francis, *Address of His Holiness Pope Francis for the Opening of the Synod*, 2021. www.vatican.va.

3 United States Conference of Catholic Bishops, *National Synthesis of the People of God in the United States of America for the Diocesan Phase of the 2021–2023 Synod* (Washington, DC: United States Conference of Catholic Bishops, 2022), 4, www.usccb.org.

4 Michele Dillon, *Postsecular Catholicism: Relevance and Renewal* (New York: Oxford University Press, 2018).

5 *Catechism of the Catholic Church*, no. 1457.

6 *Catechism of the Catholic Church*, nos. 1776–1802.

7 Pope Francis, *Amoris Laetitia [Post-Synodal Apostolic Exhortation on Love in the Family]*, The Holy See, March 19, 2016, see especially no. 300, www.vatican.va. On the discussion among high-profile cardinals and church officials as to whether

a conscientiously discerned, individualized pastoral pathway to Communion for divorced Catholics constitutes authoritative teaching, see Dillon, *Postsecular Catholicism*, 157–163.

8 Gregory A. Smith, "Just One-Third of U.S. Catholics Agree with Their Church that Eucharist is Body, Blood of Christ," Pew Research Center, August 5, 2019, www.pewresearch.org.

9 William D'Antonio, Michele Dillon, and Mary Gautier, *American Catholics in Transition* (New York: Rowman & Littlefield, 2013).

10 *Catechism of the Catholic Church*, no. 1324.

11 The number of Catholics in the United States has been fairly stable since 2005. The total number of priests—both diocesan and religious—has decreased from 59,426 in 1965 to 34,923 in 2021. Center for Applied Research in the Apostolate, "Frequently Requested Church Statistics." Accessed April 1, 2024. https://cara .georgetown.edu.

12 John C. Seitz, *No Closure: Catholic Practice and Boston's Parish Shutdowns* (Cambridge, MA: Harvard University Press, 2011).

13 Christian Smith and Michael O. Emerson, with Patricia Snell, *Passing the Plate: Why American Christians Don't Give Away More Money* (New York: Oxford University Press, 2008), 30.

14 For more on Catholics who attend Mass infrequently, see Maureen K. Day, *Cultural Catholics: Who They Are, How to Respond* (Collegeville, MN: Liturgical Press, Forthcoming).

15 *Catechism of the Catholic Church*, no. 2181.

16 *Catechism of the Catholic Church*, no. 1124.

17 "Frequently Requested Church Statistics;" and Mary L. Gautier, "Seminarians and Priests: Ordained Leadership in the Twenty-First Century," in *Young Adult American Catholics: Explaining Vocation in Their Own Words*, ed. Maureen K. Day (Mahwah, NJ: Paulist Press, 2018), 342–343.

18 Mary L. Gautier, Paul M. Perl, and Stephen J. Fichter, *Same Call, Different Men: The Evolution of the Priesthood since Vatican II* (Collegeville, MN: Liturgical Press, 2012).

19 Brandon Vaidyanathan and Cella Masso-Rivetti (co-author), "From Burnout to Flourishing: Well-Being Among Priests Amidst Crisis in the Church" (presentation at the SSSR+RRA 2022 Annual Meeting, Baltimore, MD, November 11–13, 2022).

20 Claire Gecewicz and Dennis Quinn, "U.S. churchgoers are satisfied with the sermons they hear, though content varies by religious tradition," Pew Research Center, January 28, 2020, www.pewresearch.org.

21 Pope Paul VI, *Lumen Gentium* [Dogmatic Constitution on the Church], The Holy See, November 21, 1964, 31.

22 See discussion of "injured" and "dissenters" in Robert J. McCarty and John M. Vitek, *Going, Going, Gone: The Dynamics of Disaffiliation in Young Catholics* (Winona, MN: Saint Mary's Press, 2018), 14-24.

23 General Secretariat of the Synod, *Enlarge the Space of Your Tent: Working Document for the Continental Stage* (Vatican City: General Secretariat of the Synod, 2022), www.synod.va.

24 For happiness, see the beatitudes in Matthew 5:3–12; the original Greek is typically translated either as "blessed" or "happy." For abundant life, see John 10:10.

25 Robert Wuthnow, *Sharing the Journey: Support Groups and America's New Quest for Community* (New York: Free Press, 1994), 163–188. See discussion of "communality" in Kai T. Erikson, *Everything in Its Path: Destruction of Community in the Buffalo Creek Flood* (New York: Simon and Schuster, 1976); Bernard J. Lee, *The Catholic Experience of Small Christian Communities* (Mahwah, NJ: Paulist Press, 2000), 71–73; and Jonathan Haidt, *The Righteous Mind: Why Good People Are Divided by Politics and Religion* (New York: Pantheon Books, 2012), 189–273.

26 Wuthnow, *Sharing the Journey*, 261–262; and Robert D. Putnam and David E. Campbell, *American Grace: How Religion Divides and Unites Us* (New York: Simon and Schuster, 2010), 443–492, especially 449, 453, 460, 464, 471–479, 490.

27 Smith, "Just One-Third of U.S. Catholics Agree." In fact, the three-year eucharistic renewal initiated by the USCCB was prompted by this study. See "National Eucharistic Revival: Here's what you need to know," *Catholic World Report*, June 17, 2022, www.catholicnewsagency.com.

28 D'Antonio, Dillon, and Gautier, *American Catholics in Transition*, 114.

29 Tom Gaunt and Benedict Reilly, "Do Catholics Know What Their Church Teaches? A Challenge for Interpreting National Polls" (presentation at the SSSR+RRA 2022 Annual Meeting, Baltimore, MD, November 11–13, 2022).

30 United States Conference of Catholic Bishops, "The Eucharist," no date, www.usccb.org, accessed April 1, 2024.

31 D'Antonio, Dillon, and Gautier, *American Catholics in Transition*, 114–116.

32 For a review of this, see Susan Bigelow Reynolds, *People Get Ready: Ritual, Solidarity, and Lived Ecclesiology in Catholic Roxbury* (New York: Fordham University Press, 2023), 46–61.

33 Robert N. Bellah, Richard Madsen, William M. Sullivan, Ann Swidler, and Steven M. Tipton, *Habits of the Heart: Individualism and Commitment in American Life* (Berkeley: University of California Press, 1995), 71–75.

34 Reynolds, *People Get Ready*, 10–12.

35 Pope Francis, *Evangelii Gaudium*.

36 Richard Gula, *Just Ministry: Professional Ethics for Pastoral Ministers* (Mahwah, NJ: Paulist Press, 2010), 225–226.

37 Bishops' Committee on Priestly Life and Ministry, *Fulfilled in Your Hearing: The Homily in the Sunday Assembly* (Washington, DC: United States Conference of Catholic Bishops), 20.

38 An example of this reversal of pastoral practice is explored in Robert J. McCarty and John M. Vitek's *Going, Going, Gone: The Dynamics of Disaffiliation in Young Catholics* (Winona, MN: Saint Mary's Press, 2017), 35.

39   Center for Religion and Civic Culture, University of Southern California, "Ten
      Characteristics of Thriving (Faith) Communities," January 23, 2023, crcc.usc.edu.

2. AUTHORITY

1   Lynne Abraham, "Report of the Grand Jury," In the Court of Common Pleas, First
     Judicial District of Pennsylvania, Criminal Trial Division, September 21, 2005,
     www.bishop-accountability.org.

2   Abraham, "Report of the Grand Jury."

3   Dan Stamm, "Defrocked Bucks County Priest Faces Charges for Fondling
     Altar Boys Before Mass, DA Says," NBC Philadelphia, September 3, 2019, www
     .nbcphiladelphia.com.

4   Stamm, "Defrocked Bucks County Priest." In 2004 the Archdiocese found an al-
     legation brought against Schmeer by a different victim to be credible. Schmeer ac-
     cepted a life of "prayer and penance," without ministry. Ellen Dunkel, "Those who
     are Named in the Grand Jury Report," *Philadelphia Inquirer*, September 25, 2005.

5   Paul Perl, Mark M. Gray, and Bryan T. Froehle, "Attitudes of U.S. Catholics and
     Non-Catholics About Sexual Abuse by Priests: One Year Later," Center for Ap-
     plied Research in the Apostolate (CARA). June 6, 2003.

6   Laurie Goodstein and Sam Dillon, "Bishops Proceed Cautiously In Carrying Out
     Abuse Policy," *New York Times* August 18, 2002, 1, 24.

7   Perl et al., "Attitudes of U.S. Catholics and Non-Catholics About Sexual Abuse
     by Priests."

8   Paul Perl and Bryan T. Froehle, "Attitudes of U.S. Catholics About Sexual Abuse
     by Priests," May 22, 2002, Washington, DC: Center for Applied Research in the
     Apostolate.

9   Quinnipiac University Poll, "Bishops Who Hid Alleged Sex Abuse Priests Should
     Quit, Americans Tell Quinnipiac University Poll," Quinnipiac University, April 11,
     2002, https://poll.qu.edu.

10 Patricia Rice, "Catholics Hope Policy Will Revive Church's Moral Clout," *St. Louis
     Post-Dispatch*, November 24, 2004, B1.

11 A 2018 grand jury report on clergy sexual abuse in six Pennsylvania dioceses.

12 CNN, "CNN/OSR Poll," March 19, 2013, http://i2.cdn.turner.com/cnn/2013/images
     /03/19/rel3b.pdf.

13 Jenice Armstrong, "Catholics who Choose Pets over Babies Aren't Selfish—No
     Matter what Pope Francis Says." *Philadelphia Inquirer*, Published January 6, 2022,
     www.inquirer.com

14 Andrew M. Greeley, *The American Catholic: A Social Portrait* (New York: Basic
     Books, 1977).

15 John T. Noonan, *A Church that Can and Cannot Change: The Development of
     Catholic Moral Teaching* (South Bend, IN: University of Notre Dame Press, 2005).

16 Roger Finke and Rodney Stark, *The Churching of America 1776–1990: Winners
     and Losers in Our Religious Economy* (New Brunswick, NJ: Rutgers University
     Press, 1992).

17 Pope Paul VI, *Gaudium et Spes [Pastoral Constitution on the Church in the Modern World]*, The Holy See, December 7, 1965, www.vatican.va.

18 Michele Dillon, *Catholic Identity: Balancing Reason, Faith and Power* (New York: Cambridge University Press, 1999), 45–52.

19 James Hitchcock, "The Rebellious Heart: The Unraveling of the Church Since Vatican II," *Crisis*, November 1, 1985, www.crisismagazine.com/

20 Greeley, *The American Catholic*.

21 From a personal interview conducted by one of the authors for a research project on Vatican II. Quoted with permission.

22 Pope Paul VI, *Gaudium et Spes, #43 and #62*. On hierarchical authority, see "Dogmatic Constitution," nos. 18–21, 25, in Walter Abbott, ed., *The Documents of Vatican II* (New York: Herder and Herder, 1966); the Dogmatic Constitution is also discussed in Dillon, *Catholic Identity*, 51.

23 "Pope Says Church is Making 'Profound' Birth Control Study," *New York Times*, June 24, 1964, 1, 3.

24 R. T. Ravenholt, "The A.I.D. Population and Family Planning Program—Goals, Scope, and Progress," *Demography* 5 (1968): 561–73.

25 The announcement was vague, stating only that the Vatican was "studying" the issue of birth control. Many people mistakenly inferred that Pope Paul himself had initiated the process. "Pope Says Church is Making 'Profound' Birth Control Study," 1, 3.

26 "Prelates Ask New Look at Roman Tenets," *Los Angeles Times*, Oct. 30, 1964, 3.

27 "Prelates Ask New Look at Roman Tenets," 3.

28 We do not know the month of the 1967 poll, but results were published in late March.

29 A papal encyclical is a formal pastoral letter written by the pope to an audience that can be as small as the world's bishops or as large as "all people of good will." As a pastoral document, it is an expression of the pope's ordinary teaching authority on matters of doctrine, morality, or discipline. Although the teachings expressed in an encyclical are not infallible, and hence are subject to change, "Catholics are nevertheless obliged to assent to their doctrinal and moral content." See "Encyclical" in *New Catholic Encyclopedia*, vol. 5 (Washington, DC: Catholic University of America, 1967), 332–33.

30 Greeley, *The American Catholic*; Michael Hout and Andrew Greeley, "The Center Doesn't Hold: Church Attendance in the United States, 1940–1984," *American Sociological Review* 52 (1987): 325–345.

31 Sixty percent said he asserted his authority "just as he ought to," and 13 percent that he asserted it too little. Ten percent had no opinion.

32 Full wording: "In some places in the United States it is not legal to supply birth control information. How do you feel about this—Do you think birth control information should be available to anyone who wants it, or not?"

33 A large survey conducted every one to three years since 1972 by the National Opinion Research Center.

34 The figure is limited to questions that asked specifically about *remarriage* after divorce, but the gap between Catholics and Protestants was similar for general approval of divorce itself. A 1954 Gallup question asked, "Do you believe in divorce?" Sixty percent of Protestants and 28 percent of Catholics said "yes," a difference of 32 percentage points.

35 "Tolerance on Sex is Found Growing," *New York Times*, Aug. 12, 1973, 21.

36 Tom Smith, "The Sexual Revolution?" *Public Opinion Quarterly* 54 (1990): 415–435.

37 "Tolerance on Sex is Found Growing," 21.

38 The figure omits Millennial and iGen to avoid the "messiness" of more overlapping data points with Vatican II and post-Vatican II.

39 Michele Dillon, "What do we know about how Catholics inform their consciences?" *National Catholic Reporter*, June 18, 2018, www.ncronline.org.

40 "U.S. Public Becoming Less Religious," Pew Research Center, November 3, 2015, www.pewresearch.org.

41 National Conference of Catholic Bishops, "Pastoral Message of the Administrative Committee," February 13, 1973, Reprinted in *The Catholic Lawyer* 19 (Winter 1973): 29–33, https://scholarship.law.stjohns.edu.

42 John Deedy, "CounterAttack by the Bishops," *New York Times*, February 18, 1973, 254.

43 Percentages for 1962–1969 are from Gallup, reported by Judith Blake, "Abortion and Public Opinion: The 1960–1970 Decade," *Science* 171 (1971): 540–549. Those for 1972–2018 are from our analysis of the GSS. Blake presents results for Whites only. For sake of comparison, we do the same.

44 "America's Abortion Quandary," Pew Research Center, May 6, 2022, www .pewresearch.org.

45 "Where the Public Stands on Religious Liberty vs. Nondiscrimination," Pew Research Center, September 28, 2016, www.pewresearch.org.

46 For 1972–76, the response we define as pro-life states: "Abortion should be permitted only if the life and health of the woman is in danger." Afterward, the question wording changed: "The law should permit abortion only in case of rape, incest, or when the woman's life is in danger."

47 So was McGovern's first running mate in the race, Thomas Eagleton. See James W. Antle III, "George McGovern's Pro-Life Paradox," *American Conservative*, October 22, 2012, www.theamericanconservative.com.

48 Byron W. Daynes and Raymond Tatalovich, "Presidential Politics and Abortion, 1972–1988," *Presidential Studies Quarterly* 22 (1992): 545–561.

49 Robert D. McFadden, "Archbishop calls Ferraro Mistaken on Abortion Rule," *New York Times*, September 10, 1984, A1, B9.

50 "Archbishop calls Ferraro Mistaken on Abortion Rule," A1, B9.

51 Justin Nortey and Claire Gecewicz, "Three-quarters of U.S. Catholics View Pope Francis Favorably, Though Partisan Differences Persist," Pew Research Center, April 3, 2020, www.pewresearch.org

52 Patricia Rice, "Archbishop Burke Says He Would Refuse Communion to Kerry," *St. Louis Post-Dispatch*, January 31, 2004, 25.

53 Laurie Goodstein, "Vatican Cardinal Signals Backing for Sanctions on Kerry," *New York Times*, April 24, 2004, A13.

54 Katherine Q. Seelye, "Kerry Attends Easter Services and Receives Holy Communion," *New York Times*, April 12, 2004, A15.

55 The bishops chose not to make a direct statement about abortion in the document. Tom Foreman and Kate Sullivan, "Catholic Bishops Approve Document that Falls Short of Denying Communion to Biden or Other Politicians who Support Abortion Rights," CNN, November 17, 2021, www.cnn.com.

56 "Most Catholic Americans Disagree with Hardline Positions of Church Leadership," AP-NORC Center for Public Affairs Research, June 3, 2022, https://apnorc.org.

57 Michael J. Rosenfeld, "Moving a Mountain: The Extraordinary Trajectory of Same-Sex Marriage Approval in the United States," *Socius* 3 (September 15, 2017), https://doi.org/10.1177/2378023117727658

58 Robert Nugent, "The U.S. Catholic Bishops and Gay Civil Rights: Four Case Studies," *Catholic Lawyer* 38 (1996): 1–24, https://scholarship.law.stjohns.edu.

59 United States Conference of Catholic Bishops, "The Mystery of the Eucharist in the Life of the Church," 2002, www.usccb.org.

60 Christopher White, "Pope Francis Says He Has Never Denied Communion, Warns Against Politicizing Eucharist," *National Catholic Reporter,* September 15, 2015, www.ncronline.org.

61 "Special Report: Young Adult Catholics," Center for Applied Research in the Apostolate, 2002, https://cara.georgetown.edu.

62 Codified in Pope Francis's apostolic letter "*Vos Estis Lux Mundi*" ("You Are *the Light of the World*").

63 "Americans See Clergy Sex Abuse as an Ongoing Problem," Pew Research Center, June 11, 2019, www.pewresearch.org.

64 Our analyses statistically control for frequency of church attendance. Catholics are much more likely to have heard a church leader speak out for victims if they attend often, presumably in part because they hear more homilies.

3. RACE

1 Pope Francis, "Full text: Pope Francis' apology to the Indigenous Peoples in Canada," *America: The Jesuit Review*, July 25, 2022.

2 Maka Black Elk and William Critchley-Menor, S.J., "Atoning for sins against Indigenous people begins with confronting the past. Red Cloud Indian School is showing the way," *America: The Jesuit Review*, October 8, 2021.

3 David Lopez, "Whither the Flock? The Catholic Church and the Success of Mexicans in America," in *Immigration and Religion in America: Comparative and Historical Perspectives.*, ed. Richard Alba, Albert J. Raboteau, and Josh DeWind (New York: New York University Press, 2009), 76.

4 Lopez, "Whither the Flock?," 80–81.

5 Lopez, "Whither the Flock?," 80–81.

6 Darren W. Davis and Donald B. Pope-Davis, *Perseverance in the Parish? Religious Attitudes from a Black Catholic Perspective* (New York: Cambridge University Press, 2017); Bryan Massingale, *Racial Justice and the Catholic Church* (Maryknoll, NY: Orbis Books, 2010); and Stephen J. Ochs, *Desegregating the Altar: The Josephites and the Struggle for Black Priests, 1871–1960* (Baton Rouge: Louisiana State University Press, 1990).

7 Cyprian Davis, *The History of Black Catholics in the United States* (New York: Crossroad Press, 1990).

8 John T. McGreevy, *Parish Boundaries: The Catholic Encounter with Race in the Twentieth-Century Urban North* (Chicago: University of Chicago Press, 1996).

9 Joseph Cheah, *Anti-Asian Racism: Myths, Stereotypes, and Catholic Social Teaching* (Maryknoll, NY: Orbis, 2022).

10 Richard Alba, Albert J. Raboteau, and Josh DeWind, eds., *Immigration and Religion in America: Comparative and Historical Perspectives* (New York: New York University Press, 2009); Charles Hirschman, "The Role of Religion in the Origins and Adaptation of Immigrant Groups in the United States," *International Migration Review* 38 (2004): 1206–1233; Sharon Erickson Nepstad, *Catholic Social Activism: Progressive Movements in the United States* (New York: New York University Press, 2019); Maureen K. Day, *Catholic Activism Today: Individual Transformation and the Struggle for Social Justice* (New York: New York University Press, 2020); and Pierrette Hondagneu-Sotelo, *God's Heart Has No Borders: How Religious Activists are Working for Immigrant Rights* (Berkeley: University of California Press, 2008).

11 James C. Cavendish, "Church-Based Community Activism: A Comparison of Black and White Catholic Congregations," *Journal for the Scientific Study of Religion* 39, no. 3 (2000): 371–384.

12 The racial and ethnic distribution that we observe in our sample is very similar to racial and ethnic distributions observed in other studies of U.S. Catholics, such as "America's Changing Religious Landscape," Pew Research Center, May 12, 2015, www.pewforum.org; and Mark Gray, Mary Gautier, and Thomas Gaunt, S.J., "Cultural Diversity in the Catholic Church in the United States," Center for Applied Research in the Apostolate (CARA), 2014.

13 "America's Changing Religious Landscape," Pew Research Center. To illustrate how immigration has helped fuel the increasing racial and ethnic diversity of the U.S. Catholic population, Pew reports that while only 5 percent of White Catholics in the U.S. are immigrants, 70 percent of Asian Catholics, 66 percent of Hispanic Catholics, and 24 percent of Black Catholics in the U.S. are immigrants.

14 Alba, Raboteau, and DeWind, eds., *Immigration and Religion in America*, 24.

15 James C. Cavendish, Michael R. Welch, and David C. Leege, "Social Network Theory and Predictors of Religiosity for Black and White Catholics: Evidence of a 'Black Sacred Cosmos?'" *Journal for the Scientific Study of Religion* 37, no. 3 (1998):

397–410; and Andrew M. Greeley, "Ethnic Variations in Religious Commitment," in *The Religious Dimension: New Directions in Quantitative Research*, ed. Robert Wuthnow (New York: Academic Press, 1979), 113–134.

16 Nancy Tatom Ammerman, *Pillars of Faith* (Berkeley: University of California Press, 2005).

17 "Black Catholics in America," Pew Research Center, March 15, 2022.

18 Gray, Gautier, and Gaunt, S.J., "Cultural Diversity in the Catholic Church."

19 "Black Catholics in America," Pew Research Center.

20 Cavendish, Welch, and Leege, "Social Network Theory and Predictors of Religiosity for Black and White Catholics."

21 D'Antonio, Dillon, and Gautier, *American Catholics in Transition*, 54.

22 International Theological Commission, *Faith and Inculturation*, The Holy See, 1988, www.vatican.va.

23 International Theological Commission, *Faith and Inculturation*, #11.

24 *Lead Me, Guide Me: The African American Catholic Hymnal* (Chicago: G.I.A. Publications, 1987).

25 See, for instance, William Cenkner, *The Multicultural Church: A New Landscape in U.S. Theologies* (New York: Paulist Press, 1996); and Anscar J. Chupungco, *Liturgies of the Future: The Process and Methods of Inculturation* (New York: Paulist Press, 1989).

26 James Cavendish, *A Research Report Commemorating the 25th Anniversary of 'Brothers and Sisters to Us': Looking Back Seeing Today's Reality Pressing Forward.* (Washington, DC: U.S. Conference of Catholic Bishops, Inc., 2004).

27 Davis and Pope-Davis, *Perseverance in the Parish?*.

28 "Black Catholics in America," Pew Research Center.

29 Mark Peyrot and Francis M. Sweeney, "Determinants of Parishioner Satisfaction among Practicing Catholics," *Sociology of Religion* 61, no. 2 (2000): 211. These authors speculate that Black Catholics are more satisfied in predominantly Black parishes because of the tendency of these parishes to "have a more celebratory worship style, greater outreach, and a closer sense of community." In their book *Perseverance in the Parish? Religious Attitudes from a Black Catholic Perspective*, on page 63, Davis and Pope-Davis report that approximately 76 percent of Black Catholics do not attend a predominately Black parish, even though attendance at such parishes enhances overall levels of religious engagement and diminishes exposure to racial intolerance. The Pew Research Center's "Black Catholics in America" (2022) reports that 75 percent of Black Catholics who attend Mass at least a few times a year do not attend a predominantly Black parish.

30 In our chapter "Citizenship," we also saw that these different stances on policy issues are also reflected in the political alignments of those in our sample. Specifically, White, non-Hispanic Catholics (41%) are more likely to report being Republican than are Black Catholics (0%), Hispanic Catholics (11%), or Others. Conversely, Black Catholics (85%), Hispanic Catholics (57%), and Others (42%)

are all more likely to report being Democrats than are non-Hispanic Whites (34%).

31 Among the programs which our interviewees lifted up as models of this kind of training are the Mexican American Catholic College in San Antonio, Texas, the Institute for Black Catholic Studies at Xavier University in New Orleans, Louisiana, and the immersion experiences offered at refugee camps by Jesuit Worldwide Learning.

32 In the United States, being conversant in Spanish is especially critical for ministers, considering that approximately 35 percent of U.S. Catholics are Hispanic, that their percentage of the U.S. Catholic population is growing, and that over half of those Hispanic Catholics are foreign born. Pew estimates that approximately 66% of Hispanic Catholics are foreign born. See "America's Changing Religious Landscape," Pew Research Center.

33 International Theological Commission, *Faith and Inculturation*, no. 11.

34 Some of our interviewees stated that these efforts of inculturation in parishes, schools, and universities can be supported and coordinated more effectively when dioceses have specific offices charged with overseeing these efforts.

35 The challenges of ministering in multicultural parishes have been described in detail by sociologist Brett Hoover, who, in his 2014 book *The Shared Parish: Latinos, Anglos, and the Future of U.S. Catholicism*, documents how some parishes, instead of trying to fully integrate their liturgies, have adopted a "shared parish model," in which a single church facility is shared by distinct cultural groups who retain their own separate liturgies and ministries. This model, Hoover illustrates, allows each group to retain their own language and customs within a shared church space.

36 Mark O'Keefe, What Are They Saying About Social Sin? (New York: Paulist Press, 1990); and Catechism of the Catholic Church, no. 1869. The Catechism of the Catholic Church, no. 1869, states: "Sins give rise to social situations and institutions that are contrary to the divine goodness. 'Structures of sin' are the expression and effect of personal sins. They lead their victims to do evil in their turn. In an analogous sense, they constitute a 'social sin.'"

37 Aaron Wessman, *The Church's Mission in a Polarized World* (Hyde Park, NY: New City Press, 2023). In this book, Wessman refers to people's willingness to encounter people who are different from them as "crossing over," and regards this as a form of discipleship.

38 An example that Maka Black Elk provides is the media's portrayal of the cemeteries discovered on the ground of some of the Indian boarding schools. He believes that the media portrayals lead viewers to think that all of the Native children in these cemeteries died because of abuse, or that their deaths were kept secret from their families. He states "This nuance is hard to explain without sounding defensive. But when children died in those institutions, they did most often from disease. It was too expensive, or maybe even practically impossible, to send those bodies back to their families. And so that's why graves became sort of a necessity

at those sites and why those graveyards today and back then were essentially exclusively for the children who went to school there."

39 See Day, *Catholic Activism Today*; and Paul A. Djupe and Christopher P. Gilbert, *The Political Influence of Churches* (New York: Cambridge University Press, 2009).

40 United States Conference of Catholic Bishops, "Reflections on the Movement for Black Lives (BLM)," retrieved December 3, 2023, www.usccb.org.

41 Lisa A. Keister, *Catholics in America: A Social Portrait* (New York: Oxford University Press, Forthcoming).

42 Keister, *Catholics in America*.

4. CITIZENSHIP

1 Robert N. Bellah, *Beyond Belief: Essays on Religion in a Post-Traditionalist World* (Berkeley: University of California Press, 1991).

2 David C. Leege, Kenneth D. Wald, Brian S. Krueger, and Paul D. Mueller, *The Politics of Cultural Differences: Social Change and Voter Mobilization Strategies in the Post-New Deal Period* (Princeton, NJ: Princeton University Press, 2002), 161.

3 E. J. Dionne Jr., "There Is No Catholic Vote—And It's Important," in *American Catholics and Civic Engagement: A Distinctive Voice*, ed. Margaret O'Brien Steinfels (Lanham, MD: Rowman and Littlefield Publishers, 2004), 253.

4 Elana Schor and David Crary, "Survey: Biden and Trump split the 2020 Catholic vote almost evenly," *America*, November 6, 2020, www.americamagazine.org.

5 Pope Paul VI, *Populorum Progressio* [Encyclical on the Development of Peoples], The Holy See, 1967, no. 33.

6 For a discussion of this shift, see Day, *Catholic Activism Today*. Some of the books that discuss the historical civic engagement of Catholics in public life include David J. O'Brien, *Public Catholicism*, 2nd ed. (New York: Orbis Books, 1996); Jay Dolan, *In Search of an American Catholicism: A History of Religion and Culture in Tension* (New York: Oxford University Press, 2002); and Sharon Erickson Nepstad, *Catholic Social Activism: Progressive Movements in the United States* (New York: New York University Press, 2019).

7 "*Faithful Citizenship*" is a shortened name of the USCCB document *Forming Consciences for Faithful Citizenship*. This document outlines some of the principal ideas the bishops offer Catholics in considering their engagement in public life. It begins by outlining the connection between faith and politics as well as four major themes within Catholic social teaching. It then looks at a politically diverse list of issues (e.g., peace, marriage, migration). Despite the political diversity, it does note that "Not all issues are equal; these ten goals address matters of different moral weight and urgency. Some involve intrinsically evil acts, which can never be approved." February 2020, www.usccb.org.

8 Pope Francis, *Amoris Laetitia*, no. 37.

9 For 1996 data, see J. Baxter Oliphant, "Public Support for the Death Penalty Ticks Up," Pew Research Center, June 11, 2018, www.pewresearch.org. For 2021 data, see

"Most Americans Favor the Death Penalty Despite Concerns About Its Administration," Pew Research Center, June 2, 2021, www.pewresearch.org.

10 John Gramlich, "10 Facts about the Death Penalty in the U.S.," Pew Research Center, July 19, 2021, www.pewresearch.org.

11 Numbers of Catholics who voted for Clinton or Trump will vary somewhat depending on the sources used, with the 2016 Cooperative Congressional Election Study finding that 49% of the Catholic vote went to Trump and 46% went to Clinton. Corwin E. Smidt, "Catholics and the 2020 Presidential Election," *Politics and Religion Journal* 15, no. 2 (2021): 290, 307, https://doi.org/10.54561/prj1502283s.

12 Smidt, "Catholics and the 2020 Presidential Election," 297.

13 For an overview of lay Catholics' attitudes toward climate change, see Michele Dillon, *Postsecular Catholicism: Relevance and Renewal* (New York: Oxford, 2018), 56–61; and Maureen K. Day, "Responding to the Invitation: Fostering a Bolder Response to *Laudato Si'*," *Journal of Moral Theology* 11, no. 1 (2022): 12–22.

14 Salvatore J. Cordileone, "Letter to Priests of the Archdiocese on the Notification Sent to Speaker Nancy Pelosi," Archdiocese of San Francisco, May 20, 2022, https://sfarchdiocese.org.

15 Robert W. McElroy, "Bishop McElroy: The Eucharist is Being Weaponized for Political Ends. This Must Not Happen," *America*, May 5, 2021, www .americamagazine.org.

16 This is a close replication of a Gallup poll question, which asked about religion. Seventy-seven percent of Americans as a whole believe that religion is losing its influence on public life, while 20 percent believe that religious influence is rising. This is roughly inverse to the findings when this question was first asked in 1957 (14% and 69%). Seventy-five percent of contemporary Americans say that the United States would be better off if people were more religious. Frank Newport, "Most Americans Say Religion Is Losing Influence in U.S.: But 75% Say American Society Would Be Better Off If More Americans Were Religious," *Gallup News*, May 29, 2013, https://news.gallup.com.

17 *Catechism of the Catholic Church*, no. 1939.

18 *Catechism of the Catholic Church*, nos. 1940–1942.

19 *Catechism of the Catholic Church*, no. 1905.

20 *Catechism of the Catholic Church*, nos. 1906–1909.

21 *Catechism of the Catholic Church*, no. 1912.

22 Moral theologians may use the term "imagination" rather than "interpretive lens," and sociologists are more likely to use the term "frame." For imagination, see Richard M. Gula, *Reason Informed by Faith: Foundations of Catholic Morality* (New York: Paulist Press, 1989), 71–72; and Richard M. Gula, *The Call to Holiness: Embracing a Fully Christian Life* (New York: Paulist Press, 2003), 107–144.

For an overview of literature on frames, see Maureen K. Day and Linda M. Kawentel, "Unity and Diversity: Frames of Catholicity Among Catholic Campus Ministers," *Review of Religious Research* 63, no. 1 (2021): 23–42, https://doi.org/10 .1007/s13644-020-00424-z.

23 Pope Francis, "For a Culture of Encounter" [Morning Meditation in the Chapel of the Domus Sanctae Marthae], The Holy See, September 13, 2016, www.vatican.va.

24 Christian Smith, *Resisting Reagan: The U.S. Central America Peace Movement* (Chicago: University of Chicago Press, 1996), 181; Jerome Baggett, *Habitat for Humanity: Building Private Homes, Building Public Religion* (Philadelphia: Temple University Press, 2000), 135; Bin Xu, *The Politics of Compassion: The Sichuan Earthquake and Civic Engagement in China* (Stanford, CA: Stanford University Press, 2017); and Day, *Catholic Activism Today*, 159.

25 "Political Polarization in the American Public: How Increasing Ideological Uniformity and Partisan Antipathy Affect Politics, Compromise and Everyday Life," Pew Research Center, June 24, 2014, www.pewresearch.org.

26 Kevin Enochs, "In US, 'Interpolitical' Marriage Increasingly Frowned Upon," *VOA News*, February 3, 2017, www.voanews.com.

27 Michael Lipka, "U.S. Religious Groups and Their Political Leanings," Pew Research Center, February 23, 2016, www.pewresearch.org.

28 More details on this composite variable label are provided in the Introduction. As a reminder, roughly 20 percent of our sample were classified as "high-commitment" Catholics, owing to their 1) weekly Mass attendance, 2) reporting that the Catholic Church was the most or among the most important parts of their life, and 3) selecting 1 or 2 on a 1–7 scale on their likelihood of leaving Catholicism.

29 Brian Starks, "Exploring Religious Self-Identification among U.S. Catholics: Traditionals, Moderates, and Liberals," *Sociology of Religion* 74, no. 3 (2013): 314–342, https://doi.org/10.1093/socrel/srs075.

30 Daniel Lipinski, "Confessions of a Pro-Life Catholic Democrat in a Divided Nation," *America*, October 13, 2021, www.americamagazine.org.

31 Jürgen Habermas, *The Structural Transformation of the Public Sphere: An Inquiry into a Category of Bourgeois Society*, trans. Thomas Burger with the assistance of Frederick Lawrence (Cambridge, MA: MIT Press, 1991).

32 Michael Lipka and Gregory A. Smith, "Like Americans Overall, U.S. Catholics Are Sharply Divided by Party," Pew Research Center, January 29, 2019, www.pewresearch.org.

33 Lipka and Smith, "Like Americans Overall, U.S. Catholics Are Sharply Divided by Party."

34 Authors' analysis of 2021 Pew data: "Most Americans Favor the Death Penalty Despite Concerns About Its Administration," Pew Research Center, June 2, 2021.

35 Patricia Ewick and Marc W. Steinberg, *Beyond Betrayal: The Priest Sex Abuse Crisis, the Voice of the Faithful, and the Process of Collective Identity* (Chicago: University of Chicago Press, 1996).

36 Smith, *Resisting Reagan*, 181.

37 Baggett, *Habitat for Humanity*, 135.

38 Xu, *The Politics of Compassion*.

39 Day, *Catholic Activism Today*, 159.

40 For more on cultural repertoire, see Ann Swidler, *Talk of Love: How Culture Matters* (Chicago: University of Chicago Press, 2001).

41 See Dillon, *Postsecular Catholicism*, 126–155.

42 Tricia C. Bruce, *How Americans Understand Abortion: A Comprehensive Interview Study of Abortion Attitudes in the U.S.* (South Bend, IN: McGrath Institute for Church Life, 2020).

43 The name of the initiative is Prepares: Pregnancy and Parenting Support. To learn more about these efforts, visit www.preparesforlife.org. Accessed June 2, 2022.

44 Walking with Moms in Need encourages parishes to provide support and other resources to pregnant women and mothers of young children. www.walkingwithmoms.com, accessed June 2, 2022.

45 Simon J. Hendry, "Ruined for Life: The Spirituality of the Jesuit Volunteer Corps" (PhD diss., Graduate Theological Union, 2002), 464; Dillon, *Catholic Identity*, 199; and Day, *Catholic Activism Today*, 177.

46 Tricia C. Bruce, *Parish and Place: Making Room for Diversity in the American Catholic Church* (New York: Oxford University Press, 2017); and Mary Ellen Konieczny, *The Spirit's Tether: Family, Work, and Religion among American Catholics* (New York: Oxford University Press, 2013).

47 Michael O. Emerson and Christian Smith, *Divided by Faith: Evangelical Religion and the Problem of Race in America* (New York: Oxford University Press, 2001).

48 This is discussed further in Maureen K. Day, "Polarization? Identifying What Divides and Unites American Catholics," *Religion and Politics*, 17, no. 2 (2023): 251–275.

49 Mary Ellen Konieczny, Charles C. Camosy, and Tricia C. Bruce, *Polarization in the US Catholic Church: Naming the Wounds, Beginning to Heal* (Collegeville, MN: Liturgical Press, 2016); and Mary Ellen Konieczny, *The Spirit's Tether: Family, Work, and Religion among American Catholics* (New York: Oxford University Press, 2013).

5. LOVE

1 This terminology is used in Pope Francis's apostolic exhortation *Amoris Laetitia* (which is literally translated "The Joy of Love," but is about Joy in the Family). Because putting "irregular" in quotes is the style used in this document, we consistently use quotes around "irregular."

2 Dillon, *Postsecular Catholicism*, 160.

3 "As Family Structures Change in U.S., a Growing Share of Americans Say It Makes No Difference," Pew Research Center, April 10, 2020, www.pewresearch.org. Also see "In Places where Same-Sex Marriages are Legal, How Many Married Same-Sex Couples are There?," Pew Research Center, June 13, 2023, www.pewresearch.org.

4 Danielle Taylor, "Same-Sex Couples are More Likely to Adopt or Foster Children," U.S. Census Bureau, 2020, accessed May 17, 2023, www.census.gov. Also see Shoshana Goldberg and Kerith Conron, "How Many Same Sex Couples in the

U.S. are Raising Children?" (brief), Williams Institute, July, 2018, accessed May 17, 2023, https://williamsinstitute.law.ucla.edu.

5 "America's Changing Religious Landscape," Appendix D: Detailed Tables.

6 Michele Dillon, *Postsecular Catholicism*, 165. Also see Pew Research Center's publications: "How People in 24 Countries View Same-Sex Marriage," June 13, 2023; and "U.S. Catholics Open to Non-Traditional Families," September 2, 2015.

7 Penny Edgell, *Religion and Family in a Changing Society* (Princeton, NJ: Princeton University Press, 2006); and Bella DePaulo, "More people than ever before are single—and that's a good thing," *The Conversation*, April 23, 2017, https://theconversation.com.

8 DePaulo, "More people than ever before are single."

9 "About six-in-ten Americans say legalization of same-sex marriage is good for society," Pew Research Center, November 15, 2022, www.pewresearch.org.

10 Although some commentators have described this as a new approach, we believe it is more accurately described as a renewed emphasis. In his book *Mercy and the Rule of Law: A Theological Interpretation of Amoris Laetitia* (Collegeville, MN: Liturgical Press, 2021), Catholic theologian Gerald Bednar demonstrates that the church has always had a merciful approach to family life.

11 The church's Synod on the Family (2014–2015) and its current Synod on Synodality, which began in 2021 and will conclude in 2024, are emblematic of the Pope's desire for the church to better accompany contemporary families and those who feel on the margins of the church.

12 Dillon, *Postsecular Catholicism*.

13 Francis, *Amoris Laetitia*, no. 35.

14 Francis, *Amoris Laetitia*, nos. 36–37.

15 Francis, *Amoris Laetitia*, no. 35.

16 Francis, *Amoris Laetitia*, no. 52. This echoes one of the themes presented explicitly in the midterm report of the Synod on the Family that became more muted in the final report. See Dillon, *Postsecular Catholicism*, 136–140, for a thorough description of the revisions made to the midterm report of the Synod on the Family before the final report was issued. This recognition is also evident in the Vatican's March 15, 2021, statement "Responsum of the Congregation for the Doctrine of the Faith to a dubium regarding the blessing of the unions of persons of the same sex," which states that "the presence . . . of positive elements" in "unions between persons of the same sex" are "in themselves to be valued and appreciated;" that the Church "accompanies them and shares their journey of Christian faith."

17 Francis, *Amoris Laetitia*, no. 243.

18 Francis, *Amoris Laetitia*, no. 243.

19 Francis, *Amoris Laetitia*, no. 305; fn. 351.

20 Michele Dillon, *Postsecular Catholicism*, 160.

21 A very similar breakdown in the types of families among U.S. Catholics is seen in the Pew Research Center's Religious Landscape Survey. See "America's Changing Religious Landscape," Appendix D: Detailed Tables.

22 "America's Changing Religious Landscape," Chapter 2, "Religious Switching and Intermarriage.".

23 Another factor adding to the complexity of the family lives of U.S. Catholics is the large number of Catholic families composed of immigrants. According to Pew's Religious Landscape Study, 27 percent of U.S. Catholics were born abroad, and an additional 15 percent has at least one parent who was born abroad.

24 "One-in-Five Adults Were Raised in Interfaith Homes: A Closer Look at Religious Mixing in American Families," Pew Research Center, October 26, 2016, www .pewresearch.org.

25 "The U.S. Catholic Family: Demographics," Center for Applied Research in the Apostolate (CARA), July 2015.

26 "Frequently Requested Church Statistics."

27 D'Antonio, Dillon, and Gautier, *American Catholics in Transition*, 43.

28 "Frequently Requested Church Statistics." These statistics reveal that between 1985 and 2022, enrollment in parish-based religious education and faith formation declined over 50 percent.

29 D'Antonio, Dillon, and Gautier, *American Catholics in Transition*, 50.

30 In separate analyses, we compared Catholics' responses to these questions with their responses to other items in the same battery of questions designed to show which teachings our respondents regard as core, important, or peripheral to what it means to be a good Catholic. The teachings our respondents regard as core to being a good Catholic are belief in Jesus's resurrection and belief in the true presence of Christ's body and blood in the bread and wine consecrated at Mass. These are core teachings of the faith at an institutional level, and it appears that everyday Catholics have likewise centered these items. The teachings our respondents regard as important to being a good Catholic are donating time and money to help the poor and opposing abortion. The teachings our respondents believe are peripheral, or least important, to being a good Catholic are the ones related to marriage and sexuality, as described in this chapter.

31 *Catechism of the Catholic Church*, no. 1122.

32 *Catechism of the Catholic Church*, nos. 1126–1134.

33 *Sacrosanctum Concilium* (The Constitution of the Sacred Liturgy), one of the documents of Vatican II, states that "the liturgy is the summit toward which the activity of the Church is directed; at the same time it is the fount from which all the Church's power flows" (1963, no. 10).

34 Francis, *Amoris Laetitia*, nos. 242–43.

35 The church's *Code of Canon Law* makes room for this possibility—that an individual's conscience may direct him or her on a path that diverges from the Church's public teachings—by distinguishing between the realm of the Church's public teachings, or the "external forum," and the realm of individual conscience (*Forum conscientiae*), or the "internal forum." Canon 130, www.vatican.va.

36 *Catholics in Transition*, 50.

37 Our survey also asked respondents where they would place themselves on a scale from 1 to 7, with 1 being "I would never leave the Catholic Church" and 7 being "Yes, I might leave the Catholic Church." Corroborating the findings with respect to the importance of the church in their lives, divorced and separated Catholics are more likely than married Catholics to say that they might leave the church.

38 Melissa Wilde, "From Excommunication to Nullification," *Journal for the Scientific Study of Religion* 40 (2001): 235–249; Mark Gray, Paul Perl, and Tricia Bruce, *Marriage in the Catholic Church: A Survey of U.S. Catholics* (Washington, DC: CARA, 2007); and Pierre Hegy and Joseph Martos, eds., *Catholic Divorce: The Deception of Annulments* (New York: Continuum, 2000).

39 Hegy and Martos, eds., *Catholic Divorce.*

40 Hegy and Martos, eds., *Catholic Divorce*, 23.

41 Hegy and Martos, eds., *Catholic Divorce*; and Sheila Rauch Kennedy, *Shattered Faith* (New York: Henry Holt, 1997).

42 Hegy and Martos, eds., *Catholic Divorce.*

43 DePaulo, "More people than ever before are single."

44 For a fuller understanding of these interviewees' perspectives on sex, marriage, parenting, and the mission of the family, see Helen M. Alvaré, *Religious Freedom After the Sexual Revolution: A Catholic Guide* (Washington, DC: Catholic University of American Press, 2022); Julie Hanlon Rubio and Jason King, eds., *Sex, Love, and Families: Catholic Perspectives* (Collegeville, MN: Liturgical Press, 2020).

45 Pew has also reported that 70 percent of U.S. Catholics believe that it is acceptable for a same-sex couple to live together, 66 percent believe it is okay for children to be raised by a gay or lesbian couple, and 46 percent believe that the Catholic Church should recognize the marriages of gay and lesbian couples. See "U.S. Catholics Open to Non-Traditional Families."

46 For this figure, we selected surveys that include large enough subsamples for each generation. To reduce "clutter" and show the trends clearly, we also excluded some outliers and some surveys that took place very close in time to others.

47 USCCB, *Ministry to Persons with a Homosexual Inclination: Guidelines for Pastoral Care* (Washington, DC: USCCB, 2006), 21.

48 Dean R. Hoge, William D. Dinges, Mary Johnson, Juan L. Gonzales, Jr., *Young Adult Catholics: Religion in the Culture of Choice* (Notre Dame, IN. University of Notre Dame Press, 2001), 198–199.

6. TRENDS

1 Actual in-pew Mass attendance was not truly that high; it is well-established that people exaggerate religious participation in response to surveys because it is a socially-desirable behavior. But the goal of this analysis is to draw comparisons across time. Changing responses to this question over the years probably tend to reflect, at least in part, real changes in behavior.

2 In 1987, Hout and Greeley wrote, "Catholic church attendance really has stopped falling." Michael Hout and Andrew M. Greeley, "The Center Doesn't Hold:

Church Attendance in the United States, 1940–1984," *American Sociological Review* 52 (1987): 336.

3 Jeffrey M. Jones, "U.S. Church Attendance Still Lower than Pre-Pandemic," *Gallup News*, June 6, 2023, https://news.gallup.com.

4 Frank Newport, "Catholic Church Attendance Drops This Year In Midst of Scandal," *Gallup News*, December 18, 2002, https://news.gallup.com; and George H. Gallup Jr., "Catholics Trail Protestants in Church Attendance," *Gallup News*, December 16, 2003, https://news.gallup.com.

5 Perl et al., "Attitudes of U.S. Catholics and Non-Catholics About Sexual Abuse by Priests."

6 Greeley et al., *Catholic Schools in a Declining Church.*

7 The low percentage in 2021 should be interpreted cautiously because the survey occurred very early in the year, before COVID-19 vaccines were available to most people.

8 Pippa Norris and Ronald Inglehart, "Uneven Secularization in the United States and Western Europe," in *Democracy and the New Religious Pluralism*, ed. Thomas Banchoff, 31–57 (New York: Oxford University Press, 2007).

9 Raphaël Franck and Laurence R. Iannaccone, "Religious Decline in the 20th Century West: Testing Alternative Explanations," *Public Choice* 159 (2014): 385–414.

10 Alasdair Crockett and David Voas, "Generations of Decline: Religious Change in 20th-Century Britain," *Journal for the Scientific Study of Religion* 45 (2006): 567–584; and Steve Bruce, "Christianity in Britain, R.I.P.," *Sociology of Religion* 62 (2003): 191–203.

11 Sascha O. Becker and Ludger Woessmann, "Not the Opium of the People: Income and Secularization in a Panel of Prussian Counties," *American Economic Review: Papers & Proceedings* 103 (2013): 539–554.

12 In 1972 and 2021, the GSS did not ask respondents their religion at age 16.

13 Although his book is older, Dean Hoge's *Converts, Dropouts, Returnees* is helpful in seeing the ways Catholic affiliation and disaffiliation has changed and remained similar since the early 1980s, and also contains qualitative data to complement this national survey data. Dean R. Hoge, *Converts, Dropouts, Returnees: A Study of Religious Change Among Catholics* (New York: Pilgrim Press, 1981).

14 Marc Musick and John Wilson, "Religious Switching for Marriage Reasons," *Sociology of Religion* 56 (1995): 257–70.

15 Michael Hout, "Angry and Alienated: Divorced and Remarried Catholics in the United States," *America* 183 (December 16, 2000): 10–12.

16 Mark Gray, "Welcome Sign Needed?" *Nineteen Sixty-Four* (blog), Center for Applied Research in the Apostolate (CARA), January 15, 2020, http://nineteensixty -four.blogspot.com/.

17 See https://twitter.com/ryanburge/status/1612096639644336128.

18 In the two decades before the 1990s, the percentage of the American public with no religion had increased only marginally. In the 1972 GSS, it was 5 percent; in

1991, it was 8 percent. Then in 1993, it rose slightly to 9 percent. By 1996, it was 14 percent.

19 Michael Hout and Claude S. Fischer, "Explaining Why More Americans Have No Religious Preference: Political Backlash and Generational Succession, 1987–2012," *Sociological Science* 1 (2014): 423–47; and Ryan P. Burge, *The Nones: Where They Came From, Who They Are, and Where They Are Going* (Minneapolis: Fortress Press, 2021).

20 Hout and Fischer, "Explaining Why More Americans Have No Religious Preference."

21 Carol Ann McGregor and Ashlyn Haycook, "Lapsed Catholics and Other Religious Non-Affiliates," in *Empty Churches: Non-Affiliation in America*, ed. James L. Heft and Jan E. Stets, 79–105 (New York: Oxford University Press, 2021).

22 Robert P. Jones, Daniel Cox, and Juhem Navarro-Rivera, "The 2012 American Values Survey: How Catholics and the Religiously Unaffiliated Will Shape the 2012 Election and Beyond" (Washington, DC: Public Religion Research Institute, 2012).

23 Burge, *The Nones*.

24 Darren E. Sherkat, "Tracking the Restructuring of American Religion: Religious Affiliation and Patterns of Religious Mobility, 1973–1998," *Social Forces* 79 (2001): 1,459–1,493; and Musick and Wilson, "Religious Switching for Marriage Reasons."

25 Sherkat, "Tracking the Restructuring of American Religion."

26 "The Shifting Religious Identity of Latinos in the United States," Pew Research Center, May 7, 2014, www.pewresearch.org/

27 Mark T. Mulder, Aida I. Ramos, and Gerardo Martí, *Latino Protestants in America: Growing and Diverse* (London: Rowman & Littlefield, 2017).

28 Franck and Iannaccone, "Religious Decline in the 20th Century West."

29 Linda Woodhead, "The Rise of 'No Religion' in Britain: The Emergence of a New Cultural Majority," *Journal of the British Academy* 4 (2016): 245–61.

30 Davidson et al., *The Search for Common Ground: What Unites and Divides Catholic Americans*.

31 Andrew M. Greeley and Peter H. Rossi, *The Education of Catholic Americans* (Chicago: Aldine, 1966); Greeley et al., *Catholic Schools in a Declining Church*; and Paul Perl and Mark M. Gray, "Catholic Schooling and Disaffiliation from Catholicism," *Journal for the Scientific Study of Religion* 46 (2007): 269–280.

32 Christian Smith, Kyle Longest, Jonathan Hill, and Kari Christoffersen, *Young Catholic America: Emerging Adults In, Out of, and Gone from the Church* (New York: Oxford University Press, 2014).

33 For a contrary finding see: Jonathan Hill, "Religious Pathways During the Transition to Adulthood: A Life Course Approach" (PhD diss., University of Notre Dame, 2007).

34 The table also excludes a small number of respondents with no high school education.

35 To obtain an adequate sample size of pre-Vatican II Catholics, the table combines data from both 2011 and 2017.

36 Paul M. Perl and Mark M. Gray, "Sacraments Today: Belief and Practice among U.S. Catholics," Center for Applied Research in the Apostolate (CARA), 2008.

37 Thomas P. O'Connor, Dean R. Hoge, and Estrelda Alexander, "The Relative Influence of Youth and Adult Experiences on Personal Spirituality and Church Involvement," *Journal for the Scientific Study of Religion* 41 (2002): 723–732. On the long-term predictive power of adolescent religiosity across 50 years of adulthood in a longitudinal sample of individuals, see Michele Dillon and Paul Wink, *In the Course of a Lifetime: Tracing Religious Belief, Practice, and Change* (Berkeley: University of California Press, 2007).

38 Greeley et al., *Catholic Schools in a Declining Church*; and Perl and Gray, "Catholic Schooling and Disaffiliation from Catholicism," 2007. An exception is Davidson et al., *The Search for Common Ground*, showing positive effects of parish-based religious education.

39 Eric L. Dey, "Undergraduate Political Attitudes: An examination of Peer, Faculty, and Social Influences," *Research in Higher Education* 37 (1996): 535–554; and Tamkinat Rauf, "How College Makes Liberals (or Conservatives)," *Socius* 7 (2021):1–13.

40 Moreover, this may be an overestimate of the true figure. The Association of Catholic Colleges and Universities estimates that about 10 percent of Catholic college students attend Catholic institutions.

41 Andrew M. Greeley, *The Catholic Myth: The Behavior and Beliefs of American Catholics* (New York: Touchstone, 1990); and Andrew M. Greeley and Mary G. Durkin, *Angry Catholic Women* (Chicago: Thomas More, 1984).

42 "U.S. Catholics Open to Non-Traditional Families," Pew Research Center, September 2, 2015, www.pewresearch.org/

43 For comparisons of religious practices, we limit analysis to respondents under 75. Women tend to live longer than men, so surveys obtain more elderly female than male respondents. Because older generations tend to be more religiously committed, differential mortality can lead to slightly exaggerated gender differences.

44 Note that women are not more pessimistic, generally, about change in the church. This question is from a series asking about the likelihood of change in several areas. Men and women differed very little on the others (e.g., allowing priests to marry, allowing birth control, and allowing same-sex marriage).

45 A few surveys of the general public—mostly from early years in the figure—ask if women should be "clergy" or be "ministers, priests, or rabbis." Nearly all later surveys ask specifically about support of women as clergy in the respondents "*own* religion." The figure excludes questions that asked if women should be ordained *for a particular reason*, such as the priest shortage or addressing clergy sexual abuse.

46 Dogmatic Constitution, nos. 33 & 37, discussed in Dillon, *Postsecular Catholicism*, 24, 175.

47 Analyzed in the chapter 2 section on abortion attitudes.

48 Davidson et al., *The Search for Common Ground*, 1996; and Scott M. Myers, "An Interactive Model of Religiosity Inheritance: The Importance of Family Context," *American Sociological Review* 61 (1996): 858–866.

49 Myers, "An Interactive Model of Religiosity Inheritance."

50 McGregor and Haycook, "Lapsed Catholics and Other Religious Non-Affiliates," 103.

51 Ryan Burge, "Four of the Most Dramatic Shifts in American Religion Over the Last 50 Years," Graphs About Religion, July 10, 2023, www.graphsaboutreligion .com; and Ryan P. Burge, "The Data is Clear—Episcopalians Are in Trouble," *Religion in Public* (blog), November, 23 2020, www.religioninpublic.blog.

52 Christian Smith, *American Evangelicalism: Embattled and Thriving* (Chicago: University of Chicago Press, 1998).

53 See, for example: Larry R. Petersen and Gregory V. Donnenwerth, "Secularization and the Influence of Religion on Beliefs about Premarital Sex," *Social Forces* 75 (1997): 1,071–89.

54 Ryan P. Burge, "So, Why is Evangelicalism Not Declining? Because Non-Attenders Are Taking On the Label," *Religion in Public* (blog), December 10, 2020, https:// religioninpublic.blog

55 This is aside from the effect of the COVID-19 pandemic. In the General Social Survey, weekly attendance among denominationally-affiliated evangelicals (as opposed to those merely self-labeling) peaked in 2012 and then fell through 2018.

56 Ryan P. Burge, "What Turned the Tide on Gay Marriage?" *Religion in Public* (blog), December 17, 2019, https://religioninpublic.blog

57 Ryan P. Burge, "Here's an attempt to convey just how unpopular a complete ban on abortion is," X (f/k/a Twitter), April 12, 2023, 9:23pm, https://twitter.com /ryanburge/status/1646323188253577216.

58 "A Record High Share of 40-Year-Olds in the U.S. Have Never Been Married," Pew Research Center, June 28, 2023, www.pewresearch.org.

59 Kenneth Johnson, "U.S. Fertility Up Slightly, but 8.6 Million Fewer Births Long Term," University of New Hampshire: Carsey School of Public Policy, August 9, 2022, https://carsey.unh.edu.

60 Paul Sullins, "The Effect of University Characteristics on Student Religiousness: A Meta-Analysis of Catholic Universities," *Interdisciplinary Journal of Research on Religion* 9, no. 10 (2013): 1–37.

CONCLUSION

1 Mainline Protestants were next highest, with a mere 1.7 leaving for every adult convert. "America's Changing Religious Landscape," Chapter 2, "Religious Switching and Intermarriage."

2 Stephen Bullivant, *Mass Exodus: Catholic Disaffiliation in Britain and America since Vatican II* (New York: Oxford University Press, 2020).

3 Lee, *The Catholic Experience of Small Christian Communities*, 44.

4 Cavendish, Welch, and Leege, "Social Network Theory and Predictors of Religiosity for Black and White Catholics," 405.

5 *Catechism of the Catholic Church*, nos. 1396–1397.

6 "The Religious Typology: A new way to categorize Americans by religion," chapter 2: "Attitudes toward organized religion," Pew Research Center, August 28, 2018, www.pewresearch.org.

7 Patricia Tevington, "Americans Feel More Positive Than Negative About Jews, Mainline Protestants, Catholics," Pew Research Center, March 15, 2023, www.pewresearch.org.

8 Christian Smith, *Moral, Believing Animals: Human Personhood and Culture* (New York: Oxford University Press, 2009); and Donna Freitas, *Sex and the Soul: Juggling Sexuality, Spirituality, Romance, and Religion on America's College Campuses* (New York: Oxford University Press, 2008).

9 Jesus meets needs of hunger, healing and belonging throughout the Bible, but see Mark 10:46–52 for an encounter in which Jesus explicitly asks a blind man to name his need.

10 "Credentials issued by American Pilgrims by year, 2007–2020" (graph), American Pilgrims on the Camino, August 6, 2021, https://americanpilgrims.org.

11 Hannah Arendt, *Between Past and Future: Six Exercises in Political Thought* (New York: Viking Press, 1961), 174–175.

12 Christian Smith, *To Flourish or Destruct: A Personalist Theory of Human Goods, Motivations, Failure and Evil* (Chicago: University of Chicago Press, 2015), 223–265, especially 262–263.

13 Freitas, *Sex and the Soul*.

14 Smith, *To Flourish or Destruct*, 247–254.

15 Jay P. Dolan, *The American Catholic Experience: A History from Colonial Times to the Present* (Notre Dame, IN: Notre Dame University Press, 1992); Dolan, *In Search of an American Catholicism*; and Peter Steinfels, *A People Adrift: The Crisis of the Roman Catholic Church in America* (New York: Simon & Schuster, 2003).

16 Dillon, *Postsecular Catholicism*.

17 Salvatore Cernuzio, "Synod: Laymen and Laywomen Eligible to Vote at General Assembly," *Vatican News*, April 26, 2023, www.vaticannews.va.

18 *Catechism of the Catholic Church*, no. 2358.

19 NCR Staff, "Statements by US Bishops on Orlando Shooting," *National Catholic Reporter*, June 22, 2016, www.ncronline.org.

20 Tom Faletti, "Stations of the Cross: Overcoming Racism" (handout) (Washington, DC: U.S. Conference of Catholic Bishops, 2020).

21 Note that Black Catholic liturgy can have considerable variation. Tia Noelle Pratt, "Black Catholics' Identity Work," in *American Parishes: Remaking Local Catholicism*, eds. Gary J. Adler Jr., Tricia Colleen Bruce, and Brian Starks, 132–152 (New York: Fordham University Press, 2019).

22 Theologians and official documents tend to conflate marriage and family, even though these two phenomena are often distinct in the United States, as seen in situations such as multi-generational families, single-parent families, and others.

For more on the history of Catholicism's pastoral approach to marriage, see Bednar, *Mercy and the Rule of Law*.

23 Symposium of Episcopal Conferences of Africa and Madagascar, "SECAM: 'No Blessing for Homosexual Couples in all Churches in Africa,'" *SECAM*, January 11, 2024, www.secam.org.

24 Day, "Polarization? Identifying What Divides and Unites American Catholics."

25 Dillon, *Postsecular Catholicism*.

26 Day, "Responding to the Invitation: Fostering a Bolder Response to *Laudato Si'*."

27 James Cavendish, "Religion as a Resource in an Increasingly Polarized Society," *Sociology of Religion* 84, no. 1 (2023), 1–15, https://doi.org/10.1093/socrel/srac033; and Wessman, *The Church's Mission in a Polarized World*.

28 Swidler, *Talk of Love: How Culture Matters*.

INDEX

abortion: Catholic attitudes toward, 23, 79–97, 108, 151–53, 155, 159–65, 180, 210, 222–25, 237, 258, 260, 279n43, 279n46, 289n30; church teaching on, 65, 79, 90, 93, 139, 143

abuse, of children, 13, 57–67, 97–99, 101, 122–23, 236, 240, 277n4, 283n38

accompaniment, pastoral practice of, 43, 47, 94–95, 121, 126–29, 169–74, 183–87, 192–98

aggiornamento ("bringing up to date"), 9–11

American Catholic Laity Surveys, 3–4, 6–12, 16, 87, 102, 132, 206, 213, 215; instrument for 2017 survey, 257–68

American Catholics: demography of, 7–19; mass attendance among, 32–36; religious beliefs and practices among, 25–28, 32–36; support levels for public policy activities of bishops, 79–85, 91–95, 112, 124, 139–44, 161–66, 259–60. *See also* commitment levels among Catholics

Amoris Laetitia (The Joy of Love), 140, 172–74, 184, 274n7, 287n1, 288n10, 288n16

annulments, 27, 178–80, 184–89, 258

artificial birth control. *See* contraception

Asian American Catholics, 17–19, 102–32, 281n13; disaffiliation among, 210–11; distinct historical experiences of, 102–4, 114; recommended ministry practices among, 115–29, 242–43

authority, 57–99, 173, 237, 240, 258, 278n22; of bishops, 22–23, 60–65, 89–95, 97–99; of laity, 41–43, 64–68, 88–90, 178–81; of pope, 41–43, 65–67, 246; of priests, 41–43. *See also* moral authority

baptism, 36, 195, 208, 242

Benedict XVI (pope), 13, 52

Biden, Joe, 84, 133–36, 143, 280n55

"big tent" image of church, 21, 30–32, 37–38, 40, 51–53, 113–14, 244–45, 249, 276n23

birth control. *See* contraception

bishops, U.S., 4–5, 24, 55; authority of, 60–65, 89–95, 97–99; confidence in leadership of, 60–65, 89–95, 97–99; public policy activities of, 79–85, 91–95, 112, 124, 139–44, 161–66, 259–260, 284n7; satisfaction with, 39–42, 217–18, 235–37, 259; scandal handled by, 22–23, 60–65, 89–95, 97–99, 201–2; as source for moral decision-making, 78–79, 258

Black Catholics, 17–19, 102–32, 267, 281n13, 282n29; disaffiliation among, 210–11; distinct expectations of, 104–5, 112, 123; distinct historical experiences of, 102–3, 121–26; political party affiliation of, 137–38, 282n30; recommended ministry practices among, 113–29, 242–43; religious beliefs of, 105–11; religious practices of, 111–12, 295n21

campus ministry, 46, 118–19, 188, 199–200, 225–27

canon law, 62, 289n35

ABOUT THE AUTHORS

MAUREEN K. DAY is a Research Affiliate at the Center for Religion and Civic Culture and the Institute for Advanced Catholic Studies at the University of Southern California.

JAMES C. CAVENDISH is Associate Professor of Sociology at the University of South Florida, Past President and Past Executive Officer of the Association for the Sociology of Religion, and Chair of the Board of the Franciscan Center in Tampa, Florida.

PAUL M. PERL is a sociologist affiliated with the Center for Applied Research in the Apostolate (CARA) at Georgetown University.

MICHELE DILLON is Dean of the College of Liberal Arts at the University of New Hampshire.

MARY L. GAUTIER is Senior Research Emerita at the Center for Applied Research in the Apostolate at Georgetown University and co-author of more than a dozen books on Catholicism in the United States, most recently *God's Call Is Everywhere: A Global Analysis of Contemporary Religious Vocations for Women.*

WILLIAM V. D'ANTONIO is Professor Emeritus at the Catholic University of America. The author of many books, he is also the Co-creator with the late Professor Dean Hoge, of this American Catholic Laity series.